DATE DUE

AUG 2 7 2007	
OCT 10 2007	

Edgewalkers

EDGEWALKERS

People and Organizations That Take Risks, Build Bridges, and Break New Ground

Judi Neal

Westport, Connecticut
London

Library of Congress Cataloging-in-Publication Data

Neal, Judi.
  Edgewalkers : people and organizations that take risks, build bridges,
  and break new ground / Judi Neal.
     p. cm.
  Includes bibliographical references and index.
  ISBN 0–275–98920–8 (alk. paper)
  1. Success in business.   2. Risk-taking (Psychology)   3. Entrepreneurship.
4. Leadership.   I. Title.
  HF5386.N3535 2006
  658.4'094—dc22   2006024870

British Library Cataloguing in Publication Data is available.

Library of Congress Catalog Card Number: 2006024870
ISBN: 0–275–98920–8

First published in 2006

Praeger Publishers, 88 Post Road West, Westport, CT 06881
An imprint of Greenwood Publishing Group, Inc.
www.praeger.com

Printed in the United States of America

The paper used in this book complies with the
Permanent Paper Standard issued by the National
Information Standards Organization (Z39.48–1984).

10 9 8 7 6 5 4 3 2 1

Copyright Acknowledgments

The author and publisher gratefully acknowledge permission for use of the following material:
Illustrations on pages: 1, 13, 23, 43, 67, 97, and 125 are by Quint Buchholz © Sanssouci im Carl
Hanser Verlag 2001. Used by permission.

This book is dedicated to my mother, Mildred Robinson, my brother, Daniel Lee Robinson, and my grandfather, Walter Payne, who frequently cross the bridge between the worlds to guide me from above. I also dedicate this book to my sister, Marie Wolny, and my husband, Dennis Patnode, for the loving ways they have tended the hearth while I have been out walking the edges.

Contents

ACKNOWLEDGMENTS

This book has taken several years to turn from just an idea into this actual material object that you hold in your hands. So many people have contributed to this book in so many ways. I am grateful beyond measure.

First of all, I want to thank Tom Brown, who gave me the opportunity to write an essay for *Business: The Ultimate Resource*. He encouraged me to write about something that was new and leading edge for me, something that I was passionate about. So I wrote about Edgewalkers. Then he asked me to do a series of columns for Amazon.com and suggested that I profile people who were Edgewalkers. He said, "You know, you might even turn it into a book!" You were right. Tom, thank you for providing those opportunities and for planting the seeds.

Over the years, I interviewed about 50 people for this book. I wasn't able to include all the interview material, but I was touched by each person and always learned something new. I am grateful to all of you for your time, your openness, and your inspiration. You are the pioneers in the new consciousness that is unfolding in organizations and in the world.

Ron Pevny invited me to co-facilitate a five-day leadership retreat that would incorporate spirituality, native American practices, and leading-edge business concepts. We spent two years creating our program and attracted a diverse and powerful group of Edgewalkers to join us in Sedona, Arizona, in 2005. Ron, thank you for your persistence, for the loving way you handled so many details, and for teaching me about the power of vision quests to help people learn how to walk between the worlds.

Ben Forbes learned about my work when we were together at an Organizational Behavior Teaching Conference and asked me to run a workshop for business people in the Cleveland community. That was such a great success that he has continued to suggest other opportunities to offer similar workshops in other venues. Ben, thank you for seeing the power of this work and for championing it among people you know. And thank you for sharing so openly your own Edgewalker journey with me.

I also want to acknowledge the Leadership Dialogue Group members Kay Wild, Dede Taylor, Sharron Emmons, Lynn Quinn, Deborah Cox, John Anderson, Tom Aageson, and my co-leader, David Shultz. This group was proud to call itself the Edgewalker Group before any of us had any ideas about what an Edgewalker might be.

Writing can be a lonely and arduous task, but two people helped to make the writing process fun, creative, and interesting. Roger Husbands first suggested the idea of a "Writing Day" when I was working on the book *Creating Enlightened Organizations*. Both of us were having a hard time keeping our self-imposed commitments to write, so Roger suggested that we get together one day a month, turn off the phones, ignore email, and just write. We would each go to separate parts of the living room and work individually for two hours. Then we would take a break, talk about our work, give each other feedback, and go back to writing again. We did this on a regular basis until Roger moved to California. Roger, thank you for your friendship and for helping me learn how to be disciplined about writing.

Paul Kwiecinski, my coach, helped me pick up where Roger left off. For about two years, we have had writing appointments by phone every week or two. Paul has been supporting and encouraging me from the time I first started to write the book proposal until the completion of this book. More than anyone, he knows the day-to-day victories and setbacks I have had in all the processes it takes to complete a book and get it published. Paul, you made it fun, you kept my feet to the fire, and you always knew the right things to say or ask when I got stuck. So hurry up and get your book on the Corporate Blues done so we can go on speaking tours together. Then you can teach me how to play blues guitar. I might have some spare time now!

I am grateful to my dear friends Deborah Cox, who continually sent me Reiki healing energy; Dale Finn, who kept me connected to the outside world when I was burrowed in my library; and Cheryl Tromley, who has been there through thick and thin every since we were graduate students at Yale.

I also want to acknowledge my friends and colleagues from the Solomon Group—Charles (Chuck) Manz, Karen Manz, and Bob Marx. We have such a good time writing and collaborating together and finding the deeper spiritual meaning in teaching and working with students. Chuck, I am especially grateful for the way you encouraged me to get my book proposals out, for the guidance and encouragement you have given me, and for all your mentoring around the publication process.

Nick Philipson is my editor at Greenwood/Praeger, and you couldn't ask for a smarter, more delightful person to work with. Nick, thank you for being a champion of this book at Greenwood/Praeger and for helping me to see that the concept of Edgewalkers was more encompassing than I originally thought. I am grateful for all your guidance and for your encouragement to make this book practical and relevant.

This book was written with a tremendous amount of guidance from the spiritual world. I always felt divinely guided to find the right people to interview, the right books to read, and the words to say. If I have fallen short of communicating these ideas that have come from between the worlds, it is because of my own imperfections and limitations. I am grateful for all the inspiration I have been given.

Finally, I must lovingly acknowledge the two people who have been my Hearthtenders and who made my days a little lighter because of the way they picked up the load. My sister, Marie Wolny, is truly my soul sister. Marie, I could never express in words how much all you do means to me. You have helped me keep my dreams alive and have taken up day-to-day administrative tasks with such a grace and competence. My husband, Dennis Patnode, has selflessly supported me every single day of the process of writing this book. Dennis, I am so grateful for the way you took on more than your fair share of things so that I could write. I feel so loved by all your encouragement and all of your sacrifices. Thank you for understanding what a deep calling this book has been for me.

INTRODUCTION

One of my favorite movies is a movie from 1980 titled *Windwalker*. Trevor Howard plays the dying Cheyenne warrior Windwalker. In accordance with Native American tradition, when he dies, his body is placed on a stretcher up in a tree, and the scene fades to night. The next morning, you see the wind whipping through his deerskin coverings, and his body is shaken loose from the tree. The Great Spirit has awakened him for one more task before bringing him home. At first, Windwalker is confused, not knowing which world he is in. Finally, when he realizes that he is alive and in the material world, he shakes his fist at the sky and yells, "Grandfather, this is not funny!" He then sets out to accomplish the task that the Great Spirit sent him to do. That image of Windwalker going back and forth between the worlds stayed with me.

Many years later, in 1997, I was asked to join the board of High Tor Alliance, a nonprofit organization that focused on research on contemplative practices in the workplace. The board believed that it was important to practice what we preached, and so we committed to several different contemplative practices as a group. One of those practices was to begin our meetings with a verse from Rumi, the 13th-century Persian mystic:

The breeze at dawn has secrets to tell you, don't go back to sleep.
You must ask for what you really want, don't go back to sleep.

People are going back and forth across the doorsill
where the two worlds touch
The door is round and open, don't go back to sleep.

—Rumi

There it was again! An image of people going between the two worlds.

In January 2001, seven business leaders sat in my living room for an all-day workshop. This was the kickoff for a seven-month program called the Leadership Dialogue Group series, sponsored by High Tor Alliance. I and my co-facilitator, David Schultz, would be working with these leaders to help integrate inner values, concerns, and spiritual practices into their lives and work in a nonsectarian way. Our goal was to offer them an alternative to traditional bottom-line-driven business models, one that would support healthy and productive ways to live, work, and network with others.

All of the business leaders in our group were interested in making a difference in their organizations and in making a positive contribution to the world. I told them that I had read somewhere that people who are on the leading edge of social change often live on the edge of town. These people don't identify with the mainstream and often see themselves as on the margins of things. Thinking back on the movie *Windwalkers* and on the Rumi poem, I called these change leaders "Edgewalkers." The members of the Leadership Dialogue Group liked the term so much that they began calling themselves the Edgewalker Group.

About that time, Tom Brown, former editor-at-large of *Business Week*, asked me if I would like to be involved in doing some writing for a large international project called *Business: The Ultimate Resource.*[1] I agreed to write an essay and to do some editorial work on the career-development section of the book. Tom asked me what my leading-edge interests were and what I would like to write about. I told him that I am passionate about spirituality in the workplace, which has been the focus of my work since 1992. He said that someone else had been commissioned to write about spirituality in the workplace and asked whether I had any other ideas that were emerging for me. So I told him about the Edgewalker Group and some ideas that I had regarding who Edgewalkers are and why they are important now. Tom encouraged me to write an essay, which was titled "How to Walk on the Leading Edge without Falling Off the Cliff" (Neal, 2002). He also encouraged me to write a column for Amazon.com, called "On the Edge," that highlights people who are Edgewalkers.

Since writing those articles, I have spoken at numerous conferences and meetings about Edgewalkers and have been running workshops for people who consider themselves Edgewalkers. This book has emerged from all these experiences and from the countless dialogues with people who have a natural gift for being on the leading edge and who know how to walk in many worlds. They have been my teachers.

They have taught me that a new kind of human being is emerging on the planet and that this has major implications for business, governments, religion, education, and all of our social institutions. These Edgewalkers are people who walk between the worlds. They understand that there is more to the world than just the material, visible world. They walk between the visible and the invisible. They see themselves as Global Human Beings and often have had experiences of living in more than one culture. They are bridge builders who link different paradigms, cultures, and realities.

They tend not to follow a linear career path but to listen deeply to their calling and to go where their hearts tell them to go. It's not unusual to see them make radical career changes and for them to have periods of time when they are not working, during which they listen internally for their next calling. They are strongly intuitive and are good at seeing their own future, as well as sensing major trends that are unfolding.

This book describes the forces that have led to the emergence of Edgewalkers and describes how they are our hope for the future. It describes the qualities and skills of Edgewalkers and provides you an opportunity to assess whether or not you are an Edgewalker. You will learn how to discover Edgewalker qualities and develop Edgewalker skills. Being an Edgewalker is not easy. This book describes some of the costs, risks, and difficulties of being an Edgewalker and provides suggestions on how to walk the edge without going over the cliff.

Managers and organizations need to understand the implications of having Edgewalkers as employees and as customers. Traditional management theories of leadership, strategic planning, motivation, and teamwork don't work for people who walk between the worlds. And customers who are Edgewalkers are looking for different products and services than are sought by the mainstream, as well as a different kind of relationship with the company. More and more Edgewalkers are emerging in organizations, and many of them feel like they don't fit in. Organizations and societies often don't know how to appreciate their visionary gifts.

This book describes groups of people in organizations, such as Edgewalkers, Placeholders, and Flamekeepers, who serve different functions in organizations and society, with suggestions on how to manage these differences. We also look at how we can create Edgewalker organizations—organizations that have an uncanny knack for knowing and creating what's next and that have a gift for taking counterintuitive actions that end up being outlandish successes.

This book is designed to be useful to business leaders who are looking to harness the full potential of their organization. It will also be useful to anyone who wants to make a positive difference in the world.

There are certain people who just seem to sense what is about to emerge next and who intuitively know how to create the future before it unfolds. *Edgewalkers* profiles these people and distills their wisdom in a way that can be used by people who want to reach their fullest leadership potential.

We conclude with a look at what the world might look like if organizations and institutions begin to value and develop the Edgewalkers more than we do now. I have been interviewing people who are Edgewalkers since the mid-1990s and have been writing and speaking about them since then. I always get a very strong response from people when I describe Edgewalkers and their role in the world. Many people have been relieved to have an understanding of why they feel pulled in the directions that are calling them, why they feel like they never quite fit in, and why they have such a sense of loneliness, while paradoxically feeling a great sense of joy at being a part of a global community. My hope is that if you are an Edgewalker who is reading this book, you will find that the world has a great need for the unique gifts you have to offer and that this book will enhance your ability to make a difference in the world.

Chapter One

WHY NOW? WHY EDGEWALKERS?

The complexity of the business world today is astounding. Nothing is predictable anymore. The rules of the game are changing. Just when you think you have figured out how to have a competitive advantage, a competitor develops a new technology. Just when you think you have found the right motivation tool, the values in your workforce seem to shift. Just when you think you have found the right geographic area for the expansion of your internationalization efforts, political turmoil erupts.

Yet, some people seem to have an uncanny knack for knowing what's going to happen before it unfolds. They are able to create new rules to the game instead of following the rules that everyone else follows. They are able to plan a strategy that seems absurd to most people at first and is later called "brilliant" when they are successful. They are a part of an unusual breed of leaders called "Edgewalkers."

WHAT IS AN EDGEWALKER?

An Edgewalker is someone who walks between the worlds[1]. In ancient cultures, each tribe or village had a shaman or medicine man. This was the person who walked into the invisible world to get information, guidance, and healing for members of the tribe. This was one of the most important roles in the village. Without a shaman, the tribe would be at the mercy of the unseen gods and spirits, the vagaries of the cosmos.

It took years of training under an elder to become a shaman and often required great personal risk. The shaman had to face his or her own shadow and become pure and selfless in order to serve the tribe. After a long apprenticeship and many trials, the shaman would be given amazing powers to see into the future, to speak with the spirits so that the tribe would know where the mammoth were, and to get guidance from the invisible world.[2]

Being able to walk between the two worlds was necessary for survival.

MANY WORLDS

The skill of walking between the worlds has not died out, and is probably even more relevant today. The organizations that will thrive in the 21st century are organizations that embrace and nurture Edgewalkers. These unusual leaders have learned to walk in many different worlds without getting completely caught up in any one of them. They are the bridge builders who link different paradigms, cultural boundaries, and worldviews.[3]

The leaders who walk on the edge are leaders who can appreciate and work in different cultures. These may be international cultures (such as Mexico or Thailand), functional cultures (such as engineering or marketing), or values cultures (such as humanistic or bottom-line-driven). Edgewalkers can have a foot in both worlds and walk the fine line between them. They have a unique set of valuable skills that often goes unrecognized or is undervalued in organizations.

Several years ago I gave a workshop on Edgewalkers at the Center for Creative Leadership. I asked participants to tell me what they thought the word "Edgewalkers" meant. Here are some of their free associations:

- Build bridges between old and new.
- Have a feeling for the soft edges.
- Work in the boundaries.
- Are intuitive.
- Exist at the edge of heaven and earth.
- Are shapeshifters.
- Are awake and aware—the first characteristic of an Edgewalker.
- Are able to interpret—to help others by using language that bridges two worlds.
- Hold the tension of opposites.
- Are lonely people (ring bearers in *The Lord of the Rings*).

- Feel loneliness—are in danger of disappearing forever. If someone realizes you are an Edgewalker, you can't work there anymore.
- Are visionary and meet people where they are; can see holistically; can even see the shadows in self and in an organization. Have an eye on the future.

In Chapter 3, I will describe the characteristics of an Edgewalker in more detail, but I have been amazed that these same kinds of thoughts and images of Edgewalkers come up whenever I do this kind of a workshop.

THE TRENDS

Why are we seeing Edgewalkers emerge now? What role do they play in our organizations and in our world? There have always been Edgewalkers in the world, but we are seeing an increasing number of people who are walking the fine line between different worlds. Some of the major factors that have lead to this increase are:

1. Globalization: The increase in cross-cultural business and relationships.
2. Technology: The development of high-tech communications that help people be more interconnected.
3. Less Predictability: The increasing unpredictability of the world by traditional linear and rational methods.
4. Time Poverty: The increasing pace of the world.
5. Spirituality in the Workplace: The dramatic international increase in interest in anything having to do with spirituality and higher levels of consciousness and the incorporation of spiritual values in the workplace.

Let's explore each of these trends in a little more detail.

Globalization

I have been teaching in business schools and consulting to organizations for more than 25 years. In that time, I have seen a dramatic increase in the number of international students in my classes and in the number of international employees at my consulting clients' facilities. As the cost of airfare has decreased and the economic well-being of many other countries has improved, international travel has become fairly common. People are seeing more of the world, and sometimes they like what they see in other places, and they stay. Or they find ways to go back and forth between their home country and their adopted country.

More and more corporations are investing globally and increasing business activities outside their borders in order to remain competitive. For example, U.S. engineers can work on a project during the day and then send their plans electronically to locations overseas to be worked on while they sleep.[4]

In only 10% of the 191 nations are people ethnically or racially homogenous. Never before in history have so many inhabitants traveled beyond their homelands, either to travel or work abroad, or to flee as refugees. In host countries, the social fabric is being reconfigured and strained by massive waves of immigrants, whether legal or illegal.[5]

I first became aware of the importance of this phenomenon and its implications for the leaders of the future in a conversation with Mari Ishihara. Mari is a former M.B.A. student of mine from Japan who has become a close friend. Mari loves the United States, and after graduation she began a very successful career in international banking in New York City. After several years, her company, a Japanese bank, wanted her to go back to Tokyo to work for a couple of years. She really didn't want to go, but with aging parents and a brother who had cancer, she felt it was important to be back in Japan near them.

Mari found that her U.S. education and her New York City experience were very valuable to her as she worked with the bank's international clients. She had learned how to understand and adapt to different cultures. And she was highly successful. She made enough money to put two of her brothers through school in the United States and to buy several pieces of property. However, she wasn't happy.

She didn't fit in anywhere anymore.

She was too Americanized to be comfortable in the Japanese business environment (one that does not see women as equals), and too Japanese to completely fit into the American business environment (one that does not value relationships as more important than making money). International clients loved her, but something inside her was dying.

Mari, like many Edgewalkers who don't fit in, finally decided to start her own business. She is now CEO of Feng Shui Space and loves being a feng shui consultant to organizations. Feng shui is an ancient art of placement that operates on principles of getting energy, or "chi," to flow and to be balanced. Mari grew up with the spiritual guidance of her grandmother, who was a Shinto priest. Mari's mother and father were both entrepreneurs. Her new work is a way for her to build a bridge between her Japanese heritage and her knowledge of American business.

Michael Stephen, retired chairman of Aetna International, was involved in forming joint ventures in Argentina, Brazil, Peru, Indonesia, and China. At the same time, he was responsible for nurturing existing joint ventures in Malaysia, Hong Kong, Taiwan, Chile, Mexico, New Zealand, and Canada. He found that sharing spirituality with the many different people he met was the way he could build a "universal business language." He writes in his book, *Spirituality in Business:*

> With each person I found a common ground, sometimes where I least expected one. Our shared belief system transcended politics or religion or profit. Time and again I saw a spiritual underpinning at work, which led my company and me to greater achievements. More importantly, it brought to me a more complete understanding of how all of us are connected.[6]

As a result of international travel, international business, and a growing appreciation of diversity, it is becoming more and more common for people of very different cultural backgrounds to marry and raise children. My oldest son met his Chinese wife while working at Merrill Lynch, in New York City. Their son is an Edgewalker of the future. There are many difficulties and exciting challenges that children of cross-cultural marriages face.

> Race mixing, understood by some to contribute to the threat of mongrelization, is still seen as negative. *Half-breeds, mixed-bloods, metis,* historically have found themselves objects of scorn—as if having two parents who match each other ethnically is some kind of requirement for being whole. These genetic *Edgewalkers* often identify with one side of their heritage or another rather than claiming them both.[7]

At the same time, children of mixed marriages have the experience of living in two different worlds and naturally learn how to travel between the different worldviews. Out of necessity, they must create a unique and individualized identity that is not completely of one culture or the other. The skills and qualities that they learn growing up are very much the skills and qualities needed in business, education, religion, and all our major institutions as the world becomes more and more global in awareness.

Globalization has also raised our awareness of the negative impact that business practices and governmental policies can have, not just on the local area but for the whole planet. We are interconnected. As Lance Secretan, a well-known leadership guru, says, "We are one."[8] One of the most positive images of our interconnectedness was the New Year's Eve celebration in 2000, the start of the new millennium. Millions of people all over the planet sat in front of their televisions watching as the New Year's Eve celebrations unfolded around the world, hour by hour. The cameras would switch from celebrations in the streets of New York to celebrations in China, in Thailand, and in Venezuela. The whole human race was celebrating together. For that one 24-hour period, we were truly aware of our oneness.

People are increasingly concerned about the growing threat of human extinction (and extinction of other life forms) due to war, disease, environmental degradation, and abrupt climate change. Edgewalkers, because of their unique perspective and role in the world, tend to be concerned about larger issues and about the systemic and long-term impacts of business and political decisions and actions.

> The next frontier in our global perspective is personal and emotional, not geographic. It will take all of us stepping beyond current boundaries to affirm the enlightened values by which our world must go forward.[9]
>
> —*Nina Boyd Krebs*

Technology

Computers, the Internet, and cell phones have, over the past 10 years or so, dramatically changed the way large numbers of people communicate and interact. And they have contributed significantly to our ability to interact globally with relative ease.

Locke, Levine, Searls, and Weinberger[10] go so far as to say that the Internet has revolutionized business and democracy. Managers and political leaders are no longer the ones with all the information; it is available to anyone who has online access to the Web. Formal authority no longer holds the cachet it had in the past, because anyone at any level of an organization can have access to networks and important information from around the world. And anyone can create a network. You don't need formal permission from someone else to create a Web site or a listserve.

Virtual teams are ubiquitous, with members frequently interacting with others from different countries and in different time zones. The Internet and cell phones make connection relatively easy, as people are on the go. People who will be successful in this high-tech world are the ones who understand the technology but are also able to build relationships across cultures, who are able to communicate across different functions,[11] and who are able to inspire others to commit energy to something that will make a positive difference in the world.[12]

The new technologies, especially the Internet, provide a way for Edgewalkers to have a foot in the mainstream while also being able to maintain their interest in what's on the leading edge. Information is available to them, and it is relatively easy to create a forum and a way to connect with other people who might share their ideas and interests. With the new technology, Edgewalkers are less likely to be marginalized.

Less Predictability

The world is getting less and less predictable by traditional linear and rational methods. I first became aware of this when I went to a National Training Labs (NTL) course in the 1980s and spoke to a colleague who was attending a different course that week on nonlinear approaches to strategic planning. He told me that the course leaders believed that traditional strategic planning had reached its limits because there is so much discontinuous change in the world. You can no longer predict the future from the past (if we ever could!). Thus the saying, "If you want to make God laugh, tell Him your plans."

No one could predict the fall of the Berlin Wall or the sudden collapse of communism. And we certainly weren't ready for the terrorist attacks of September 11 and the significant impact that this event had on the economy, on our sense of interconnectedness in the world, and on our questions around the meaning of work and the power of capitalism.

We are learning that the old linear models of planning don't work in a world that is changing rapidly and often in turbulent ways. Mathematicians, scientists, logistics managers, forecasters, and others are finding that nonlinear models are more helpful in guiding us in preparing for an uncertain future. Jaworkski notes in his book, *Synchronicity,* that he was fortunate to work with scenario planning at

Royal Dutch Shell as a way of helping the organization prepare for the unpredictable. He writes:

> I realized that small changes at just the right place can have a system wide impact because these changes share the unbroken wholeness that unites the entire system. A seemingly insignificant act in one part of the whole creates nonlocal results that emerge far away. Unseen connections create effects at a distance—"quantum leaps" in places quite surprising to us. This model of change comported with my daily experience much more so than the traditional model of incremental change.[13]

Time Poverty

Many of these forces combine to have many of us feeling that we have more to accomplish in less time than ever. Technology is partly to blame. Our increased ability to communicate with each other anytime, anywhere, is both a blessing and a curse. We need to answer emails, answer phone calls, check our cell phones, our Blackberries, and our Dick Tracy wristwatches. We feel like we are on call 24/7, or, as the Beatles so aptly put it, "eight days a week." Because of the Internet, world news channels, email, and other technology, we can communicate quickly with others all over the world.

This barrage of information and communication means that we are always responding to input. Or we are taking advantage of our ability to reach larger numbers of people more quickly, which creates more responses, which creates the need for more action on our part. I have noticed that the harder I work to answer emails, the more replies I generate, and thus the more emails I need to answer.

Being fast and being first gives you the competitive edge. But it can also be exhausting.

It used to be that you couldn't make completely informed decisions because you didn't have access to all the information available. While to some extent that is still true, it is now becoming equally difficult to make informed decisions because there is just too much information out there and not enough time to make sense of it all.

For that reason, there is a strong demand in organizations for people who have the ability to quickly scan immense amounts of information and to make sense of it in a way that can inform business decisions. Dave Duffield, founder of PeopleSoft, is well known for his ability to quickly pull diverse threads of information together to guide the strategic direction of his organization. PeopleSoft was acquired by Oracle in 2005, and Duffield quickly moved on to form a new company, utilizing his early strategy of creating software that emphasizes ease of use, as well as extraordinary customer service. He seems to have an intuitive sense of what the market needs and a gift for when to get in and when to get out. Jeff Carr was one of PeopleSoft's first 50 employees and rose to the presidency of a PeopleSoft division. "Dave Duffield was a visionary who could look around corners and see trends before anyone else," Carr says. "He bet the company on client/server and Windows at a time when others still saw it as risky technology."[14]

PeopleSoft's employees are in great demand because of the innovative and responsive culture that was created. As a result, Oracle has its hands full with competitive pressures. PeopleSoft was much more than just a technology firm with good marketing. "It was a company built in large measure on customer service, hitting the market at the right time and utilizing the risk-taking entrepreneurial spirit of Duffield and people he brought into the company."[15]

Edgewalkers like Duffield rely on intuition, right-brain thinking, and a gut-level sense of what's emerging in their markets. At the same time, there is a core commitment to deep values of serving people and creating products that make their lives and work better.

One of the major complaints in the workplace these days is that there is not enough time to do everything. Dr. Stefan Rechtschaffen tells a story of a man who showed up in his emergency room suffering from an apparent heart attack. Two days later, when Dr. Rechtschaffen returned to check on him, he discovered that the man had checked himself out against doctor's orders. Ten days later, he was back in the hospital with a second heart attack. When asked why he had checked out before, he responded, "I don't have the time to be laid up in a hospital. I have so many important things to do."[16] Rechstschaffen goes on to say, "Happy people seem to live less frenetically. They have more time in their lives. They are more in the moment. This happiness is available to all of us."[17] Edgewalkers have learned the ability to do what Rechtschaffen calls "time shifting," an ability to become aware of the present and to sense the particular rhythm and flow of the present moment.

Richard Barrett is a friend of mine and a wonderful role model. He was the vice president of logistics for World Bank and the founder of the Spiritual Unfoldment Society at the World Bank.[18] He is now CEO of the Values Centre and helps corporations to enhance corporate consciousness. Recently, at a conference, he shared with me how well things were going in his life and work. He described his daily practice of sitting on the side of a hill on his property in North Carolina, just sitting with his dog and gazing at the countryside—not thinking, not doing, just sitting and enjoying the view. This is a man who has created an international network of consultants and who speaks at conferences all over the world. He's incredibly successful, and, for him, one of the marks of success is being able to sit for an hour each day in the sun with his dog. He is an excellent example of an Edgewalker who has the gift of "time shifting."

Spirituality in the Workplace

Daniel Pink, in his book, *A Whole New Mind,* says that the abundance in American society and other industrialized countries "has brought beautiful things into our lives, but that bevy of material goods has not necessarily made us much happier." He adds:

> The paradox of prosperity is that while living standards have risen steadily decade after decade, personal, family, and life satisfaction haven't budged. That's why more people— liberated by prosperity but not fulfilled by it—are resolving the paradox by searching for meaning. As Columbia University's Andrew Delbanco puts it, " 'The most striking feature of contemporary culture is the unslaked craving for transcendence.' "[19]

Ray and Anderson estimate that 26 percent of the U.S. and European populations have strong values related to spirituality, personal development, organizational transformation, ecology, and social justice. That's more than 50 million adults in America and 86 million adults in Europe! Their research shows that this is the fastest growing and most influential demographic group.[20]

But the strong interest in spirituality and consciousness in the United States began in the late 1960s and early 1970s, with the advent of the Beatles. The turning point came when the George Harrison influenced the Beatles to go to India to spend time with the Maharishi Mahesh Yogi, which had a major impact on their lives and their music. Because of their popularity, spiritual seeking and studying the mystical traditions became the "in" thing to do. Over time, thousands of people learned that practices such as meditation, contemplative prayer, yoga, and t'ai chi had significant positive effects on their well-being and effectiveness.[21]

There have been five major trends that have led to an increased interest in integrating spirituality and work: (1) the changing psychological contract for work; (2) changing demographics and the aging of the workforce; (3) the Millennium Effect; (4) increased interest in self-help groups and personal growth; (5) the impact of the attacks on September 11, 2001, and terrorism.[22]

The first trend, the changing psychological contract, is a result of the mergers, acquisitions, and resultant downsizing in the late 1980s and throughout the 1990s. It used to be that the psychological contract with an organization was that if you performed reasonably well and stayed out of trouble, you would have a job for life. There is now a new employee contract. This contract states that, to paraphrase Jack Welch, former CEO of General Electric, "we can't guarantee you a job for life, but we will try to ensure that you are marketable." The result of this is that people can no longer depend on the organization to provide stability and security. In an evolutionary sense, this means that instead of looking externally for something to provide meaning, people are beginning to look within. In some cases, this means that people are examining their inner lives, their core values, and their purpose in life and finding that meaning comes from within, from their spirituality.[23]

The second major trend is demographic. In the United States and many other Western countries, baby boomers—who make up the largest age segment of the population—are all reaching middle age at the same time. So, in a sense, it is as if these societies are all having a midlife crisis. Middle age is a time when many people look back at where their lives have come from and look forward to the kind of life they want to live in the future. It is a time of self-assessment and can be a time of recommitment to deeper values.

For this reason, spirituality has become a mainstream interest, as evidenced by the number of best-selling books on the topic as well as its emergence as the theme of many popular movies and television shows. All of this has a spillover effect into the workplace, as people who are interested in spirituality look at ways that they can apply their principles and practices in all parts of their lives, including work.

The turning of the millennium drove the third trend toward an interest in spirituality. As human beings, we tend to set aside certain holidays, anniversaries, and other special times as opportunities for contemplation on who we have become and what we have done poorly that we would like to change. New Year's is traditionally a time in the secular Western culture for New Year's resolutions and for looking back at the past year and making predictions about the future. The recent millennium celebration multiplied that "New Year's Effect" and raised it to a global level of consciousness. As the human race, we spent time looking back at our history and evaluating how far we've come. We also spent time thinking about this new millennium and what we would like to see for ourselves on this planet. These are basically spiritual questions, questions that get at the heart and the meaning of life.

The fourth trend is the increasing interest in personal growth and self-help groups. One example of this is the dramatic growth in programs like Alcoholics Anonymous. Twelve-step programs offer a very practical, nonreligious, everyday kind of spirituality. Some magazines, such as *Utne Reader,* encouraged the creation of local salons where people could discuss personal growth in the midst of a dramatically changing world. *Fast Company,* a very popular and hip U.S. business magazine, supports the development of "Fast Company Cells."

The fifth trend is a result of September 11, 2001, and other terrorist attacks around the world. On the tragic day of September 11, thousands of people kissed their loved ones goodbye and went to work, never to return. In the midst of the terror and the chaos, those with phones called their families to tell them they loved them. In the aftermath, those who lived held each other and cried, and prayed, and made commitments to place love over work. Many quit their jobs and moved or went into business for themselves to complete unfulfilled dreams. People learned that life can be short and fragile and that it's not worth it to sell your soul for the almighty dollar (or euro). A Time/CNN poll offers the following statistics:

- 81% of respondents think that the terrorist attacks of September 11 will impact their lives in the future.
- 57% have thought more about the spiritual part of their lives since the attacks.
- 55% have experienced a greater focus or purpose in life since the attacks.[24]

Tragedy and difficult events tend to lead us to ask deeper questions, what I would call the three key spiritual questions:

- Who am I, and what are my deepest values? What do I really care about?
- What is my purpose in life? Why am I here, and what am I meant to do?
- If I am true to myself, what should I be doing next?

Many of the trends we have discussed led people to ask these spiritual questions of themselves and to seek answers for all the different parts of their lives—for their relationships, their families, their health, their community, and their work.

 It should be noted that this increasing interest in spirituality in the workplace is an international phenomenon, but it is focused in industrialized countries, such as the United States, Canada, Mexico, Norway, the United Kingdom, Sweden, Australia, and New Zealand. There have been some activities in developing countries such as India, the Philippines, and Brazil, but they are not yet widespread. The reason for this is that in industrialized countries, we have had a materialistic and scientific philosophy that has split off and often denied the spiritual side of life. We are only now trying to reintegrate the two. However, in countries that are less industrialized, and in cultures such as the African American, Latin American, and Native American cultures, spirituality is already more a part of everyday life.

Health care is leading the way on the practical integration of spiritual values and practices in the workplace. In 2001, John Renesch and I created the International Spirit at Work Award, formerly called the Willis Harman Spirit at Work Award. More than one-third of the organizations that have received this award have been large health care systems. The award was created to honor Willis Harman's vision of business as the primary institution for helping to bring about a positive and healthy "Global Mind Change."[25] The reason health care is so far in the forefront of integrating spiritual values is the life-and-death nature of the work done in these organizations.

The National Institutes of Health was funded in 1991 to create the National Center for Complementary and Alternative Medicine. It has done significant research on the power of prayer and other spiritual intervention in the healing process.[26] The mainstream public has increasingly been turning to alternative healing methods and practices such as reiki, acupuncture, prayer, meditation, t'ai chi, and yoga, and it is becoming more and more common to see these practices incorporated in health care organizations for patients and employees alike.

Patricia Aburdene, author of several books on megatrends, states in her latest book, *Megatrends 2010: The Rise of Conscious Capitalism,* that "the quest for spirituality is the greatest megatrend of our era."[27] Her book describes seven megatrends:

1. The power of spirituality.
2. The dawn of conscious capitalism.

3. The move toward leading from the middle.
4. Spirituality in business.
5. The values-driven consumer.
6. The wave of conscious solutions.
7. The socially responsible investment boom.[28]

Edgewalkers are the people who are leading these megatrends. The leaders you will read about in this book all have a deep commitment to their own spiritual development and to living by spiritual values. Spirituality is the primary characteristic that gives Edgewalkers their "edge."

MAY YOU LIVE IN INTERESTING TIMES

The Chinese have a curse: "May you live in interesting times." Well, we may be cursed to live in these interesting and challenging and perhaps even dangerous times. But another way to look at it is that we may be blessed. Jerry Wennstrom, a rising New York artist who destroyed his work and gave away all his belongings, believes that the best way to live in today's complex world is to trust in the Divine, in something unseen that guides us on our journey. He says,

> To allow life to happen when we are engaged in a full and unexpected encounter with danger is to trust with our lives the magic, still place of safety that is always available. The conscious, perfect order of creation fully equips each encounter with everything we need to survive. To get a glimpse of this perfect order and let it work on our behalf, we must agree at a deep level to accept the possibility of death in every dangerous event. We must be willing to die at any time, exactly where and when death occurs.[29]

Edgewalkers know how to walk the line between that place where life is challenging, creative, and full of potential and the place where life is dangerous and there is the potential for failure and even death. This is not to say that Edgewalkers court death but to say that they are willing to "bet the farm" on things they believe in. And they are willing to let go of what doesn't work anymore.

Five trends in today's world have led to the increasing need for Edgewalkers in our organizations: (1) the increase in globalization, (2) the ubiquitous use of technology, (3) the unpredictability of the world events and of business trends, (4) the speed at which we live, and (5) the hunger for spiritual purpose and meaning and the rise of spirituality in the workplace. These trends have all contributed to workplaces that can be described as uncertain, chaotic, and difficult. And they have contributed to the emergence of a new kind of leader.

Edgewalkers are the leaders of the future. They are the corporate shamans who walk into the invisible world and bring back wisdom and guidance for their organizations. It is not an easy role to play, but it is one that can make people feel fully alive and one that is essential to the success of our organizations.

Chapter Two

WHO ARE THE EDGEWALKERS?

Out on the edge, out on the line
That's where I spend most of my time
Seachin' for something before the fear returns
Found that I had a lot to learn
I'm on the borderline, borderline[1]

—Lars Bogucki
"Borderline," June 14, 1989

When I was eight years old, my family moved from California to Hawaii, which was a dream come true for my father. And it was probably my first experience with being an Edgewalker. We moved to a small village called Waimanalo that was predominantly Hawaiian, but there were also a number of families who were Japanese, Chinese, Portuguese, and Filipino. No one race was a majority.

In my school, I was the only child with blue eyes. Hawaii is a friendly place, so the other kids thought my eye color more a curiosity than anything else. But still, I wanted to fit in. So I learned to speak "pidgin English," a polyglot language based on English and filled with words from all the different peoples who have settled in Hawaii. I toughened up my feet so I could walk barefoot on the tiny ironwood pinecones on the path to the beach. And I learned to open a coconut with my bare hands and to drink the sweet coconut milk. I learned to do the hula, play the ukulele, and sing songs in Hawaiian. Over time I did fit in, sort of, but I always knew that I was different. The word for people of Caucasian descent in Hawaiian is "haole." Its everyday meaning refers to a person with white skin, but the literal meaning of the word is "foreigner." I learned to function in the Hawaiian culture, but I would always be a foreigner.

RESEARCH ON EDGEWALKERS

Edgewalkers always feel like foreigners, no matter how much they seem to fit in. For the past several years, I have been interviewing and studying people who are Edgewalkers. My primary focus has been on people in leadership positions, because of their ability to have a powerful impact on organizations. Something they all share in common is an experience like the one I have described, where they were taken out of an environment that was comfortable and familiar and had to adapt to a very different environment. This chapter profiles several of the Edge-walkers I interviewed and summarizes the "Edgewalker Qualities of Being" and the "Edgewalker Stages of Development" that are common to most Edgewalkers.

I began each open-ended interview with a definition of an Edgewalker as "someone who walks between the worlds." I told each participant that I believe that a new type of leader is needed in the world today—someone who is effective by all the traditional measures but who also has the ability to sense the future, to build bridges between different paradigms, and to create what has never been created before. I emphasized the importance of the ability to walk between the visible and the invisible world and the importance of spirituality. Each interview lasted approximately an hour and a half.

Some typical questions asked in the interviews were these:

1. Thinking back on your life, what are some early examples of when you have "lived in two (or more) different worlds at once"?
2. When do you think you first became an Edgewalker, and how did that happen?
3. What attracts you to living in two (or more) different worlds?
4. What is difficult about living in two (or more) different worlds?
5. What personal qualities help you to live in two (or more) different worlds?
6. What skills have you developed as a result of living in different worlds?
7. What gifts or benefits have you received from living in different worlds?

(A full list of interview questions is presented in Appendix A.)

As the research unfolded, I also became aware of people from the past who fit my description of an Edgewalker. Igor Sikorsky, inventor of the helicopter and founder of Sikorsky Aircraft, is one fascinating example. I'll talk more about him shortly, but first I'd like to review the history of the term "Edgewalker."

HISTORY OF THE TERM "EDGEWALKER"

When I first started talking about Edgewalkers, I thought I had invented the word. Rupert Sheldrake talks about the "Morphic Resonance Field"[2] and describes the way in which ideas and new discoveries emerge simultaneously in several different parts of the planet at almost the same time. So it is with the term "Edgewalker." As I described in the preface, I began using the term in 1997. A search for the term on Google in December 2005 unearthed an article titled "Being an Edge-Walker," written by Melissa Michaels in 1992. The search also revealed that an artist named Tom White created a beautiful bronze sculpture of a Native American he named "Edgewalker" in 1994; in addition, a movie made about the life of an artist interested in Mayan art titled "Edgewalker: A Conversation with Linda Schele" was produced in 1998. An album by a German band called "Edgewalker" was released in 2005. And there were multiple references to an online game called "Edgewalkers."

A search on Amazon.com resulted in a link to a book by Nina Boyd Krebs, published in 1999 and titled *Edgewalkers: Defusing Cultural Boundaries on the New Global Frontier*. This book focuses primarily on the experience of children who come from bicultural or multicultural backgrounds and on the struggles that they face in finding their own identity in a mainstream world. Many of the findings of Krebs's research are similar to the findings of my own research, even though she focused more on multicultural issues and my research has focused on leadership, spirituality, and organizational transformation.

In 2002, I met a woman named Cynthia Kemper at a conference. She had created an organization called Edgewalker International and wrote a monthly newsletter called "Edgewalkers Insight." The emphasis of her work seemed to mostly be on innovation, creativity, and new ideas in business and politics, but she also recognized the importance of spirituality in Edgewalking.

Like many ideas whose time has come, the concept of Edgewalkers has emerged in art, music, literature, business, and even the online game world. No one owns it, but many people seem to resonate with it.

AN EDGEWALKER FROM THE PAST

Edgewalkers, like the shamans of old, have always been in our midst, and there is much that we can learn from them in today's complex world. We have needed them to "go where no man has gone before" and to break new ground and inspire us. As mentioned earlier, Igor Sikorsky is a quintessential example of an Edgewalker.

Igor I. Sikorsky: Mystical Designer

Money Lost—Nothing Lost; Health Lost—Little Lost; Spirit Lost—Everything Lost
Igor Sikorsky

Perhaps it was because he came from a long line of priests in the Russian Orthodox Church. Perhaps it was because his father, Ivan Sikorsky, was the first to break with family tradition and became a psychology professor. Or perhaps it was his ability to listen to his own inner intuitive urgings and to passionately follow his calling. But Igor Sikorsky, inventor of the helicopter and founder of Sikorsky Aircraft, was an Edgewalker before his time. He learned early on to walk between two worlds, which he called the Material Universe and the Heavenly Universe. He learned how to navigate the visible and invisible realities. As a result, he was a highly successful businessman and leader who was loved by those who worked for him.

I learned about Igor Sikorsky when I taught an Organizational Development M.B.A. course to 14 Sikorsky employees. None of the young engineers and managers had ever met Mr. Sikorsky. He had died more than 30 years earlier, at the age of 83. Yet, when they spoke of him, their voices were filled with awe, and a few had eyes that glistened with tears. You could feel a deep sense of love and respect for the man who had founded the company they worked for. One student wrote, "I was not fortunate enough to have meet Mr. Sikorsky, but the old timers I've met that knew him speak of him with the highest of esteem. He was a gentleman in the truest sense of the word. His vision was that the helicopter to be used for humanitarian efforts. He'd be proud to see his dream as he envisioned it."

In all my years of working with organizations, I have never again come across this intensity of feeling for an organizational founder that people had never met.

What was it about him that engendered this sense of awe? Sergei Sikorsky, his oldest son, says that Igor was a deeply religious person, but in no way did he try to sell anyone on his beliefs.[3] He quotes his father as saying, "There is a great deal of wisdom in all the great religions in the world." Igor believed that it was a sign of immaturity to say "my religion is the only religion." Anne Morrow Lindbergh said, "The thing that's remarkable about Igor is the great precision in his thought and speech, combined with an extraordinary soaring beyond facts. He can soar out with the mystics and come right back to the practical, to daily life and people. He never excludes people. Sometimes the religious minded exclude people or force their beliefs on others. Igor never does."[4]

Sergei says, "My father had a deep humility as a scientist. When you realize what a tiny speck we are on the Earth, and what a tiny speck the Earth is in the

Universe, you have to realize that there is a very high statistical probability that there are other civilized cultures out there."[5] He explained that this awareness kept his father quite humble and always open to new possibilities.

Igor's father, Ivan, was a strong influence on him. Ivan demonstrated a thirst for knowledge at a very early age. Sergei says that Ivan, his grandfather, would walk three miles a day to school in Kiev, Russia, and then go to the library afterwards and make handwritten copies of the books that interested him. He began building his library this way as a child, and when he died, just before the Bolshevik revolution, he willed his personal library of more than 6,000 books to the Kiev Library. Ivan was friends with Freud and Jung and wrote more than 250 books on medicine and psychiatry, including a book titled *Soul of the Child.*

Igor's mother was the one who gave him a deep love of science. She was a doctor and home-schooled him in his early years, teaching him much about science. She was deeply interested in the work of Leonardo da Vinci and described his work on flying machines to young Igor, igniting his imagination.

Young Igor followed in his parents' footsteps with his love of knowledge. By the age of 12, he was very intellectually open. It was at this time that he read a book by Jules Verne titled *The Clipper of the Clouds,* published in 1887, about a flying machine with propellers on the top. As a child, he began to work with pieces of wood, rubber bands, and even whalebone stays that he would steal from his older sister's corset in order to make models of propellers and helicopters.

At the age of 19, he began working professionally in the field of aviation and tried to design a helicopter that would fly. All the early experts in aviation told him that what he was trying to do was theoretically impossible, but he never believed them and never gave up the dream. After two years of failure, he put his helicopter design ideas temporarily on hold and began designing very successful fixed-wing aircraft. He became fabulously wealthy and then lost it all in the Bolshevik revolution.

When I asked Sergei if there had ever been a spiritual crisis in his father's life, he replied that the revolution turned his father's life upside down. He had to leave his beloved Russia and his friends and lost all his wealth. He eventually ended up in the United States and, after years of struggle and starvation, founded Sikorsky Aircraft.

His faith, wisdom, and spiritual intuition kept him focused on his vision of building helicopters that would keep their pilots alive and would help in humanitarian efforts. There is still a bulletin board at Sikorsky Aircraft that is updated daily with the number of lives saved by Sikorsky helicopters. Each time there is a rescue or an evacuation, the number goes up, and all employees in the company are aware and proud of the good that these helicopters do.

Igor I. Sikorsky © Igor I. Sikorsky Historical Archives.
Used by permission.

He was called a "mystical designer" and was described as having "scientific intuition." Igor believed that the mind can travel through time into the future and bring back useful ideas. His hero, Jules Verne, certainly had done that, and it appears that Igor had the same ability.

Charles Lindbergh was one of his closest friends, and, when Igor died, Charles wrote a note of condolence to his widow, saying:

> When I start to write about Igor, it is hard to know where to begin for he was such a great man and his life covered such a broad expanse of the intellectual, material and spiritual worlds. I know of no man who so merged these worlds together or who could so move from one to the other to the benefit of all. His scientific designs gained from his spiritual awareness just as his spiritual awareness was enhanced by his scientific knowledge, and he understood as few men do the essential relationships involved.[6]

His son, Sergei, says, "Dad could look at an airplane on the ground and could visualize the flow of air around the airplane as well as if it were in a wind tunnel. He could describe whether it was a good airplane or a pilot's nightmare."[7]

One story about Igor's scientific intuition has to do with a small fighter aircraft he designed. In those days he was his own test pilot. The night before he was to fly it, he walked around the aircraft and had an uneasy feeling. Everything looked fine, but he had an intuition about the tail. He left on note on the plane, saying, "Test flight canceled." He provided drawings of how the tail should be redesigned. Two weeks later, the test flight was successful.

One year later, Igor was in France and went to an aircraft "graveyard" to see what he could learn from planes that had crashed. He saw one badly smashed French airplane that had a tail design just like the original one that he had rejected. When he asked what had happened, he was told that the pilot was killed on the first flight because of a flaw in the tail design that no one had foreseen. Was it just luck that Igor decided not to take that test flight a year before, or was there some kind of divine guidance that kept him alive?

As a leader, Igor is described as always polite and respectful. He never raised his voice, never got angry, even with his children. He knew most of the people in Sikorsky Aircraft by name. There are many stories of him walking around the shop floor and the engineering department and stopping to observe employees at work. He would ask people to describe their work and would sometimes make suggestions in the gentlest of ways.

Once, when a design engineer was working on a battery platform for aircraft to be used in Greenland, Igor visited with him and said, "I presume you've already made allowance for the fact that whoever works on this will be doing so in the Greenland winter, and of course will be wearing gloves. So of course you've designed a bigger access door so that the workmen won't have to work in bare hands in the freezing cold." The engineer hadn't thought of it, but the suggestion was given with such caring that he was eager to make the design changes.

Even though he passed away in 1972, Igor Sikorsky left a legacy and a spirit that are alive and well in the company, and he continues to inspire the people who work there. We can learn a great deal from his life, his vision, and his values.

Igor Sikorsky had many of the characteristics of an Edgewalker. He grew up in one country and later moved to other countries, having to adapt to new cultures. He had an unusual combination of interests, especially engineering and theology. He was intuitive and at the same time very scientific and precise. He was very detail oriented and also was a caring and warm leader. He had the ability to transcend polarities and to integrate seemingly opposite ways of being. He had a deep religious faith that he lived by and strong leadership skills. Most interesting, he had the ability to travel into the future to see what was emerging, and he knew how to use that information to make design decisions and business decisions. All of these gifts contributed to his success, and to the sense of respect and awe that he engenders in people who never even met him.

MEET THE EDGEWALKERS

In Chapter 1, you read about four Edgewalkers—Mari Ishihara, Michael Stephen, David Duffield, and Richard Barrett. This next section offers brief profiles of several more Edgewalkers from my interviews. These people come from a wide variety of different fields. However, they do share some common characteristics that will be described in depth in the following two chapters.

Tom Aageson is the former executive director of Aid to Artisans (ATA) and is now an independent museum consultant. When Tom reached his fiftieth birthday, he was a highly successful executive at the Mystic Seaport Museum Store in Connecticut. He and his family went on a week's retreat for his birthday while Tom contemplated the rest of his life. He realized from his process of journaling, prayer, contemplation, and time in nature that his mission was to do whatever he could to eradicate poverty in the world. That led him to a position as the executive director at Aid to Artisans, a group that helps artists and craftspeople in third-world countries to design and market products that respect their cultures and improve their economic situation. He left that post to become the executive director of the New Mexico Museum Foundation and continues his work with helping artists in third-world countries. He is particularly proud of the work he has done with the United Nations on these issues. Tom walks among the business world, the artist's world, and the world of social justice. Tom believes that his contemplative practices and his strong spiritual commitment to reducing poverty have helped him to find work that gives him great meaning and allows him to make his best contribution.

Bill Catucci is the CEO of Regulatory Data Corporation and former CEO of AT&T Canada. Bill has learned to walk between the worlds of bottom-line demands and humanistic management. When Bill first came to work for AT&T Canada, the company was losing a significant amount of money. His first act was to send a check for $75 to the home of every employee, saying that this wasn't much but that it was a token of appreciation for what the employees had already contributed to the company, that he looked forward to working with them to turn the company around, and that there would be more where that came from if they were successful. (A Placeholder would have figured out how to cut costs instead of spending "frivolously" on each employee.) The company was very successful, and people were rewarded well. He turned AT&T Canada from a company losing $1 million a day into a winner—and inspired his people as part of that process. Then he turned around Equifax, raising the value of the company by more than $3 billion during a time when the stock market was stagnant.

John Lumsden is the CEO of Metserve, in New Zealand. John is originally from Scotland and served as an executive in Canada for a number of years; he's truly learned how to walk in different cultural worlds. The first day of every professional meteorological training course for new Metserve employees begins with a Maori welcoming ceremony that focuses on Tawhiri-Matea, the God of the Winds. John holds regular "advances" (as opposed to retreats) for his management team, at which people spend

Mural of Tawhiri-Matea, the God of the Winds. Used by permission of The Meteorological Service of New Zealand Limited.

time reflecting on deeper questions of life and work. They aim to have a "lean and meaningful" organization—lean to be competitive, meaningful in the services it provides for the users as well as in the environment it fosters for the employees.

Darwin Gillett is executive director of the Institute for Human Economics, dedicated to helping business owners and corporate executives engage the full power of human talent and spirit. He is also co-director of the Business Breakthrough Institute and of Conscious Business Solutions, a program that helps healers in the wellness field and other professional practices launch, manage, and expand their practices, bringing spiritual light to the "business" side of their practices. As an M.B.A., a former Fortune 500 director of corporate planning, and a CEO of a small manufacturing company in the United States, Dar learned how to integrate the world of practical finance and economics with the world of spirituality and human values. After a powerful spiritual experience, he had a vision that companies and their leaders could achieve far greater success once they understood the connection between economics and human energy, including spiritual as well as intellectual energy—and he has been writing and speaking about this vision ever since.

Jennifer Cash O'Donnell was the director of organizational strategy for AT&T—Asia Pacific. She walks among the worlds of operations, organizational development, and spiritual values. She has helped AT&T achieve great business results through a focus on human relationships and team building, using the Team Spirit process developed by Barry Heermann. Her success at AT&T Solutions with this team-based program brought her several promotions and eventually took her to the position of director of the leadership team in the Asia Pacific division, where she was responsible for the professional and personal development of more than 1,300 people in 13 countries. She is now a full-time mother and a part-time leadership coach and consultant, and she is just beginning in the journey of partnership with four incredible partners—called Noble Purpose Partners— in an LLC dedicated to helping individuals seek out and reestablish their noble purpose in life, through Barry Heermann's latest book, *Noble Purpose: Igniting Extraordinary Passion in Life and Work.*[8] Jennifer has a strong spiritual life and has found that living in alignment with her deepest values has helped her to be much more effective in her consulting work with clients.

WHAT CAN WE LEARN FROM THESE EDGEWALKERS?

The common career wisdom is that a person should specialize in one field and really go into depth and become an expert. That makes you invaluable to the company and helps to create greater job security. The more irreplaceable you are, the better. Good leaders are thought of as the ones who fight for the most resources and power for their particular unit. The prevailing belief is that it's a highly competitive, dog-eat-dog world and that the only the strongest prevail.

But Edgewalkers show us that a new way of being is emerging in organizational life, one that offers a more positive view of reality. This view is based on a systems perspective that holds that we are interconnected and that what affects one can affect many. Edgewalkers believe that the greatest creativity comes from walking in different worlds and blending different paradigms, which is what creates your leading edge. And they have a deep commitment to expanding their own consciousness to a point where they become more and more committed to the greater good.

Chapter Three

The Edgewalker Qualities of Being

I would rather be ashes than dust! I would rather that my spark should burn out in a brilliant blaze than it should be stifled by dry rot. I would rather be a superb meteor, every atom of me in magnificent glow, than a sleepy and permanent planet. The proper function of man is to live, not to exist. I shall not waste my days in trying to prolong them. I shall use my time.

—Jack London

All of us have some of the characteristics an Edgewalker, but not all of us are Edgewalkers, and thank God for that! Can you imagine a world where everyone was eagerly pursuing the next, new thing, where no one was ever satisfied with the status quo, and where each person was hungry for whatever it is that is just over the horizon? The world needs these kinds of people, but it also needs people who can help to maintain systems that are functional and who have some level of contentment and appreciation for the way things are on a day-to-day basis.

However, in organizations, we tend to have far too many people who are uncomfortable with change and who are not utilizing their full abilities and energy. While we don't need organizations that are completely filled with Edgewalkers, we need more Edgewalkers than we usually have if our people and our organizations are going to reach their full potential.

Are you an Edgewalker? Take this simple quiz to see. And if you are not an Edgewalker, take heart. Chapter 6 will describe two other effective organizational roles—Hearth Tenders and Flamekeepers—and the importance of their contributions to organizational effectiveness. This chapter describes the five Edgewalker "Qualities of Being."

But, first, I invite you to take this short Edgewalker Quiz to get a sense of how much of an Edgewalker you might be.

EDGEWALKER QUIZ

Check the statements that you agree with. If you agree with 12 or more, you are probably an Edgewalker—and a higher score increases the odds.

1. I have a strong spiritual life.
2. I frequently feel different from most people.
3. I seem to have an ability to sense coming trends before they emerge.
4. I have an unusual combination of interests and passions
5. I have had mystical or spiritual experiences that have provided guidance in my everyday life and/or work.
6. I speak more than one language or have deep familiarity with more than one culture.
7. I have made, or am contemplating, a major career shift that no one would have predicted.
8. I often find myself being a bridge or "translator" for people from very different backgrounds.
9. I have this feeling that I was called to do something very special and important in the world.
10. I find myself attracted to and wanting to learn from people who are very different from me.
11. I am strongly aware of the problems of the whole planet (global warming, destruction of rain forests, overpopulation, exploitation of people in poorer countries) and want to see some more action on them.
12. People often see me as a leader, even though I am different from most of the people who have been leaders in that organization.
13. I have the ability to listen beyond the words that are spoken.
14. I consciously tune into something higher than myself for guidance and inspiration.
15. It is extremely important to me that my work be aligned with my deepest values.
16. I have artistic abilities or unusual gifts that I combine with down-to-earth practical skills.
17. I tend to break the rules if I think it is for a higher purpose.

18. People often see me as a risk-taker, but the things I do don't seem risky to me. Somehow I just know they will work out.
19. I have a strong sense of adventure.
20. I find myself exploring new ideas and wondering about what the next new thing is in my field or area of interest.

This is not a scientific questionnaire, but I have found that it seems to have reasonable face validity and does seem to differentiate among groups. The first time I used this questionnaire was when I was giving a talk to a group of women who were all of the same faith. Most of the women were retired and were in their sixties. Very few of these women scored more than 12 on this questionnaire, and they did not feel that they were Edgewalkers. On another occasion, I did a workshop on Edgewalkers at the World Business Academy Conference, a conference called "The Global Mind Forum." As people were filling out the questionnaire, I started to hear chuckles, and this baffled me. I didn't think there was anything particular humorous about the questions. When I inquired about the laughter, someone said, "You made up this questionnaire just for us, right?" I responded that I hadn't and asked why they thought that. It turns out that almost everyone in the room had a score of 19 or 20. The people attracted to this conference tend to be people who are on the leading edge of social change and who have strong spiritual values.

Only you can decide if you are an Edgewalker or if it is attractive to you to be one. Edgewalkers have the excitement of being on the leading edge, but they also pay a high cost in terms of feeling disconnected. Edgewalkers feel different because they *are* different, and that can be lonely. We'll explore this more in Chapter 6.

CHARACTERISTICS OF EDGEWALKERS

Up to this point, we have been talking about Edgewalkers in fairly general terms. Now let's get more specific. In the leadership field, there has been an ongoing debate about whether leaders are born or made. Most leadership experts now agree that leaders are made—not born—and that it is worthwhile to invest in leadership development activities because they do help people to be more effective leaders. We could ask the same question about Edgewalkers—are they born or made? However, I think we would get a slightly different answer.

Almost anyone can be a leader, given the right circumstances and the right training and support. But not everyone can be an Edgewalker. They are a rare breed. Only a few are called to be pioneers and to travel into the future in the way that Igor Sikorsky did.

The rest of this chapter focuses on five Edgewalker Qualities of Being that seem to be an inherent part of the makeup of Edgewalkers.

FIVE EDGEWALKER QUALITIES OF BEING

There are five Edgewalker Qualities of Being that I have found are inherent in those people who are always on the leading edge. Most of us have the seeds of these qualities in us, but some people more naturally have been able to develop and integrate them. These qualities are an integral part of the Edgewalker's nature, without the person's even having to think about it. They come with no effort. They are inherent strengths or gifts.

From a managerial perspective, it is easier to select for these qualities than to try to develop them in people. In other words, if you were trying to increase the number of Edgewalkers in your organization, you would want to create ways to identify people who already have these qualities. These five qualities are (1) self-awareness, (2) passion, (3) integrity, (4) vision, and (5) playfulness. Read through these descriptions to assess your own characteristics as an Edgewalker.

> 1. *Self-awareness*: Awareness of your thoughts, values, and behavior and a commitment to spend time in self-reflection with the goal of becoming a better person.
>
> We are the mirror as well as the face in it.
> We are tasting the taste this minute of eternity.
> We are pain and what cures pain, both.
> We are the sweet water and the jar that pours.
>
> *—Rumi*

The most important Edgewalker quality is *self-awareness*. When I teach leadership courses or workshops, I always begin with these words from the Delphi Oracle: "*Know Thyself*." Let Davidson describes self-awareness as one of the key qualities of an awakened leader and goes on to say, "It opens the eye of the storm, the clarity needed in the midst of unpredictable change and increasing ambiguity."[1]

All great spiritual and contemplative traditions encourage the development of self-awareness. At the heart of these traditions is the knowledge that we are one with God, the Allness, the Universe, or something greater than ourselves. Our true nature is divine, and Edgewalkers know and cultivate this aspect of self, an aspect so often denied or repressed in our busy, materialistic society. Self-awareness comes from asking the questions "Who am I?" and "Who is the seeker that is asking this question?"

Journaling is an excellent tool for increasing self-awareness.[2] It allows you to explore the important questions in your life about who you are, what you value, and how you want to be in the world. In the mid-1990s, I interviewed hundreds of people who were integrating spirituality and work and asked them about their spiritual practices. Journaling was near the top of the list. Being in nature was the number one spiritual practice.[3] Patricia Aburdene says that journaling is her most significant spiritual practice. When I asked her about how she did her research for *Megatrends 2010,* she told me that journaling and receiving guidance from her spiritual guides were her primary research tools.[4]

Tom Aageson, the executive director of the New Mexico Museum Foundation, intentionally set an extended period of time aside when he turned 50 so that he could increase his self-awareness. By dedicating time to inner reflection, he was able to clarify his new path of reducing poverty in the world through helping artists in less-developed countries.

John Lumsden, CEO of MetServe, in New Zealand, so deeply believes in the importance of self-awareness that he holds an annual "advance" where he and his managers take time for personal and collective self-reflection. About a month before the advance, John gives each manager a packet of spiritual and inspirational books and tapes to study before they go away together. All participants are asked to think about the implications of these writings for themselves personally and for the leadership of the organization.

People with a high degree of self-awareness are in touch with body, mind, emotion, and spirit, and they experience the interconnections among these elements of the human self. They take the time to check in with themselves and to notice what they are thinking and feeling. The body has an inner wisdom, and Edgewalkers know how to understand its messages.

Tami Simon, CEO of Sounds True, a recording company that is committed to preserving spiritual wisdom, is one person who is very committed to self-awareness and to checking in with her inner self to get guidance about business decisions. At the end of the 1990s, the company was going through a great deal of financial difficulty, but Tami has been very committed to the company's practice of profit sharing. She says, "The way I decide how much profit sharing that we are going to give employees each year is that I give until I feel like throwing up." Talk about visceral decision making!

Shri G. Narayana is the chairman of Excel Industries, in Mumbai, India, and a lifetime practitioner of yoga. He is affectionately known by his employees as Guruji, beloved teacher. He has spent a lifetime honing his self-awareness through diet, exercise, and meditation. He told me that he has become very sensitized to energies in food and how they affect his emotions. For instance, he has learned that when he eats onions or garlic, he tends to get more easily irritated with others, so he has eliminated them from his diet.

The reason self-awareness is so important is that awareness of self leads to awareness of others. Mr. Narayana's sensitivity to his own responses helps him to be incredibly sensitive to others. He has been able to develop a strong intuition about others and their needs. This intuition and empathy have created compassion in him for others, especially for others who are not as fortunate, such as the elderly and the rural farmers in India. Excel Industries has created a number of foundations to help the less fortunate and to make a difference in rural India.

Through self-awareness, Edgewalkers come to trust their inner responses and inner knowing about people and situations. They also tend to have a greater understanding of, and compassion for, others. They are able to very quickly find the points of commonality, even though someone on the surface might appear very different.

2. *Passion*: An intense focus on your purpose or the use of your gifts in a way that adds value to your life and the world.

Only passions, great passions, can elevate the soul to great things.

—*Denis Diderot (Good Earth tea bag)*

There is nothing halfhearted about an Edgewalker. Many people would describe them as intense. That intensity comes from their passion about a cause or issue or value that is greater than themselves.

On a cold, windy day in December 2005, I walk from the subway across Broadway and 25th Street in New York City to go to visit Peter and Monika Ressler. They are partners in a highly successful Wall Street search firm that specializes in institutional debt and equity, sales, and trading. They are also the coauthors of *Spiritual Capitalism: What the FDNY Taught Wall Street about Money.*[5] The elevator takes me up several floors to a very large office suite, where I am ushered in to Peter's office. I have just a few moments to enjoy the view out the large windows and to appreciate the black leather couches and other quality furnishings before Peter charges in with his jacket over his shoulder and an unlit cigar in his mouth.

One look at Peter and you know he fits right in with the hard-driving Wall Street executives. He grew up in Brooklyn, and there is still something of the tough Brooklyn street kid beneath the polished and sophisticated look of a successful businessman. Peter would be the first to tell you that the word most people use to describe him is "intense." His wife, Monika, jokes that he scares most people off with his intensity. But it doesn't take long in a conversation with Peter and Monika to realize that their intensity comes from a real sense of calling about helping to transform capitalism and about helping to change the culture of Wall Street organizations. When they talk to you, their eyes are directly and unwaveringly on you, and you can feel their focus. They don't make small talk. They jump right into a conversation with challenging deep questions or with stories that have a meaningful message. This is the hallmark of an Edgewalker. They have no patience with superficial conversation and immediately move a conversation to deep, challenging, and provoking questions and issues.

Edgewalkers know who they are, and they have a strong sense of their purpose in life. If you were to dig a little deeper into their life histories, you would find that many of them lived through some kind of traumatic or life-threatening event. Although I don't have actual statistics, on the basis of my interviews, I have come to think that an unusually high percentage of Edgewalkers have come from homes with an alcoholic or abusive parent, a parent with mental illness, or a parent who died early. That kind of experience often forces the child to temporarily shut down from the current reality and to go somewhere else. It may be an inner place, or an imaginary place, or even an out-of-body experience. It is the way they psychologically survive a difficult situation.

Other Edgewalkers may have had a near-death experience, which is probably the most profound experience of walking between the worlds. Near-death experiencers report a strong sense of being in a different and much more beautiful reality and often don't want to come back into their bodies. Yet they do come back and find themselves wondering why. Most of them realize that they must have come back for a reason, and they begin to seek that sense of purpose.[6]

Lance Secretan writes, "The greatest leaders in history all saw a beacon beckoning to them from the future—a Cause. They had a clear vision of the world they sought to create and a burning passion to bring that world into existence. For them and many others, their Cause defined a future world brightened by the light of their dream."[7] Edgewalkers all have a strong sense of Cause, and they are passionate about making a difference.

Sometimes this passion comes about as a result of an interaction with a significant person who says or does something to awaken us to our inner purpose. This is the case for J. Robert Ouimet, the chairman of O.C.B. Holding Company, in Montreal, Canada. I am going to go a little more in detail about his story because he is one of the major leaders in the spirituality-in-the-workplace movement. He is a very successful businessman and is also committed to deepening his spiritual life. He would be the first to tell you that his connection to God provides the guidance that he lives by in his business and his life.

The O.C.B. Holding Company is "active in the production and sale of frozen and sterilized food products, and also investment management, employing around 400 people."[8] Robert has always been very spiritual, and the source of his spirituality is a deep involvement in the Roman Catholic Church. His family spent summers in Magog, Quebec, and each day, as a child, he would go to the Benedictine Monastery of St. Benoit-du-Loc. The Benedictine motto is "Ora et Labore," which means "to work is to pray." That motto has influenced Robert his whole life. He is now in his seventies and is passionate about the integration of spiritual and economic values in the workplace.

I had the privilege of first visiting one of his plants, the Tomasso Corporation, in 2004. My friend and colleague Thad Henry, former vice president of academic affairs at the University of New Haven, where I taught management, accompanied me. Robert is a thin, wiry man, and he takes your hand in his when he meets you and looks you straight in the eye. You know you are being sized up, and you wonder how deep he can look into your soul. If it weren't for that twinkle in his eye, you might find him very intimidating. Instead, with his warm French-Canadian accent, you find him totally charming and engaging.

Robert's father, Rene Tomasso, founded the food-processing company that Robert now runs. Rene Tomasso was also a religious man, and he ran the company in ways that were very much in alignment with his faith and values, working hard to create a family environment. Robert followed in his father's footsteps, but a real turning point came for him when he met Mother Teresa in 1983, in Calcutta. He was a great admirer of hers, and when he had the chance to meet her, he had one question for her: "Should I give everything I have, Mother?"

She answered, "You cannot give it, it has never been yours. It has been loaned to you by God. If you want, you can try to manage it . . . with Him . . . which is very different than 'for Him.' And if you want to manage 'with Him,' you have to follow His hierarchy of Love. You are married. I am not married. So, for you, His hierarchy of Love is: First, your wife. Second, your four children. Third, the four hundred employees and their families. And in that order. Not first the employees, and last the wife."[9]

After this experience with Mother Teresa, Robert became passionately committed to creating his company as a laboratory for spirituality in the workplace and to managing "with God." He now travels to business schools and conferences around the world to share his experiences with implementing spiritually based practices in his company. He also holds an annual conference on spirituality in the workplace in Montreal to which he invites CEOs, academics, and consultants, as well as priests, monks, and nuns.

His company is very successful, and Robert is known throughout Montreal for his generous philanthropy to many organizations. But what impresses me most about him is his moment-to-moment dedication to being in prayer. Everything Robert says and does is "with Him." Robert has become a true friend and a spiritual mentor, and on every occasion when I have been with him, we begin with several minutes of silence so that we can feel the connection to the Transcendent. And Robert will often begin praying in the middle of a conversation, as he includes Jesus in whatever dialogue might be going on. If there is any kind of decision to be made, he always asks that we pray for guidance before we take any action.

From this description, one might think him a religious fundamentalist, but I think there are two main differences between Robert's deep religious spirituality and the rigidity of fundamentalists. The first is that you can feel love and acceptance emanating from him. The second is that he insists that anything that is a spiritual activity be offered in a "true climate of freedom." He is very aware that the workforce is very diverse and that there must be a strong respect for individual differences and for the "primacy of human dignity," as he calls it.

A principle that Edgewalkers understand is that each person is a microcosm of the whole. A leader who is an Edgewalker knows that if a vision or dream or hunger is arising in him or her, it is most likely arising in others. The challenge for the Edgewalker is to find others who have the same passion and to band together to make a difference. Edgewalkers are particularly good at heeding Joseph

Campbell's exhortation to "follow your bliss." The leader who is an Edgewalker has a strong sense of being connected to something greater than himself or herself.

Igor Sikorsky is a wonderful example of someone who followed his bliss, despite incredible hardships and loss. He had the dream of creating flying machines and had a vision of the helicopter from early childhood. He had a strong awareness that this was his calling, as well as a deep commitment to create something that would support humanitarian efforts in the world.

Chip Conley is the CEO of San Francisco's most successful hospitality business, Joie de Vivre, and is the author of a book called *Rebel Rules: Daring to Be Yourself in Business*. He writes:

> Unlike visionary leaders who can arouse cult like followings, passionate leaders create loyalty to an organization more than to an individual. This is especially valuable at a time when employees tend to identify more with their work than they do with their company. A passionate leader is able to create "sticky people," employees who don't bolt for the revolving door. Consequently, turnover in a well run, passionate rebel company is far lower than the industry standard.
>
> Passionate leaders are great team builders. They've mastered the left-brain/right-brain tango. They use both their analytical skills and their salesmanship to create a wonderful work climate. Along with their big heart, they may also have big ears, all the better to listen with. Passionate companies are the ones that are always described as having "a family environment." The passionate rebel is often Mommy and Daddy all rolled into one.[10]

3. *Integrity*: A commitment to live in alignment with your core values, to align your words and your behavior, and to keep your word.

Meditate.
Live purely. Be quiet.
Do your work with mastery.
Like the moon, come out
from behind the clouds!
Shine.

—Buddha

One of the primary things that gives Edgewalkers their "edge" is integrity, and I mean that in two ways. First, people who walk on higher ground, and who hold you to a higher standard, can seem to have a hard edge to them. It's a lot easier to be around people who don't ask too much of themselves or of us. No pressure. Second, integrity is actually the source of long-term competitive edge. We trust people with integrity, and we want to do business with them, to work for them, or to buy from them. We know where they stand, and we know we can count on them. Integrity provides that sustainable edge, as we have learned the hard way from organizations that have committed fraud and have lacked integrity. The media have been filled with news about the collapse of many of these organizations whose leaders lacked integrity.

Where does integrity come from? I really don't know. Most people believe that you learn it from your parents, and perhaps from your religious upbringing. But I'm not sure about that. In any set of siblings, you are quite likely to find different levels of integrity. Integrity has become a central value for me in my life, but it wasn't always that way. Let me tell you a story that changed my life.

Lessons from the Universe. In the 1980s, I worked for Honeywell as the manager of organizational development and training at the Joliet Army Ammunition Plant in Joliet, Illinois. My job was to foster team building, leadership development, quality improvement, and employee communications and to help support our very progressive self-managing work teams. It was a great job because Honeywell would let us experiment with all the leading-edge management programs before implementing them at other facilities.

One day my boss, the manager of human resources, asked me to do some team building with the ballistics team, a team that was experiencing low morale. Several members of the team were asking to transfer, and that was very puzzling. This team had the highest-paid factory jobs at the facility, and the team members had significantly more autonomy than the production workers. Their job was to test the ammunition that we built for the U.S. Army, Navy, and Air Force by shooting the ammunition through machine guns at targets down a long testing tunnel. Lots of fun, right? It's not my cup of tea, but it was something the team members seemed to enjoy.

I went out to the ballistics area to interview the team members about the morale issues and discovered that they were being told by management to alter ballistics data and to say that the ammunition met government specifications when it did not. As a result of my investigation, I decided to call the company ethics hotline and became a whistleblower. Once I had discovered that our faulty ammunition could be putting our servicemen's lives in danger, there was no question that I had to take action. It was frightening, but I couldn't have lived with myself if I didn't do something. And the people on the ballistics team were looking for a safe way to change what the company was doing, and they wanted help.

Unfortunately, when I called the hotline, my anonymity was not protected, and my name was given to several high-ranking Honeywell executives, as well as to the plant manager where I worked. I had specifically asked them not to let the plant manager know that I was making the report, because I suspected that he was one of the people who was condoning the alteration of test data and that he might cover up his actions. I was also worried about negative repercussions for myself and for the team members who had provided me information.

As you can imagine, my life became utter chaos. My boss knew I was the whistleblower and forbade me to leave my office and to do any work with employees, management, or teams. Many people in top management at the plant were temporarily removed from their jobs during the investigation and put in my training room right outside my office. Within a few days after I blew the whistle, I started to hear rumors of threats against "the whistleblower" from people in management.

At the time, it was my practice to read inspirational literature before I went to sleep each night. During the weeks immediately following the hotline phone call, I was reading a book called *Living in the Light,* by Shakti Gawain.[11] One evening, about three weeks after I had called the hotline, I was reading the chapter titled "The World as Our Mirror." The basic premise of the chapter is that we create our own lives and that everything that happens to us is a reflection of what we need to learn. There are no accidents; everything has purpose and meaning. Gawain writes, "If I see or feel something, if it has any impact on me, then my being has attracted or created it to show me something. If it didn't mirror some part of myself I wouldn't even be able to see it. All the people in my life are reflections of the various characters and feelings that live inside of me."[12]

As I read this that night, I asked myself, "Okay, if this is true, what am I seeing or feeling in my life right now that has an impact on me?" My answer was that I was seeing a lack of integrity in the top management of the company I worked for. Integrity was the key issue in everything I saw around me. Gawain continues, "If there are problems in your life, that's the universe trying to get your attention. It's saying, 'Hey, there's something you need to be aware of, something that needs to be changed here!'" I thought, if the universe is indeed a mirror and is trying to show me something here, what is it I need to learn about integrity? That was a very difficult question.

Frankly, I was feeling pretty self-righteous that I had been the one to take the step to stop the bad guys, the ones without integrity. But if I drew this experience into my life for some important lesson, what was my lesson about integrity?

After a lot of soul searching, I realized that I lacked integrity in a number of ways. I tended to be afraid of arousing the wrath of some of the top managers (our plant manager was known to have pounded the table with his fist when someone disagreed with him or told him something he didn't like hearing). I wanted people to like me, so I told them what they wanted to hear. I was afraid of conflict, so I wouldn't speak my truth. I worked hard at being nice, but the price was my own integrity. I realized that I was selling a piece of my soul every time I was inauthentic or did not say what was really in my heart. With that realization, and with a strong motivation to not attract another experience like this whistle-blowing experience, I made a personal commitment to—as much as I possibly could—live in alignment with my core values and to always speak my truth, no matter what the repercussions might be.

One morning during that time, I was thinking about the need to be clear about my core values and sat down and wrote up a list of my "Guiding Principles." These principles came from lessons I had learned when things got tough and were the core values that got me through difficult times.

It is difficult to walk between different worlds and still hold on to your soul. Aaron Feuerstein, CEO of Malden Mills, in Lawrence, Massachusetts, is one of the best-known examples of a business leader who has done this. Many people are familiar with his actions and decisions after Malden Mills burned down one night in December 1995, on Aaron's seventieth birthday.

Malden Mills produces, among other things, Polartec and Polarfleece for such companies as Lands' End and L.L. Bean. Rather than take the insurance money from the fire and retire—as his advisers recommended he do—he committed to rebuild the factory in Lawrence so that his employees and the community would not be hurt. He paid all his employees their salaries and benefits for the next three months, a cost of more than $25 million, even though most of them would not be working until the mill was rebuilt.

This incredible act of generosity and commitment to his employees and his community was completely in line with Aaron's character and behavior. Although this was one of his more dramatic acts, he was always known by his employees and the town as someone who cared.

For Aaron Feuerstein, integrity is the bottom line. And the guiding light for that integrity is his Jewish faith. He has memorized the Psalms, reads the Torah daily, and says, "The Old Testament is in my innards."[13] He often quotes his grandfather, a rabbi, in Hebrew and then translates: "You cannot oppress the wage earner. Each day you must give him his wages." Aaron puts people before profits. And if you ask him why he did what he did, he says simply, "Because it was the right thing to do."

Aaron, now a very popular speaker, is fond of telling audiences that before the fire that Malden Mills produced 130,000 yards of material per week. Thanks to the commitment of his employees to save the plant, within 10 days it was up and operating again in a partially burned building. Within six weeks, it was producing more than 200,000 yards per week.

While speaking to the Hillel Society at University of Massachusetts-Amherst, he said, "It was unthinkable to bring these towns to economic ruin. It was unthinkable to put 3,000 people out of work. The moral imperative is critical, and it must be taken without regard to the consequences. Once I made the decision, my work was over. My people took over. They did it."[14]

I consider integrity to be a lifelong goal and a never-ending challenge. In order to live with integrity, you need to be constantly clarifying what your values are and, as Miguel Ruiz says, in *The Four Agreements*,[15] be impeccable about holding yourself accountable for how well you are living in alignment with these values. Gary Boelhower has designed a wonderful values exercise that helps people do this, which you will find in Appendix C.

4. *Vision*: The gift of being able to see what others cannot—possibilities, trends, the future, guidance from the spiritual world—and the ability to take steps to make the vision a reality.

The most exciting breakthrough of the 21st century will occur not because of technology but because of an expanding concept of what it means to be human.

—*John Naisbitt and Patricia Aburdene, Megatrends 2000*

Leadership literature is full of writings about the importance of vision in running a successful organization. But usually these discussions are in the context
of strategic planning. "You must have a vision if you are going to rally the troops
to head in the same direction," they typically say. They exhort you to look 5, 10,
and 20 years into the future to envision what your organization will look like.
What business will you be in? Whom will you serve? How large will your company
be? What challenges will you face?

This is a useful exercise, but I am talking about an even more profound sense of
vision here. Edgewalkers, like prophets of old, truly have visions. They see things
from a different level of consciousness, from "other worlds" or "other realities" that
help to guide them. They take the time to retreat from the material, day-to-day
world to seek a kind of vision and guidance for the future that can't be found in
sterile hotel rooms with high-priced consultants. These visions are more likely to
be found in quiet places in the mountains or by the sea, or in sacred places such
as monasteries and spiritual retreat centers, than in the concrete and steel jungle
of corporate life.

The kind of vision I am talking about here is at the deep level of "Presence" that
is described in the book by the same title. The authors state that they believe that
the "core capacity needed to access the field of the future is presence." Presence is
defined as:

> deep listening, of being open beyond one's preconceptions and historical ways of
> making sense. We came to see the importance of letting go of old identities and
> the need to control and, as Salk said, making choices to serve the evolution of life.
> Ultimately we came to see all these aspects of presence as leading to a state of "letting
> come," of consciously participating in a larger field of change. When this happens,
> the field shifts, and the forces shaping a situation can move from re-creating the past
> to manifesting or realizing an emerging future.[16]

We live in a time when business is building a pragmatic bridge between science and mysticism. Complexity theory helps us to understand that there is an
underlying order in chaos and that the role of the successful business leader is to
sense those underlying patterns. Creativity emerges at the edge of chaos, and we
learn not only to tolerate ambiguity but also to embrace chaos as the birthplace
of what is needed in the world. Quantum physics teaches us that the world is full
of potentiality and that what we focus on becomes manifest. In other words, we
create our own reality by what we pay attention to.[17] Doesn't it make sense to pay
attention to what we would like to see unfold in the world? Sheldrake's Morphic
Resonance Field theory[18] posits that the entire universe is a living, evolving, and
conscious system that is simultaneously learning from itself and co-creating itself.

This idea is similar to Carl Jung's idea of "collective unconscious." We are interconnected by a field of consciousness that is available to those who use attention and intention to envision what wants to emerge in the world. Edgewalkers tap into this Morphic Resonance and ask, "What wants to emerge through me?" This is the source of vision.

One of the more traditional forms of seeking a vision, of tapping into this field, is the vision quest process used by many indigenous peoples. As a rite of passage, young men and sometimes young women are sent into the wilderness for several days and nights to fast and to seek a vision of their life's purpose. All the elements of nature are seen as sources of wisdom and guidance, and the young person is taught beforehand how to pay attention to the signs. These days, people in the industrialized world seem to have lost the ability to even notice the signs, much less have the skill and wisdom to interpret the messages of these signs.

In May 2005, 11 of us gathered at the Angel Valley Retreat Center, in Sedona, Arizona, for a five-day workshop on "How to Walk the Bridge between the Worlds," a workshop designed for Edgewalkers. The central part of this workshop was a 24-hour vision-quest experience in the wilderness. Ron Pevny, an expert in vision questing, was my co-facilitator for the workshop. Ron is passionate about taking the gifts of the vision-quest process into the corporate world, and we had several business leaders in our group who felt called to go on their own vision quest for life and work.

Ron writes:

> I serve as a vision quest guide because, like the growing number of others who feel called to this work, I am deeply committed to helping create a world where soul comes first. And my own soul, as best I know it, has brought me to the point where I believe that the workplace must be seen in a new light by those of us who share this commitment. For too long, I feel many in the vision questing community, guides and questers alike, have seen the business world as the arch-enemy of soul, as something that must be endured while we do our soulwork elsewhere or until we are lucky enough or fed up enough or inspired enough or courageous enough to strike out on our own as new age entrepreneurs. There is no doubt that in many, many cases business has crushed soul. But the need for cultural transformation is too urgent now for us to basically write off the most powerful institution in the world as unredeemable,—especially given the hope catalyzed by and reflected in the growing Spirit at Work movement. It's time for the light of the vision quest to be focused on the work world.[19]

Vision quests are a wonderful way for people who are in transition in their life and/or work to take time out to walk between the worlds to gain a clearer perspective on what their next steps might be. In our retreat, most people were at some kind of crossroads in their lives and work. Judy S. came to the retreat because she was feeling somewhat burned out from her years of running a volunteer organization in Florida. She had been quite successful, even receiving national recognition for her work, but was feeling that her work at this organization was probably complete and that it was time for something new. A woman who was used to the good life and high-quality hotels, she found the idea of sleeping overnight in the desert very intimidating, but she courageously headed out across the river and up the trail that led to the place where she would be doing her questing.

The next morning, when she returned, she was dusty, disheveled, and positively shining. As a result of her vision quest, she realized that she was now very committed to staying right where she was in her organization and to deepening not only her own sense of calling about her work but also that of the volunteers and volunteer administrators she works with. She writes:

> This retreat delivered a powerful experience that has resulted in a new feeling of peace and calm within; an affirmation of life choices that enable me to confidently press forward; and the knowledge that my decisions are guided by powers greater than my own bounded rationality. I have returned to my daily life refreshed and renewed, with an expanded appreciation for the ability to access the power of the spiritual world through deeply connecting with like-minded individuals, the natural world, and the depths of my own being.[20]

Several well-known corporations, such as Xerox, Honeywell, Microsoft, and Motorola, have utilized the vision-quest experience as a way of helping employees to find their own personal vision, as well as a way to help the organization to clarify its vision. One Xerox facility, in Rochester, New York, was the most systematic in its approach and saw the vision quest as a way to revitalize and to change the culture of the organization. There will be more about its story in Chapter 6, when we explore ways that organizations are creating Edgewalker cultures.

Vision is a funny thing. It is deeply personal, emerging from your unique history, your woundedness, and what James Hillman calls your "Soul's Code."[21] Edgewalkers are willing to walk on the leading edge because they are driven by a compelling vision of meeting an important need in the world. Lance Secretan describes a process of finding your vision as beginning with an understanding of why you are here. He has a series of questions about Terrathreats—"threats to the planet and the future of humanity."[22] He asks such questions as "What Terrathreats do you feel interfere with or degrade the potential of humanity and our planet? What makes you sad when you think about the human condition? . . . What excites you and draws you to make a difference?" Vision comes from turning Terrathreats into Terrafixes. "Which of these Terrathreats are uniquely calling to you for resolution? Which ones are inviting your attention? How can you reframe these statements into Terrafixes? How will these Terrathreats be lessened by your presence on Earth?"[23]

The fact is that most people in the world don't ask these kinds of "Big Questions." People with vision do. They care about something greater than themselves, and, by asking the questions, and by walking between the worlds, they get answers. Other people often think they are crazy. Chip Conley, the CEO of Joie de Vivre, says, "The visionary rebel is an experimenter and is willing to tolerate a certain amount of chaos. He must be willing to occasionally sound like a kook, for visions often can start out as delusions. Ultimately the rebel's enthusiasm, persistence, and simple, precise direction make the dream tangible and give it momentum. His naiveté can be refreshing and inspiring. People are drawn to his presence and amazed by his clairvoyance."[24]

> 5. *Playful*: A joyful sense of fun and creativity, and an ability to keep everything in perspective.

> The creation of something new is not accomplished by the intellect but by the play instinct acting from inner necessity. The creative mind plays with objects it loves.

> *—Carl G. Jung*

One of my favorite places in the whole world is the Byodo-In Temple, in Kaneohe, Hawaii. This Buddhist temple is an exact replica of the Byodo-In Temple in Kyoto, Japan, and is nestled at the foot of the steep mountain cliffs on the island of O'ahu. Whenever I go home to visit Hawaii, I always make a stop at this temple, for the sense of peace and beauty I find there.

On one bright, sunny day (is there any other kind of weather in Hawaii?), I was wandering around the koi fishponds with the other tourists. On the far side of the temple grounds I saw a group of Buddhist monks in simple brown cloth robes walking slowly across the grounds. Suddenly, one monk broke from the group and dashed delightedly over to the koi ponds near me, laughing and jumping for joy at the fish as they came to the surface scarfing up food that the tourists threw. In that moment, I had this flash of knowing that playfulness and joy were the hallmarks of someone who was enlightened. He was the kind of monk that I would have loved to have learned from.

This understanding of playfulness was reaffirmed at an advisory board meeting I attended for the Spirit in Business Institute in 2001. I had the privilege of meeting Robert Thurman, who was also on the advisory board. Bob Thurman is a scholar, an author, a former Tibetan Buddhist monk, the director of Tibet House, in New York City, and a close personal friend of His Holiness the fourteenth Dalai Lama. Like many Edgewalkers, he found it hard to live a conventional life. This is from his bio on his Web site:

> He managed to get himself kicked out of Exeter just prior to graduation for playing hooky in a failed attempt to join Fidel Castro's Cuban guerrilla army in 1958. Harvard University admitted him anyway, but a deep dissatisfaction and questioning led him to drop out and he traveled on a "vision quest" as a pilgrim to India. Returning home to attend his father's funeral, he met a Mongolian monk, Geshe Wangyal, and thus began Thurman's life-long passion for Tibetan Buddhism.
>
> In 1964, Geshe Wangyal introduced Thurman to His Holiness the Dalai Lama and described Robert as, " . . . a crazy American boy, very intelligent and with a good heart (though a little proud), who spoke Tibetan well and had learned something

about Buddhism [and] wanted to become a monk. . . . Geshe Wangyal was leaving it up to His Holiness to decide." Thurman became the first Westerner to be ordained as a Tibetan Buddhist monk. He was 24 and the Dalai Lama 29.[25]

In 1987, Bob Thurman and the actor Richard Gere founded Tibet House, in New York City, to help preserve the living culture of Tibet. It was in his role as director of Tibet House, and as an eminent Buddhist, that he had been invited to be on this advisory board, and we were all in awe of him. The leader of the group, Anders Ferguson, respectfully asked him if he would be willing to lead us in a meditation before we began the tasks of the meeting, and Bob agreed. I was sitting directly across the table from him and watched him close his eyes and lower his head. We were silent for a minute, and then he quietly led us through a beautiful meditation that reminded us of our connection to all the beings on the planet and reminded us of the importance of the work that we were called to do together. This was followed by more silence.

I was feeling very peaceful and centered when I suddenly heard him say, playfully, "Ding!" I looked up at him, and there was a huge grin on his face and a twinkle in his eye. Usually meditations of this sort are brought to completion by the sound of a bell or chimes, and, none being available, Bob became his own chime! I knew I was in the presence of a special person, and I liked him immediately.

It is not that uncommon to find playful Edgewalker leaders in organizations. My first experience with this kind of leader came in the 1970s, when I had been invited to the board meeting of Jackson Newspapers, in New Haven, Connecticut, to talk about the quality training I was doing with my colleague Bob Beaudoin with members of their press team. We were all assembled in the impressive boardroom overlooking Long Island Sound, but Stewart had not arrived yet.

All the seats were taken when Stewart walked in a few minutes later, and he looked around and assessed the situation. He went over to the phone and made a call, and I assumed that he called his secretary or someone nearby to ask that another chair be brought in. He stood there talking to someone for a minute when the phone rang. He picked it up and listened and then pointed to one of the board members and said, "It's for you." The board member got up to come to the phone, and no sooner had he left his chair than Stewart grabbed his chair and sat down with a look on his face like that of a cat with a mouthful of feathers. We all burst into laughter at the practical joke that had just been played on the board member. Stewart's playfulness permeated the rest of the board meeting, and wonderful work got done by a team of people who genuinely seemed to like each other and who cared about the newspaper.

Humor itself is a fine line to walk. I once worked as the organizational development manager for a family-owned circuit-board business, and the humor there was sarcastic, biting, and competitive. There wasn't the sense of innocence and naiveté that Chip Conley talks about in rebel leaders. The company had a climate of fear, and laughter was rare. Edgewalkers know how to use playfulness to create a culture of fun, of creativity, and of celebration.

Kenny Moore has a natural sense of how to do this. Kenny is the corporate ombudsman for Keyspan Energy, the largest energy company in the New York/New England area. As a child, he felt called to the priesthood, and eventually he became a monk in a strict monastic order in New Jersey. In his thirties, he realized that this was no longer his calling, and he found himself working in human resources at Brooklyn Union Gas, the predecessor to Keyspan.

Kenny says that he noticed three trends: nobody trusts, nobody believes in top management, and everyone is too stressed to care. Bridging the world of the monastery and corporate life, he calls this a crisis of faith, hope, and charity. He says, "Maybe that's the realm that I work in. A wise leader realizes that if you can engage not just employees' physical energy but their emotional, mental, and spiritual energy as well, you've got something powerful."[26] Kenny engages employees through play, creativity, and caring. One way he does this is that each week he buys a bouquet of flowers and puts them on the desks of two employees with an unsigned card that says, "Don't ever think your good efforts go unnoticed." Signed: "From someone who cares."

Kenny tells the story of the first time he did this:

> On Tuesday I made it a point to pass by the desk of the woman who worked on my floor. I said, "Hey, nice flowers. Is it your birthday?
>
> "No," she said. "Somebody sent them to me. Look. Here's the note." By this time, all her co-workers were crowded around, telling me the sequence of events. They also knew that an executive got the same flowers delivered. One of them even called the florist to find out who sent it. Nobody seemed to know. They all continued to speak in utter giddiness about the strangeness of the delivery and what made this woman so special. They also spent considerable time trying to figure out what she had in common with the executive, and who might have sent the flowers.[27]

He still sends weekly flower arrangements to two coworkers, and no one but the CEO knows who sends the flowers. Kenny says he may not have revolutionized the corporate culture of Keyspan Energy, but some things are a little different. Not the least of these is that Kenny looks forward to coming into work on Monday mornings.

The key element in humor and playfulness is whether or not your intention is to uplift colleagues or to embarrass and humiliate them. The first helps a company to be creative and on the leading edge. The second causes people to withdraw, to be self-protective, and maybe even to leave.

ORGANIZATIONAL IMPLICATIONS

The Edgewalker Qualities of Being discussed in this chapter are not the kinds of things you can send someone off to charm school to learn. Sure, you can send people to leadership development courses in the hopes that they will increase their self-awareness, but if they don't hunger for personal growth, not much of the training will stick. You can send people to ethics training in the hope that they will act with more integrity, but if integrity is not one of their core values, you might just as well put in better control systems and create strong disincentives for unethical behavior. And you can send people off to comedy workshops or to playshops, but if they don't have a funny bone to begin with, you are wasting your time.

If you want to have more Edgewalkers in your organization, it is much better to hire for these qualities of being than to try to develop them in people. Robert Ouimet, CEO of O.C.B. Holding, developed a managerial practice that might be useful in this context. When his organization is seeking a new manager, potential hires are given a copy of The Golden Book, which was written by Robert Ouimet and which outlines the key corporate values and the practices that support those values. Two of the key values the company seeks in managers are "authenticity" and "humility." When someone is a finalist for a position, that person is invited to dinner with his or her spouse and with the plant manager and his wife. It is called "Dinner for 4," and it is consciously designed as a way for everyone to assess whether or not there is a good alignment in values.

A similar practice could be used if you are seeking an Edgewalker. During the dinner, you, as the hiring manager, could ask yourself questions such as these:

- Self-awareness: Does this person seem to be aware of his or her impact on others?
- Self-awareness: Does he or she seem to be tuned into you in an attentive and respectful way?
- Self-awareness: Is he or she able to articulate core values and give examples of tough situations where those values were helpful in guiding decisions?
- Passion: How passionate is he or she about his or her work? Does this person seem to have a sense of calling?
- Passion: Is there any evidence of intensity or clear focus?
- Integrity: Do you feel that you can trust this person? Why?
- Integrity: Will this person take the high road when there is a tough business decision to be made?
- Vision: Does this person seem to have a strong sense of what is possible and what can be created? Has he or she demonstrated clear vision in the past?
- Vision: Is this person committed to a vision of something greater than just making a profit? Is so, what is that, and does it fit with your organization's vision?
- Playfulness: You know a playful person from the very first minute the two of you meet. It is the way the person begins a relationship. Did this person engage you with humor or a twinkle in the eye when you first met?
- Playfulness: Is there any evidence that this person will create celebrations and a climate of creative fun?

Two other questions to ask yourself when you are considering hiring an Edgewalker are (1) Did I feel energized by being in this person's presence? and (2) Did I feel slightly challenged or uncomfortable because this person pushed the edges of some boundaries? If so, you probably have a bona fide Edgewalker on hand, and if the person has skills and experience that are a fit for your organization, you will probably want to grab this person before your competitor does.

If the shoe is on the other foot and you are an Edgewalker seeking a new position, these questions can be just as useful to you. They can help you assess whether or not the leadership of this organization is supportive of someone who is an Edgewalker.

GUIDANCE FOR EDGEWALKERS

As an Edgewalker reading this, you probably have resonated with most of the Qualities of Being described in this chapter. You may be concerned that you are not as strong in some of these qualities as others. But don't be. You are who you are, and it is important to build on your strengths rather than to focus on qualities you might lack. After years of reviewing Gallup poll research on effective leaders and effective organizations, Marcus Buckingham and Donald Clifton concluded that it is much more effective to enhance your strengths than to try to correct or improve your weak areas.[28] I think this is very true for Edgewalkers.

SUMMARY

There are five primary Qualities of Being that you will find in most Edgewalkers. These qualities are the essence of the way these individuals live and interact in the world and are the result of important life experiences and, in some cases, significant spiritual transformation experiences. Edgewalkers tend to have high degrees of self-awareness, passion, integrity, vision, and playfulness. They would never define themselves as conventional, and they pride themselves on their uniqueness. And integral to all of these qualities is a sense that they are here for some larger purpose and a driving need to make a positive difference in the world.

Each year, on Labor Day, Lois Hogan writes an essay on a topic related to work. The following quotation from her 2002 essay beautifully sums up what it is like to be an Edgewalker:

> Edges are about choices and decisions. They define the territory between the familiar and the unknown; hence they are also about learning and the willingness to be temporarily disoriented. We may find ourselves in a place where it takes all our courage to imagine taking another step. We worry there will be no solid footing; we fear we will lose something or be hurt. Yet there are times when facing the brink is less a threat to life than the refusal to step out into our own truth. Something calls us to move out into the darkness, illumined only by an inner vision that draws us like the moon, to an urge we can no longer ignore. Surrendering certainty to step out into the path of no path doesn't mean there is no path—only that we cannot yet see it.[29]

Chapter Four

THE FIRST STAGE OF EDGEWALKING:
THE SKILL OF KNOWING THE FUTURE

Here's to the crazy ones. The misfits. The rebels. The trouble-makers. The round heads in the square holes. The ones who see things differently. They're not fond of rules, and they have no respect for the status-quo. You can quote them, disagree with them, glorify, or vilify them. But the only thing you can't do is ignore them. Because they change things. They push the human race forward. And while some may see them as the crazy ones, we see genius. Because the people who are crazy enough to think they can change the world, are the ones who do.

—*Jack Kerouac,* On the Road

If you are in a leadership position and have any Edgewalkers working for you, you either love them or hate them. As Kerouac says, "they're not fond of rules, and they have no respect for the status quo." It would be just about impossible to run an organization with everyone breaking the rules and trying to change things constantly. If you love them, hooray for you! You are on your way to helping create an Edgewalker culture in your organization. As I said earlier, organizations that embrace and nurture Edgewalkers are the ones that will be on the leading edge in the competitive market. If you want your organization to have an edge, you have to let your people have an edge.

How do you create an Edgewalker culture? Through understanding the stages of Edgewalker development and helping your people develop the skills at each stage. Most organizations are far too stodgy and rule-bound, and an Edgewalker culture breaks out of that and moves toward greater innovation, creativity, and integrity.

There is the "Being" element of an Edgewalker, that is, their inner qualities and their essence. These qualities were described in Chapter 3. Edgewalkers are people who take risks, create the future, and thrive on the edge. They crave newness and love to create what has never existed before. They are restless, innovative, edgy, and different.

In addition to the "Being" aspect of an Edgewalker, there is the "Doing" element of Edgewalkers, that is, the actions, behaviors, and skills that help an individual or an organization to be on the leading edge. This "doing" element is the focus of the next two chapters.

There are five Edgewalker skills that can be developed step-by-step through training, attention, and practice. These skills, practiced throughout the organization, help to develop the Edgewalker organizational culture. Anyone can develop these skills, although people with Edgewalker Qualities of Being tend to develop them more easily. These skills are acquired through five stages of development. They are: (1) knowing the future, (2) risk-taking, (3) manifesting, (4) focusing, and (5) appreciating.

Chapter 4 focuses primarily on the first stage of Edgewalker development, the skill of Knowing the Future, because this is the foundation skill for the other skills of Edgewalking. Without this skill, the other skills will not be very effective. The skill of "Knowing the Future" creates the context out of which all the other stages of development emerge. The remaining four stages of Edgewalker development are described more in depth in Chapter 5.

As you read the descriptions of each stage of Edgewalker development, think about your own life and work and about which of these skills are most relevant to you. To get the most out of these next two chapters, make a commitment to yourself to take at least *one* action to enhance at least *one* of these skills. If you are in a leadership position in an organization, you can do the same kind of assessment for your team or department. And then commit to taking at least *one* action that will enhance at least *one* of these skills in your team. Chapter 6 goes much more into detail about how to develop an Edgewalking Organization, but these steps will get you started on your Edgewalker Journey.

THE DEVELOPMENTAL PROCESS—SOME BASIC PRINCIPLES

Marcus Buckingham and Donald Clifton, in their best-selling book *Now Discover Your Strengths,* describe the Gallup interviews that were conducted with more than 80,000 managers. The goal of the interviews was to discover what the world's best managers had in common. But their most significant finding was that most organizations are built on two flawed assumptions about their employees:

1. Each person can learn to be competent in almost anything.
2. Each person's greatest room for growth is in his or her areas of greatest weakness.[1]

Competency

While Edgewalkers tend to have high-level competency in more than one area, they are not trying to be competent in everything. They focus on their strengths, their passions, and their values. They tend to really excel at two or maybe three fields, but they have no interest in being well-rounded or in being a generalist. They also have no interest in being a specialist in just one area. They thrive on being able to walk between different worlds. This is often quite a frustration to their managers, who think that they may be providing desirable and valuable growth opportunities by offering projects or promotions that are outside the person's area of passion or who expect them to focus only on their particular functional area. They don't understand why the Edgewalker turns down lucrative "opportunities for development."

In an Edgewalker Organization, all the employees, whether or not they are Edgewalkers, have an awareness of which Edgewalking skills they are most competent in. The organization is committed to helping them further these competencies through training and other developmental opportunities.

Greatest Weakness

Edgewalkers tend to ignore their weaknesses and put their time and energy into only the things they are passionate about. This doesn't mean that they don't try to learn new skills. On the contrary, they are thirsty for new knowledge, new skills, and new information. But it's always in the service of those things that they are passionate about. Through their self-awareness, they know their weaknesses, and they either steer away from those areas or find someone who has a strength in their area of weakness to support them.

An Edgewalker Organization is also aware of its weaknesses, but it focuses on its Edgewalker Strengths, not its weaknesses. It may hire people who have the strengths that are needed, or it may partner with other organizations that have these Edgewalker Strengths.

Buckingham and Clifton identify two assumptions that guide the world's best managers:

1. Each person's talents are enduring and unique.
2. Each person's greatest room for growth is in the areas of his or her greatest strength.[2]

They define "strength" as "consistent near perfect performance of an activity."[3] When they studied excellent performers, they found that they were rarely well rounded. They advise people this way: "you will excel only by maximizing your strengths, never by fixing your weaknesses. This is not the same as saying 'ignore your weaknesses.' The people we described did not ignore their weaknesses. They found ways to manage around their weaknesses, thereby freeing them up to hone their strengths to a sharper point."[4]

As you read through the Edgewalker stages of development in this chapter and in Chapter 5, you already have strengths in some of these areas. These are the areas to pay attention to and to develop further. As a leader interested in developing Edgewalking Skills in your people, remember to honor each individual's uniqueness and to create developmental activities that build on his or her passions and strengths.

OVERVIEW OF THE FIVE STAGES OF EDGEWALKER DEVELOPMENT

Reflect back on the trends described in Chapter 1. We live in a world that is rapidly globalizing, and, as Peter Russell says, becoming aware of itself as an interconnected and conscious being.[5] Technology is ubiquitous. There is less predictability. Strategic planning and other linear tools are not able to make accurate predictions about the future. Everyone is experiencing a sense of "time poverty," and there are demands for results to happen "yesterday." And, finally, there is a growing hunger for purpose and meaning in the workplace, as evidenced by the spirituality in the workplace movement.

The five stages of Edgewalker development can help us individually and collectively to see the opportunities in these trends and the creativity that exists at the edge of chaos. When I interviewed people who are Edgewalkers and asked them what they do that helps them to have their "edge," these are the things that they told me they do:

1. Knowing the Future: The ability to understand and embrace the future.

This includes the ability to gather relevant data, either logically or intuitively, and to be able to make sense of that data in a way that provides a reasonably accurate picture of what's likely to unfold. It also includes the ability to envision and create a desired future. This skill lays the groundwork for all the other skills. Edgewalking is by definition about being on the leading edge, and the only way you can be on the leading edge is to have some sense of the future and the part you will play in helping the future become reality.

2. Risk-Taking: The ability to try what hasn't been tried before, to trust your instincts, and to break new ground.

Once you have a sense of the future and your role in it, you are moved to take action. You feel courageous and inspired to go beyond what you have known and to attempt to do things that you may not think you have the skills, knowledge, or ability to do.

3. Manifesting: The ability to take a thought, idea, or vision and take practical steps to bring it into being.

When you have fully committed to action and taken the risk required to get things moving, you need to find ways to bring the future into the present and to make it real. This is a two-step process consisting of "mental work" and what 12-Step programs refer to as "footwork."

4. Focusing: The ability to be very centered and to give all your attention to an action or project that has significance and importance.

It is very easy, in this complex, multitasking world, to get pulled off track with the creation of something that has never existed before, whether it is a new product, a new business, an innovative marketing campaign, or a unique style of leadership. The forces of entropy conspire to keep you and the world in a state of equilibrium. It takes tremendous skill and discipline to stay on track and to stay on the leading edge, where it is often less than comfortable.

5. Appreciating: The ability to value others, to see their uniqueness, and to draw out the best in them.

The Edgewalker's unique gift is to be able to bridge different cultures, worldviews, functions, and paradigms. They do this through looking for commonalities and connectedness while at the same time holding sacred the uniqueness of others.

STAGE ONE: KNOWING THE FUTURE

The future enters into us, in order to transform itself in us,
long before it happens.

—Rilke

There are three basic ways that people know and understand the future. Each takes a unique set of skills and represents a distinct and different form of consciousness. First, there is the rational, data-gathering, mathematical-modeling method of understanding the future. This is the "Traditional" method of knowing the future. The key skill is being able to gather and analyze concrete data.

The second approach is the gut-level, shamanic, divination approach to embracing the future. The key skill is being able to read the subtle signs of what is unfolding. This is the "Intuitive" approach to knowing the future.

The third way to know the future is to be actively involved in creating it. This is the "Co-Creative" approach to knowing the future. The key skills are to be able to have a vision of what you want to have unfold and to take action to begin to make it real.

All these ways of knowing are legitimate, and all have their drawbacks. They are not mutually exclusive, and leaders can draw on any combination of these ways of knowing.

WAYS OF KNOWING THE FUTURE

Type:	Traditional	Intuitive	Co-Creative
Skills:	Data-based	Reading the Signs	Vision-Action

Can we truly ever "know" the future? This is an esoteric question that is far too deep to discuss here. Quantum physicists and mystics talk about the illusion of the space-time continuum and about how all points in time exist in the "Now." Each of us has had experiences where we just "knew" what was going to happen. Perhaps we knew it through logic and analysis, or perhaps we knew it though some non-rational process. Even if we cannot know *exactly* what the future will bring, we are more likely to find ourselves in a positive, desired future if we enhance our skills in understanding probable futures and preparing for what we would like to have unfold.

Traditional Ways of Knowing the Future

I once worked for a human resources manager who strongly believed in the mathematical model of embracing the future. Our department kept all kinds of data on employment trends and had formulae for predicting manpower needs and training needs. We knew we were going to get a contract for a new product line, which would require building a new factory and hiring the factory managers and employees. Our HR manager interviewed current production and engineering managers, as well as support staff managers, to get a sense of how many people would be needed and what skills would be required. We then worked with this team of managers to assess how many people from current product lines might be able to move to the new product and how many people would need to be hired. The HR manager had a formula that said that no more than 10 percent of current employees could move to the new product line, because moving more than that would cause too much disruption to the current manufacturing lines. We put together a manpower plan from all this data that told us how many people needed to be hired and by what dates. It also told us what kind of technical, team, and leadership training we would need to provide and by what dates.

This is common business practice, and it works in a stable environment. This Traditional approach to embracing the future also work for inventory planning, for sales forecasting, for asset management, and, to some extent, for new product or service development.

Synchronistically, as I was working on this chapter, there was an article in the *Wall Street Journal* that provides a perfect example of the Traditional approach. The article stated that life insurance companies are extremely concerned about the possibility of a bird flu pandemic and are trying to do statistical analyses in order to predict their readiness to handle an outbreak. A study pinpointed MetLife and Reinsurance Group of America as being the most exposed to potential losses if an outbreak were to occur. The article reports on estimates from the Insurance Information Institute that a pandemic could cost the industry $133 billion in additional death claims. "According to Morgan Stanley, that amounts to more than half of the industry's $238 billion in capital, which is an insurer's assets minus its liabilities. A more modest outbreak could amount to a little less than 15% of capital, the report notes."[6] The article concludes with a quote from RGA of Chesterfield, Missouri, which is primarily a life reinsurer. The company "continually evaluates all aspects of mortality, including pandemics such as the avian flu, as we manage our portfolio of risk."[7]

Many people who are good at embracing the future are voracious readers. They read everything they can get their hands on in their field and also make it a point to read material that is outside their field as a way of getting a broader perspective on things. Sheldon Hughes is a very successful consultant, and co-owner, with his partner, Halina Bak, of Capricorn Consulting, which has offices in New York and California. Sheldon reads all the latest books and articles in management and organizational development and is particularly interested in Appreciative Inquiry and other approaches that require a positive shift in consciousness. He is well versed in the latest change-management technologies. But he also finds himself drawn to philosophical, religious, spiritual, and futurist books and articles and reads everything he can get his hands on. He finds himself seeking evidence of positive transformation in the world, whether it is political, educational, scientific, or social systems transformation. As a result, he is on the leading edge of management change technologies and has a gift for helping clients to create a positive future.

Another key way to gather data about emerging trends is to attend conferences and to be involved in professional organizations in your field. People who speak at these conferences have often just published a book, or are about to publish a book, so you are able to be exposed to new thinking and the latest research before it hits the mainstream. A colleague of mine once did some informal research on what inspired CEOs to initiate change in their organizations. The number one factor was hearing an inspirational presentation at a conference. The CEOs then bought the book and often invited the speaker to come in and consult with their organizations. They felt that adopting this new technology or change-management system would give them a leg up on the competition.

In my academic career, I attended the Academy of Management conference, the Eastern Academy of Management Conference, the Organizational Behavior Teaching Conference, and regional conferences run by these national organizations. I got involved in the governance structure of each organization, which allowed me to build relationships with some of the leaders in my field and to learn from them. Often I would get more out of informal, exploratory, "what if" types of conversations with these leaders than I would from their formal presentations. Also, being a speaker at conferences in your field is a great way to meet other speakers, who are usually people who have their finger on the pulse of what is emerging. Sometimes I am invited to speak at conferences that are for organizations that are totally outside my field. I've spoken at conferences for manufacturing, for volunteer administrators, for hospice administrators, and for faith-based organizations. It's a great opportunity to find out what other professions are thinking about and to see if there are any parallels to your own work. I am constantly amazed to find that we have far more similarities than differences.

When you are immersed in information from all these sources—gathering facts, reading in your field as well as outside it, and being involved in the professional organizations in your field—you begin to form a gestalt of the trends that are emerging. If you are looking for them and thinking about them, patterns will begin to emerge, and somewhere in the midst of all this information will be something that sparks your energy and creativity.

> Leadership through command and control is doomed to fail. No one can create sufficient stability and equilibrium for people to feel secure and safe. Instead, as leaders we must help people move into a relationship with uncertainty and chaos. Spiritual teachers have been doing this for millennia. Therefore, I believe that the times have led leaders to a spiritual threshold. We must enter the domain of spiritual traditions if we are to succeed as good leaders in these difficult times.
>
> —Meg Wheatley [8]

INTUITIVE WAYS OF EMBRACING THE FUTURE

Fast Company is a business magazine for Edgewalkers. It is always looking for what is just over the horizon, and it actively seeks to uncover new and innovative ideas. In a recent issue, three *Fast Company* interns were given the assignment to "fill five pages with 'illuminating' (our editor's word) statistics on the state of demographics, technology, health and other stuff." [9] They went to all the experts to get statistics, and no one could give them a straight answer about things like the number of landfills, the number of retirement communities, or terrorism. When they interviewed the statisticians about the difficulty of getting explicit statistics, they found that part of the problem is the "sheer and growing complexity of our world and the speed at which it changes."[10] They conclude their article by saying, "If we're condemned to ever-increasing statistical fuzziness, individuals and businesses alike must become a lot more flexible about the way we consider the future. Rather than mapping strategy around a relatively certain future, we have to be able to accommodate a range of possible outcomes."[11]

In an environment that is rapidly changing and that defies linear prediction, it is becoming more common to use the "Intuitive" approach to embracing the future. There are many ways to use intuition to help identify this "range of possible outcomes." It is not unusual to find successful business people who use approaches ranging from astrology to journaling to meditation and prayer as a way of receiving guidance in an unpredictable world. People are afraid to talk about it because they fear being labeled superstitious, flaky, or, worst of all, New Age. But humans have been using intuition since the beginning of time as a way of understanding the present and embracing the future. Intuition is a way of "reading the signs," and there are many ways to do this. This skill is far more common than we think.

Some people describe this skill as ESP, and there has been quite a bit of research demonstrating that ESP is a real phenomenon even though we may not understand how it works. Robert Rivlin, a linguist, and Dr. Karen Gravelle, a biopsychologist, conclude:

> ESP is exactly what its name suggests: *extra*-sensory perception, truly a "sixth sense" about things, or, perhaps, a sixteenth or seventeenth sense. Not the result of hidden forces from an unknown source. Not the mystical claptrap that has been associated with ESP and psychic ability throughout the ages. Not a weird blend of magic and witchcraft. But a very human experience in which sensory signals are transmitted and received by the body that are either below the normal threshold of a known sensory system or else are a form of energy that is being detected by a sense that we are unaware of at present. In other words, just because the various forms of ESP lie outside our current ability to describe them does not mean that they will not, one day, be as rational and "scientific" as acupuncture is today.[12]

In 1935, Carl Jung gave a series of lectures at the Tavistock Institute, in London, to about 200 doctors. In describing intuition, he said:

> [I]ntuition is a sort of perception which does not go exactly by the senses, but it goes via the unconscious, and at that I leave it and say "I don't know how it works." I do not know what is happening when a man knows something he definitely should not know. I do not know how he comes by it, but he has it all right and he can act on it. For instance, anticipatory dreams, telepathic phenomena, and all that kind of thing are intuitions. I have seen plenty of them, and I am convinced that they do exist. You can see these things also with primitives. You can see them everywhere if you pay attention to these perceptions that somehow work through the subliminal data, such as sense-perceptions so feeble that our consciousness simply cannot take them in.[13]

Joann Stein is completing a study of intuition in the workplace and offered this summary of her findings:

> When in doubt, follow your intuition if it is coming from your "heart" rather than your "head." The more you trust and follow your intuition, the stronger that skill becomes. Like a muscle, the more you exercise it, the stronger it gets. No one I interviewed was sorry they listened to their intuition, they were sorry they hadn't listened to it more![14]

Dr. Marcia Emery, author of *Intuition Workbook*,[15] provides examples of how intuition can act as a powerful tool in business:

- Decide who to hire, who would be "right" for the job.
- Discover errors in your product that have gone undetected by others.
- Mend hurt feelings when you have unintentionally offended coworkers or friends.
- Use that same inner radar to help you find the best way to approach coworkers for a favor or a helping hand.
- Find the right words to motivate a child or young person to reach his or her goals.
- Lesson the risk of going into new markets by guiding you to just the right audience for your product.

You wouldn't think that Wall Street, the heart of capitalism, would be a place where people would use intuitive and spiritual approaches to running their businesses, but that's only because people aren't talking about what they are really doing. As Jung said, "you can see them everywhere if you pay attention to perceptions."

Astrology

For example, the field of high finance is a world that can turn on a dime. Mergers, terrorism, corporate fraud, and so many other events can change a hot industry into a dud overnight and can change the requirements for new executives faster than the speed of light. Two very successful human resources professionals that I talked to told me that they never make a major business or personal decision without consulting their astrologers. Even more amazing than that, they report that their astrologers were never wrong. They also work very hard on developing their own intuition through contemplative practices and seem to have an unerring sense of judgment about people, as well as about what they are being called to do in the world.

Contemplative Practices

Michael Stephen and Robert Ouimet, two Edgewalker CEOs mentioned earlier, make prayer and meditation a part of their daily practice and firmly believe that their businesses would not have been as effective if it weren't for the spiritual guidance they received from their connection to the Transcendent. They know that this time spent in interior silence and contemplation is extremely helpful in strengthening their intuition and their ability to sense the future. Both Michael and Robert focus on being of service to something greater than themselves and instill that value as a primary value in their respective organizations.

Angels

Some people are guided by angels in life and work. Ruby Vine is not shy about telling you about the two angels who sit on his shoulders. Ruby is a million-dollar donor to the University of New Haven, and Thad Henry and I paid a call to him to thank him for his generosity to the University. Nearly 80 years old, Ruby has the joy and presence of a child, and he delighted in showing us around his Florida condo, which overlooks the Atlantic Ocean and a beautiful beach in Fort Lauderdale. The cruise ships sail right past his building, and Ruby installed a ship's bell on the side of his veranda. Right at 2:30 P.M., Ruby jumped up and insisted that we all go out to the ship's bell because it was time for the cruise ship to sail out of the harbor. He delightedly clanged the bell and waved to the passengers, who waved back. He invited me to clang the bell, too, and grinned like the Cheshire Cat when I pulled on the rope to make the bell ring. Life is good to Ruby these days, but it wasn't always so.

Thad had wanted me to talk to Ruby because of my interest in Edgewalkers and had told me a little bit about Ruby and his angels. I asked Ruby to tell me about how he first met his angels, and he began a tale of World War II and described a close call that he had during an ambush by the Germans in occupied France. He says that he shouldn't have survived that attack, and the only way to explain it is that there were angels watching over him. He tells several more harrowing tales of the war, including a description of his many months as a prisoner of war in Germany, and the illness, frostbite, and starvation he faced. At each point in the tale, he talked about how the angels guided him to safety.

When he was rescued and returned home, he did not have any idea what he was going to do with his life as a civilian, but wonderful synchronicities kept occurring, and he ended up creating a company called Railroad Salvage, the first large-box store to sell nothing but salvaged goods. Ruby went on to become a multimillionaire, a significant community leader, and a major philanthropist. He takes great joy in being an angel to others and in investing in their businesses, so he is now part-owner of many successful businesses. In every business decision and in every major change in his life, at every turn, his angels have guided him to his next steps. Ruby is certain that his life was saved for a reason, and he has been trying to give back to the world ever since that fateful day at a crossroads in France.

Dreams

People who use intuition to sense the future are likely to rely on their dreams as part of their guidance. The most common stories of the use of dreams are from creative people—writers, musicians, scientists, and inventors. Robert Louis Stevenson wrote in his autobiography that whether he was awake or asleep, what he called "the little people" of his dreams were occupied in creating stories for the market. Another famous literary piece that is a product of dreaming is Coleridge's poem "Kublai Khan."

A musical example is the dream of the Italian violinist and composer Giuseppe Tartini (1692–1770). In his dream, Tartini hands his violin to the devil. He recounts:

> But how great was my astonishment when I heard him play with consummate skill a sonata of such exquisite beauty as surpassed the boldest flights of my imagination. I felt enraptured, transported, enchanted; my breath was taken away, and I awoke. Seizing my violin I tried to retain the sounds I had heard. But it was in vain. The piece I then composed, the "Devil's Sonata," was the best I ever wrote, but how far below the one I had heard in my dream![16]

According to Emery, Thomas Edison used to keep a pencil and paper on his bedstand so that he could write down ideas that came to him while he was sleeping.[17] The physicist Niels Bohr visualized the model for atomic structure while dreaming about the sun and the planets.[18]

The structure of the chemical benzene was revealed in a dream to the German chemist F. A. Keule in 1890. He writes:

> Again the atoms were juggling before my eyes ... my mind's eye, sharpened by repeated sights of a similar kind, could now distinguish larger structures of different forms and in long chains, many of them close together; everything was moving in a snake-like and twisting manner. Suddenly ... one of the snakes got hold of its own tail and the whole structure was mockingly twisting in front of my eyes. As if struck by lightning, I awoke. .... Let us learn to dream, gentlemen, and then we may perhaps find the truth.[19]

Perhaps one of the oldest business examples of dreams—my colleague Carman Brickner calls this dream an example of long-term strategic planning—comes from the Old Testament:

> This may seem a strange reference, but it is the first that came to mind so you get it. ... in history, dreams have long played a role—at least in biblical times. Joseph (of the many colored coat) may be one of the earliest businessmen who dreamed the future, with the 7 fatted cows and the 7 lean ones. He then went to the Pharaoh who saved up the food for the 7 good years as Joseph predicted and then Egypt was able to survive for the 7 lean years.[20]

Another oft-repeated story is that of Elias Howe, an inventor who created the eye-pointed needle. Howe dreamed that he had been captured by savages, who threatened to kill him if he did not invent the machine. These dark-skinned painted warriors surrounded him and led to a place of execution. While he shook with fear, suddenly he noted that the head of the spears held by his executioners had eye-shaped holes.

It was as if the dream was giving him a message: unlike the conventional needles, the needle for the sewing machine should have holes in the front.[21]

I wonder how many business leaders would trust a dream like this now?

Paula Raines, J.D., Ph.D., used a powerfully symbolic dream to help her decide to leave her law practice and to start a new career.

> Many years ago (1994) I was trying to make the decision of whether to close a private law practice and take a leap and go into practicing as a therapist and workshop leader. The question had been banging around in the back of my mind for several months when I had the following dream:
>
> I am at the beach with a number of friends. I am surrounded by a number of items including my briefcase. Someone yells that there is a massive tidal wave coming. Everyone runs but me. I stay where I am and watch the water come at me. It hits and carries me and all the stuff around me into the ocean. We travel way, way out and then the ocean brings me back to shore and puts me right back where I was sitting earlier. I am unharmed and surrounded by all the stuff that was with me before the wave. The only thing missing is the briefcase which I know will never be located.
>
> At the time I had this dream, I was working with a Jungian analyst. We both agreed the dream (with the brief case removed from my life) was an indication that my life would go on with all the "stuff" I was used to having if I closed down the law practice and lost the "briefcase." I set a date to close the practice about a week after having the dream and have never regretted the decision.[22]

The Tibetan Buddhist teacher Tarthang Tulku says:

> Dreams are a reservoir of knowledge and experience, yet they are often overlooked as a vehicle for exploring reality. In the dream state our bodies are at rest, yet we see and hear, move about, and are even able to learn. When we make good use of the dream state, it is almost as if our lives are doubled: instead of a hundred years, we live two hundred.[23]

If you are interested in increasing your Edgewalking skill of knowing the future, begin to pay more attention to your dreams. There are many good books[24] on the practical use of dreams in every day life, as well as courses and dream groups.

Other Uses of Sleep

Science is only beginning to understand the secrets and the power of the mind and to learn about our different states of consciousness. Wise people have known how to use the subtle state (that "edge" state between waking and sleeping) as a source of solving problems and developing creative ideas.

It has never been called dreaming, but Einstein is famous for taking short naps when he hit a wall in his theories or calculations. Also, Edison knew that his best ideas came just before and after sleep, when he was in that theta state. Since the art of meditation and awake/trancing had not been shared by the East with the West at this point, he would place his head on his hands, which held small pebbles over a bowl of water. That way he would try to go to "that" state, and the moment he fell into a deeper sleep, his hands would open and the water would splash up and awaken him. He'd get the pebbles out and do this over and over on his way to inventing many wonderful things.[25]

Any dream expert will tell you that if you are going to use dreams as a tool to get guidance for the future, you must keep a notepad by your bed to record your dreams. But what if you don't remember your dreams, or the idea of intuition and dream interpretation seems a little too woo-woo for you?

That's the way it is for Mark Rosenberg, CEO and CIO of a very successful investment firm called SSARIS Advisors LLC, located in Stamford, Connecticut. The COO, Jim Tomeo, is very committed to nurturing the human spirit in their organization and is quite comfortable with discussions about spirituality and consciousness. Mark, on the other hand, prefers to focus more on the power of the mind. When I told Jim that I was writing about intuition and dreaming in this book, he suggested that I talk to Mark because Mark has a different approach to the use of sleep.

For Mark, it started about 35 or 40 years ago.[26] He describes himself as an A-type personality, and it seemed to him that eight hours of sleep was a huge waste of time. He wanted to find a way to get work done while his body was resting. So he would say to himself at bedtime, "I'm going to sleep now. I want my mind to work on this while I'm sleeping." He would think of a problem or opportunity that was challenging him at work and would say to his mind, "You work on it. Let my brain work on the problem." Right from the beginning, he would wake up with the question and answer on his lips. "I can almost hear the brain saying, 'Get up, get up. We've got it!'"

Recently, Jim Tomeo received an email from corporate headquarters asking if someone from their office could visit and see one of the SSARIS programs for clients. When he told Mark about it, Mark was frustrated, because there were other programs that he would much rather have corporate look at, and he didn't know what to say to corporate. Mark went to sleep that night and gave his brain this problem to work on. He woke up at 4 A.M., with the words clear as a bell in his mind: "Yes, we want you to see our program but we also want you to see these other programs—they are more important." He was given guidance by his sleeping brain to use this visit as an opportunity to redirect the people visiting from corporate.

How well does this process work for him? "I've never come up with a better answer than the one I wake up with," he replies. "Other people may come up with a better answer, so my answer might not be the best one in the final analysis. But it's always the best one I, personally, am able to come up with."

Mark has also used this "sleep" approach to working out strategies for negotiations. He gives his brain the assignment to work out a strategy, and when he wakes up, he knows how to handle the negotiation. "It's almost as if I've gone through the whole dialogue ahead of time, he reports. In my sleep I see them and hear them say something that they actually say in the negotiation."

So, regardless of whether you believe in the "little people," like Robert Louis Stevenson, or in the miraculous power of the human brain, like Mark Rosenberg, the time we spend sleeping can be a powerful time for developing our sense of the future.[27]

ADAPTIVE UNCONSCIOUS AND THIN-SLICING

Mark uses his brain in sleep to solve problems and is also working on ways to use it while awake. One of the newest fields in psychology that helps us to do this is the study of the "adaptive unconscious." Malcolm Gladwell, author of the best-selling book *Blink: The Power of Thinking without Thinking*, describes adaptive unconscious as "a kind of giant computer that quickly and quietly processes a lot of the data we need in order to keep functioning as human beings."[28] He says that our unconscious has the ability "to find patterns and behavior based on very narrow slices of experience."[29]

Gladwell cites research by John Gottman that concludes that with very little training, people can be taught to observe a three-minute video of a conversation between a husband and wife and have an 80 percent accuracy rate in predicting whether or not the marriage will result in divorce. In a study in which Gottman asked more than 200 marital therapists, marital researchers, pastoral counselors, and graduate students, as well as newlyweds, people who were recently divorced, and people who have been happily married for a long time to watch these videotapes, the group guessed right only a little more than 50 percent of the time. These 200 experts had a lot of expertise in marriage but were not trained in thin-slicing. So they tended to focus on too many details and did little better than chance in their predictions of marital failure.

Gottman uses thin-slicing by focusing on whether or not there are expressions of contempt in that three-minute discussion. Rather than focus on lots of other details, just this one factor can tell you very important things about the future of a relationship. If one partner expresses contempt for the other, there is very little likelihood that the relationship will last. It's like the "Butterfly Effect" for marriages.[30]

Gladwell explains:

> I think that this is the way that our unconscious works. When we leap to a decision or have a hunch, our unconscious is doing what John Gottman does. It's sifting through the situation in front of us, throwing out all that is irrelevant while we zero in on what really matters. And the truth is that our unconscious is really good at this, to the point where thin-slicing often delivers a better answer than more deliberate and exhaustive ways of thinking.[31]

I recently participated with family members and friends in an online telepathy study on Rupert Sheldrake's Web site in which you guess which of four possible senders is actually sending you a message.[32] My sister and I did little better than chance, but my friend Deborah Cox was able to correctly guess the sender's identity about 50 percent of the time. We talked about our thought processes in sending and receiving online telepathic messages and discovered that most of our errors arose when we let logic override what we were intuitively sensing. We would say in our minds, "Well, I've just received two messages in a row from that source, so the next message must be coming from a different source." Deborah tended to do better because she didn't second-guess the process as much. She would sense a vibration or warmth in her heart area that would provide her the information about the sender. She trusted this information and ignored logical thoughts about who the next sender might be. In a sense, she was thin-slicing.

The trick in thin-slicing is figuring out what one or two things to focus on that will provide you the best prediction of the future. We tend to make things much more complicated than they need to be, and we also tend not to trust our intuition nearly as much as we could.

CO-CREATING THE FUTURE

What this power is I cannot say; all I know is that it exists and it becomes available only when a man is in that state of mind in which he knows exactly what he wants and is fully determined not to quit until he finds it.

—*Alexander Graham Bell*

A couple of years ago I was in an airport when I walked past a large advertising sign that stopped me in my tracks. It was the picture of a man doing a t'ai chi pose on the top of a building, with the New York skyline behind him. I said to myself, "There's an Edgewalker if I ever saw one!" At closer examination, the sign said "Tony Visconti, David Bowie's producer." Well, I just knew that I had to interview Tony. He seemed, from the photo, to be an interesting juxtaposition of the world of martial arts, the world of business, and the creative world of music. It turns out that he is all that, and so much more. Tony's e-mail answers to my interview questions are presented in Appendix B. Tony also offered to do a follow-up telephone call if I had any questions, and there were lots of things I wanted to follow up on. He is an example of someone who is able to sense the future by working to create and manifest his visions.[33]

Tony had been interested in the supernatural and in esoteric topics from an early age and had studied with a genuine spiritualist named Ellen Resch. She did soul readings and spirit writing and taught Tony about meditation and spirit guides. Tony recounts that through Ellen he learned a lot about the mind and the power of the spiritual world. She said, "Talk to your spirit guides and ask them for things. They want you to have evidence that they are there, that they exist. If you want a taxi, just ask your spirit guides."

I was pretty well conscious of doing these kinds of things. And it worked. It really did. My biggest wish in 1967 was—New York was a horrible place to make the kind

Tony Visconti advertisement. © Anthony Visconti. Used by permission.

of music I wanted—I thought, "I want to go to London." And she says, "Well ask your spirit guides." So I asked my spirit guides, and within weeks, I met the guy that was to be my future boss for the next three years. By a water cooler in my music publishers' office. He introduced himself to me. He had an English accent and was the first Englishman I had ever met. He started talking, and within minutes we understood that we both did the same kind of work. I was a record producer for my boss. He was a record producer in London for the same company. And he called me "my American cousin." It was fantastic. . . . I was working with him within an hour on a recording session.

And that led me to London. I had saved the day. He couldn't read music, and he had eight musicians that demanded that you put music in front of them. I whipped something together within an hour. We literally ran down to the studio to get the music to them, and the session went flawlessly. I saved them a whole bunch of time. If those guys had had to listen to the demo and chart their own parts, it would have taken hours.

In those days Tony was very much in touch with his spirit guides, and he knows that they put him together with this man.[34] He goes on to say:

The most miraculous thing was that one of the first people I meet in London is David Bowie, and he's nineteen years old. And we're supposed to meet each other because we want to talk about the prospect of working together. Within an hour we're talking about everything but music, and one of the first things to come up are the Lobsang Rampa books.[35] He read them all, and he said, "I've met a Tibetan Lama." I said, "My God! Don't tease me like that!"

In London, Tony tells me, there is a Buddhist Society near the British Museum that sometimes hosts Tibetan monks who are visiting. David Bowie walked in there one day to buy a greeting card with a Buddhist message, as he had already at that time declared himself to be a Buddhist. The lady behind the counter told David that there was a Tibetan Lama visiting at that time and asked him if he wanted to meet him. And of course David did, so she led him downstairs. And there was a very young Chime Rinpoche, and he was meditating. He broke his meditation to speak to David, and David spent an hour with him.

David Bowie spoke so much about Chime Rinpoche that Tony really wanted to meet him, but he didn't get that opportunity for several years. The first time Tony met Chime Rinpoche, Chime gave him a meditation and a visualization. The second time Tony met with him, he took the three refuge vows, and he has been a Buddhist ever since. Tony is certain that his desire to go to London led to these two life-changing events—the opportunity to help David Bowie get his career off the ground and the discovery of Buddhism as the answer to his spiritual seeking.

I asked Tony about intuition and the role it has played in helping him to create the future that he desires. He began by describing what intuition means to him:

> Intuition is the way you focus without focusing . . . the way you go blurry in your mind, yet to have it in your view. It's like eyesight—like using your peripheral vision as well as your central vision at the same time. . . . Intuition is the ability to see all dimensions at once of one particular subject. . . . This could be a melody, it could be a business plan, it could be your next move in t'ai chi. When you are in the middle of the t'ai chi form, you see yourself at the end of the posture doing the closing posture. You see the river that you're on. It's the ability to be in many places at once.
>
> I've analyzed it over the years, and I know I have it. It's funny at the beginning of a business venture. I have to check myself all the time, you know, that impulse to grab something now because it looks good, without seeing the future of that. It's a big mistake that everyone makes. They find themselves six months down the road in debt or really kicking themselves for that decision. I think you can make decisions based on intuition, and you shouldn't make decisions on anything else but intuition. Get all the facts. Then it's visualizing. See yourself six months down the road. Work out all the scenarios. But the impulse of the moment, is something we have to resist
>
> . . . The impulse of the moment could be pure greed or selfishness. We see a piece of cheesecake and we say, "I gotta have it." Intuition can begin with an impulse. Like in martial arts. A fist is coming towards your face—you have to be very, very quick to not get hit. That's okay, but you might walk up to that person before they even take a swing at you and say, "This is going to lead to a fight. How do we avoid this?" So intuition is at many levels. And it could start with an impulse, but usually if you are really intuitive, you are aware that something's going to happen before it happens.
>
> The big mistake in the music business, or in any business that involves trends or fashion, is that unimaginative people tend to jump on the bandwagon when something is currently trendy. So, in other words, if Britney Spears is popular, within a month there's going to be about 50 clones of Britney Spears with blond hair and

exposing their navels and singing songs that are worse than the ones she sings. And foolishly people throw millions towards "my Britney Spears clone." And this is why the music business has one of the worst returns today. People in the music business follow trends today more than ever.

In the seventies, there was a small group of us that would make the trends rather than follow the trends. And you would do it in a time when something was currently popular and you would boldly do something that no one had heard before. . . . I was one of the group of people that said, "We're gonna get the next big thing. I'm out beyond this. I'm not going to make records that are currently popular."

I think people who are really intuitive are true to their own experience. They'll say, "I might be the only person that likes this now. It's so good, I know other people will like it, too." I know I'm an archetypal human. Humans—we all have the same experience in the form of emotions. We all have anger, we feel love, we feel sadness, and all that. And I'm no different, really. Architecturally, I'm like everyone else. I'm just more in touch with my feelings.

Tony has been extraordinarily successful in his career as a music producer, and even more so in life. He exudes a sense of inner calm and a real joy about being alive. There is an ease about him, a sense of flow, but also a sense of the power of creativity. He has learned the power of co-creating the future.

You never change things by fighting the existing reality. To change something, build a new model that makes the existing model obsolete.

—*Buckminster Fuller*

I have two dear friends who are futurists. I often turn to them to check out my own sense of the future and my vision for what I want to co-create with the Universe. The first one, Patricia Aburdene, is internationally known for her work on the *Megatrends* books. Her list of the Megatrends for 2010 was discussed in Chapter 1. I recently interviewed her for a teleconference series I run with leading-edge authors, thinkers, and leaders. In this interview, one of the participants, Rob Katz, a consultant from South Africa, asked Patricia how she used her intuition in discovering the seven Megatrends described in her book. She replied:

Imagine me sitting there in morning journaling with my fountain pen and my candles are burning and asking for guidance all the time. It's my best research tool. It's absolutely miraculous. You know, it's like, ask for something, and this book comes to you that's the exact answer to what you've been asking for. There's no question whatsoever that my intuition has guided me through this entire process. More than my intuition. An army of researchers [referring to her spiritual guides].[36]

Patricia is an example of someone who has co-created with the Universe. Co-creation begins with a sense of calling or a sense of yearning for something. You become a co-creator when you actually take action to respond to that calling or yearning. As many have said, "The best way to predict the future is to create it." Patricia had a sense of calling to write another book, and she originally began writing about spirituality in Silicon Valley. The dotcom bust occurred while she was in the process, and no publisher was interested in the book. She began another book, and it, too, went nowhere. So she went inward to sense what really needed to emerge in her, and she looked outward to see what the signs were telling her. She walked the edge between the material world and the spiritual world and then knew with a certainty that she was supposed to write another *Megatrends* book.

The book is doing extraordinarily well, and Patricia is traveling all over the country speaking at conferences and is also doing well financially. She co-created her own future. And, more important, by describing the seven Megatrends and providing solid information about the trends that are unfolding, she gives people the courage to join in the movement toward conscious consumerism, spirituality in the workplace, social responsibility, social investing, and the other trends that she describes in the book. She saw the future, and, by reporting about it, she is helping it to emerge.

My other futurist friend is John Renesch, who describes himself in his earlier years as an "entrepreneurial cowboy." In the 1960s, he and a partner started a successful event-production company. In 1968, he started his own public relations and advertising firm. He was making money and enjoying the good life. Then, in the 1970s, through a series of crises, he became introspective and began to examine his life and began to ask questions about the meaning and purpose of his life. After several years of very intense questioning, he decided to commit himself to something much bigger than himself and to get involved with visionary people who seemed to be doing important work for the future of the world.

Willis Harman, author of several books, including *An Incomplete Guide to the Future*[37] and *Creative Work: The Constructive Role of Business in Transforming Society,*[38] became a mentor to John. John writes about the impact that Willis had on him:

> He knew we humans were on the wrong track—acting as if we are separate from each other when we are all really interconnected, to each other and to a higher power of some sort. He was very sure that the future could be quite different from the way it was shaping up if we would only change the way we view reality, the way we think about everything.[39]

John says, in his book *Getting to The Better Future:*

> I learned about consciousness creating reality. I learned how *material* reality is the product of *immaterial* beliefs, concepts, and ideas about how things are supposed to be. . . . This is the way we create lives that largely comply with our beliefs. Hence our consciousness "causes" our reality (the way we perceive/experience it). And the system continues to reinforce itself as we live our lives *unless we challenge it!*[40]

I asked John what he actually *does* to know the future, how he actually goes about co-creating the better future that he describes in his book. First, he pointed me to the epilogue, titled "The Great Dream," that he wrote five years after the publication of his book. He describes the Great Dream as an extension of the original American Dream to the whole world. John looks to the American founding fathers for inspiration, saying, "As Thomas Paine, possibly the closest to being the 'father' of modern democracy, told us in the mid-1770s: 'we have the power to start the world over again.'" He goes on to say, "Indigenous shamans teach: 'the world is as you dream it.'"[41]

One way John worked to co-create the future was to gather a group of leading-edge thinkers to create a document called "The 21st-Century Agenda for Business: A Global Resolution for New Corporate Values and Priorities."[42] The preamble begins to lay out this vision:

> Business has become the most dominant institution on Earth. Within the global business community, there is a spiritual renaissance fermenting. Many people are calling for "conscious organizations"—companies that embody principles of interconnectedness, stewardship, compassion and global ecology in their business dealings.[43]

This Great Dream, this extension of the American Dream, is what John calls "humanity's dream." He says that it can serve the world, because America is a microcosm of Earth because of our diverse population and because we are the first nation to be founded on the principle that "people deserve to be free to find their own happiness, in whatever form that takes."[44]

I told John that it was my hope that this book would help people learn how to increase their ability to know and to co-create the future, and I wondered if he had some words of wisdom based on his own skills as a futurist. He responded:

> For me that sense is not one I know how to increase. It is a vision of what's possible that comes through ... perhaps it is more an issue of allowing it to come through. But that isn't an "action." It is being, not doing, willingness not furthering, developing, sharpening, acting upon, etc. ... maybe some subtle "shaping" but not doing!!! I suspect it isn't all that rare if people could allow themselves to really dream, to be labeled as crazy, to let their intuition run rampant, to dare to dream.[45]

If John is right, that co-creating the future is more about "being" than "doing," then we have come full circle in this chapter. We began by looking at the "doing" skills of Edgewalkers, in contrast to the "being" qualities of Edgewalkers. Perhaps, in the end, it always comes down to "being" rather than "doing." As Lao Tzu said 2,500 years ago, "Tao abides in non-action, yet nothing is left undone. If kings and lords observed this, the ten thousand things would develop naturally."[46]

The key elements of co-creating the future are (1) the ability to listen to your own inner calling, (2) the ability to envision a desired future (more about this in Chapter 5), and (3) the ability to enlist help from both the physical world and the spiritual world in order to make the future a reality.

> Do not follow where the path may lead.
> Go instead where there is no path and leave a trail.
>
> —Harold R. McAlindon

ORGANIZATIONAL IMPLICATIONS

Just about any CEO, entrepreneur, or executive would tell you that if she could predict the future, she would be able to ensure outstanding success for her organization. This chapter has described three ways that Edgewalkers embrace and come to understand the future: (1) Using Traditional ways of knowing the future, (2) Using Intuitive ways of knowing the future, and (3) Co-creating the future.

Tami Simon, CEO of Sounds True, who is mentioned in Chapter 3, is a wonderful example of someone who has developed the skill of knowing the future using all three ways.[47]

One example is how her company approaches product development. She says that it is really an issue of self-awareness, which is a key principle in spiritual development. "If I feel a need for a product, I know that others feel that need too," Tami explains. "I used to be afraid that this was ego, but now I know that it's much better to come from a place of what you want than to guess what others want." It is also knowing that since we are all interconnected, if you are feeling drawn to spiritual growth or spiritual teachings in a certain area, most likely others are too.

Intuition is one of the powerful outcomes of having a spiritual practice. Tami states, "Intuition is basically my entire existence." She studies with a meditation teacher named Reggie Ray. Reggie's teacher taught him how to "read the signs," and Reggie passed these teachings on to Tami.

"It's an art form," she says. "And an indigenous survival skill. If you were on a hunt, you would watch for the tracks. That's how we pick projects. We read the signs. How many people are talking about it? How many requests do we get for a particular author? And what are our inner feelings about the project? That's very important, too."

The profit-sharing discussion mentioned in Chapter 3 focused on how the company could be fiscally responsible while also offering positive rewards. People made rational arguments, but Tami says that in the final go-round, they just went with their feelings. She says that they used group intuition and asked everybody "What does your gut tell you?"

If your organization wants to have more of an Edgewalker culture, encourage discussions about the future. Explore scenario planning. Support data gathering from external sources, but begin to value data that come from internal sources, as well—gut-level feelings, intuition, and a sense of calling. If you really want to be on the edge, consider bringing in a consultant who is an intuitive, a channeler, or a corporate shaman.

GUIDANCE FOR EDGEWALKERS

Edgewalkers have strong intuitive skills. They are natural futurists. Because they are avid readers, they are constantly integrating information from many sources and looking for underlying themes and patterns. Like the shamans of old, they have learned to pay attention to subtle, perhaps invisible, signs of potential change. They have an uncanny knack for making the right decisions, often taking action that seems counterintuitive to others. But when asked how they knew what to do in a particular situation, they have difficulty explaining. They respond, "I just *knew*." Intuitive skills are gained through the practice of "deep listening." When listening to others, Edgewalkers listen as much for the unsaid as the said. They also look for coincidences, patterns, or synchronicities that might provide clues to guide them in their decision making. They learn how to thin-slice.

Intuition, a sense of the future, and the ability to thin-slice are not strange, mystical, New Age weirdness. What Gladwell says about thin-slicing can be more broadly applied to the concept of sensing the future:

> Thin-slicing is not an exotic gift. It is a central part of what it means to be human. We thin-slice whenever we meet a new person or have to make sense of something quickly or encounter a novel situation. We thin-slice because we have to, and we come to rely on that ability because there are a lot of hidden fists out there, lots of situations where careful attention to the details of a very thin slice, even for no more than a second or two, can tell us an awful lot.[48]

Each of the stages of Edgewalker development requires a certain mindset or level of consciousness. In order to learn how to sense the future, you must first be interested in the future. You find yourself asking, "What's over the horizon?," "What wants to emerge here?," "What will the next hot trend be?," "What is my next step in my life and work?" It is this basic curiosity about the future that fuels the heightening of the senses and allows you to gather better data, to be more intuitive, and to get better at co-creation. It drives you to learn the analytical skills, to network, to read the signs, to pay attention to your dreams, and to take action to develop your desired future.

If you wish to develop your abilities to know the future better, there are courses and books on all three ways of knowing, from forecasting and trend analysis to intuition workshops to courses on co-creation. And I believe that these skills develop faster if you are around people who already have them, so it helps to spend time with other Edgewalkers who may have stronger skills in this area. They can support the legitimization of these skills, they can inspire you, and there is an energy connection that usually helps to speed up your skill development.

The key, however, is to be true to yourself and to your own calling. If you immerse yourself in what matters to you, keep yourself open to possibilities, and make a commitment to act on what is calling you at the deepest level, you will be shown the future.

Chapter Five

FROM INVISIBLE TO VISIBLE: THE FOUR STAGES OF CREATING WHAT HAS NEVER EXISTED BEFORE

Excellence is the result of caring more than others think is wise; risking more than others think is safe; dreaming more than others think is practical; and expecting more than others think is possible.

—Source unknown

The first stage of Edgewalker development is focused on expanding and deepening our ways of knowing the future. There are three skills that can be developed in knowing the future: (1) Traditional ways of knowing, (2) Intuitive ways of knowing, and (3) Co-creating. Once these have been mastered to some degree, the Edgewalker can move on to the four stages of creating what has never existed before. Edgewalkers, like the shamans of old, have the ability to walk into the invisible world to see the future or to see what's needed for the "tribe" (Stage One).

They bring that awareness back into the present-day, visible, material world through the next four stages:

Stage Two: Risk-taking
Stage Three: Manifesting
Stage Four: Focusing
Stage Five: Appreciating

All creation begins with a thought. "In the beginning was the Word." Thoughts are invisible, and without thought nothing would get created. Edgewalkers pay attention to their thoughts and ask questions about what is needed in the world. As we discussed in Chapter 3, Lance Secretan has described his view of what Edgewalkers do: they become aware of what Terrathreats are most important to them, and they find ways to use their gifts to create Terrafixes.[1] This always leads Edgewalkers into new creative territory, and they find themselves growing and becoming more of what they were meant to be, as a result.

STAGE TWO: RISK-TAKING: THE ABILITY TO TRY WHAT HASN'T BEEN TRIED BEFORE, TO TRUST YOUR INSTINCTS, AND TO BREAK NEW GROUND

A man may fulfill the object of his existence by asking a question he cannot answer, and attempting a task he cannot achieve.

—*Oliver Wendell Holmes*

Edgewalkers have a strong sense of adventure and experimentation. They are always attracted to the next new thing. Like entrepreneurs, Edgewalkers are easily bored with stability and are always attracted to what's over the horizon. They are constantly asking, "What's next?" and trying to figure out how to be a part of it. Because they are able to walk in two worlds, the world of practicality and the world of creativity, the risks they take to jump into the next new thing are based on information and intuition. Having a clear vision guided by strong values helps the Edgewalker to take risks that might not make sense to others.

Igor Sikorsky is the quintessential example of an Edgewalker who took risks that didn't make sense to others. As a child he had a vision of a helicopter and spent hours of childhood play trying to design a machine with propellers on the top that would fly. He took a circuitous route through a career as an airplane designer as a young man because no one thought that his idea for a helicopter would work. But he couldn't let the vision go.

The irony is that behavior that seems foolhardy or daring or crazy to others makes perfect sense to the Edgewalker. Edgewalkers have an inner knowing and a sense of trust about where they are going and what they need to do. So, as the Nike slogan urges, they "just do it!" They trust that they have the inner strength and resources to do whatever it takes to make their vision a reality.

Tony Visconti has the ability to do this when he decides what new music to produce. In Chapter 4, he is quoted as saying, "I think people who are really intuitive are true to their own experience. They'll say, 'I might be the only person that likes this now. It's so good, I know other people will like it' too.'"[2] His discovery of Mark Bolen and the band T. Rex is an example of Tony's being true to his own experience. He heard Mark playing in a club, was entranced by him and his sound, and just knew that Mark could be a star. Everyone he worked with told him he was crazy and that Mark's unusual voice would turn people off. But Tony trusted his instincts and took a risk, and T. Rex became an international success.

> There was a time . . . Between fall 1970 and late 1972, Marc Bolan and T. Rex were just about the biggest band in the world. A chain reaction of UK chart-toppers, mass hysteria in Australia and Japan, monster best-sellers all across Europe, they even scored an era-defining smash hit in America, storming the Top 10 with the album *The Slider.* Quite simply, everywhere you turned, the T. Rex sound thundered out to greet you—and then drag you into the wildest party of the age.[3]

Tony was a young producer at the time, and he basically put his career on the line by taking on T. Rex. But he trusted his judgment, and he trusted his producing skills. He knew that he had both the inner resources and the outer connections to make Marc Bolen and his band a success.

Jerry Wennstrom is another person who trusted his judgment and took huge risks in his life, although I doubt he would call what he did a "risk." Jerry, the rising artist mentioned in Chapter 1, felt compelled to destroy all his art, to give everything away, and to live on the kindness of strangers. Perhaps this is the ultimate risk (and maybe even our ultimate fear—that we might go "over the edge"). This need to let go of everything came upon him right after he heard a spiritual speaker at the Cathedral of St. John the Divine in New York City. He didn't know why he needed to do this; he just knew that he did, and he acted upon it. For 10 years, he lived in poverty, not working, not creating, but completely trusting that there was a meaning and purpose to this way of life. In his book, *The Inspired Heart: An Artist's Journey of Transformation,*[4] he describes the many wonderful synchronicities that occurred because of this trusting way of life.

Throughout the book, Jerry tells stories that illustrate how he was able to touch other people's lives and of his own growing spirituality. There came a point when he just "knew" that this time of basically being homeless and owning nothing had served its purpose, and he felt called to move to Whidbey Island, in Puget Sound. There he rediscovered art, yet in a totally new form, met his wife, and began his work helping other people on their transformational journeys. He had come full circle, but the circle was fuller.

When the gift of the inspired heart is given, there is no longer a separation between art and any other aspect of our lives. We come full circle when we are fully and equally attentive to everything in our lives. . . . We begin to see the patterns that connect our actions to those of others, centered in their own unique circles. The universal circle that emerges as we interconnect is the creative energy that holds our world in its new form. We become, with those we are connected to, the inspired heart of creation itself.[5]

It's very important to pay attention to the artists, the poets, the musicians, and the dramatists. They are the canary in the mine. Because of their sensitivity and their propensity to tell the truth about what is emerging in society, they point the way and help to give the rest of us courage to take our own risks. Jerry says:

Artists and mystics are often the first to discover beautiful new directions in consciousness. That these new directions inevitably takes us through our worst fears is the reason most of us avoid the landscape completely. This is also why so many of the men and women who are the first to point the way for us—the bushwhackers of consciousness—have been misunderstood, condemned, or, worse, killed! Death will always look like death even if it is only the death of a way of life that is no longer working for us, personally or collectively. It seems to me that our collective consciousness is up against that moment in which new expression and healthy change demand our attention.[6]

Our culture lacks imagination, and those in authority positions are invested in having the future be pretty much the same as the present. Walter Brueggemann is an Old Testament scholar and has studied the role of prophecy in religion and politics. He says that, historically, those in power shrink from imagination because

imagination is a danger. Thus every totalitarian regime is frightened of the artist. It is the vocation of the prophet to keep alive the ministry of imagination, to keep on conjuring and proposing futures alternative to the single one the king wants to urge as the only thinkable one. Indeed, poetic imagination is the last way left in which to challenge and conflict the dominant reality.[7]

Prophets, artists, poets, and Edgewalkers take incredible risks because they are deeply concerned, perhaps even horrified, by the current reality of our institutions and our society. They cry, "The Emperor has no clothes." They offer alternative visions of what is possible, and that always challenges those who are benefiting from the current paradigm. They ask that people let go of what is no longer working so that a new reality can be embraced.

Recently, I was on a reunion conference call for people who had taken my Four Gateways to Spirit at Work program. One of our participants, Carolyn Wilson-Elliot, founder of Quantum Spirit International, told us that she had been profoundly affected recently by a question asked in a workshop she was attending. There was a myth about a narrow gate in the wall around Jerusalem that was called the "eye of the needle." In the New Testament, a rich man asked Jesus, "What is required for eternal life?" Jesus replied, "Follow the commandments."

The man told Jesus that he had always kept the commandments and wanted to know what else was required. Jesus then told him, "If thou wilt be perfect, go and sell that thou hast, and give to the poor, and thou shalt have treasure in heaven: and come and follow me" (Mat. 19:21). The man walked away very sad because he was wealthy. Jesus told His disciples, "And again I say unto you, it is easier for a camel to go through the eye of a needle, than for a rich man to enter into the kingdom of God" (Mat. 19:24).[8]

The myth of the "eye of the needle" related that when the main gates to Jerusalem were closed at night, there was only a narrow passage in the wall open to travelers. In order to get through, the camel would have to be unloaded of all its baggage so that it would fit through the narrow passage. Although there is no evidence that any such passage actually existed in the wall of Jerusalem, the message is still a profound one.

Participants in Carolyn's workshop were asked, "What do you need to let go of in order to go through the eye of the needle—to fulfill your personal mission?" For Jerry, the answer to that was "everything," including his identity as an artist. For Igor Sikorsky, it was his country, his fortune, and his identity as a Russian. For Carolyn, it was some household chores, like shopping and cooking, that she outsourced. But all risk entails the willingness to let go of something, however big or small that might be.

One of my favorite movies is *Close Encounters of the Third Kind*. In this movie, several unconnected people in different parts of the world have the same vision of an unusual rock formation in Wyoming, known as Devil's Tower. They feel an undeniable pull to get to Devil's Tower, even though they don't know why. They overcome all kinds of hardship and travail just to be there. It seems that nothing can stop them.

In the movie, the government tries to scare them away by saying that a poisonous gas has been accidentally released in the area, so they buy gas masks and keep on keeping on. The government finds ways to capture those who get through the barriers and barbed wire and trucks them out of the area. But some of them escape and continue to make their way to the mountain. In the end, the two people who prevail are able to witness the first human contact with beings from outer space, and one of them is even chosen to board the spaceship and return with the gentle, childlike aliens.

This movie captures the feeling of what it's like to be an Edgewalker. You have a vision. It may not be a clear one at first, but it's an urging, a calling, a restlessness and unease that will not go away. Like Roy Neary (played by Richard Dreyfuss), in *Close Encounters*, you feel the need to turn the vision into something concrete, even if it is only to make an image of Devil's Tower out of mashed potatoes or dirt from the garden.

Risk-taking inherently means that there is a possibility of failure. Edgewalkers have a different way of responding to failure than others. They are able to stay in the flow of unfolding events and to see failure as a temporary setback, as a lesson to be learned. They are able to stay centered in the midst of difficulty because of their contemplative or spiritual practices. Jeffrey Satinover, a psychiatrist, treats many successful individuals who have floundered when they are confronted with setbacks and who consider themselves failures. He says that he has learned the following lesson:

> *Truly successful people, the most successful, have a very checkered track record,* peppered with what they consider many serious "losses." Success for them is defined not by any external, objective standard unvarying from one person to the next but rather by that level of accomplishment that the individuals themselves experience as unequivocally satisfying (and that often happens to, but need not, coincide with what others consider successful too).[9]

What do you do if you have taken a big risk and you end up in the midst of a very difficult situation as a result? Satinover reports that only 10 to 20 percent of people can stay calm in the midst of great difficulty. People who stay calm are the ones who can perceive the situation clearly and can plan the best steps to take. These are the people who, when confronted with a changing and unpredictable environment, are the ones who are best at adapting. He describes this calmness as a key element in survival.[10]

Risk-takers understand that the feelings of fear are natural, but they have learned how to not let fear take over. Gonzales, in a study of who survives risky situations and who doesn't, from pilots who land fighter jets on aircraft carriers to people who fall into the water when whitewater rafting, found that stress short-circuits the brain's ability to act in a rational way. "You see less, hear less, miss more cues from the environment, and make mistakes. Under extreme stress, the visual field actually narrows. (Police officers who have been shot report tunnel vision). Stress causes most people to focus narrowly on the thing that they consider most important, and it may be the wrong thing."[11]

One of Gonzales's findings is that humor, especially dark humor, is one of the skills that separate the survivors from the nonsurvivors.

Laughter stimulates the left prefrontal cortex, an area in the brain that helps us to feel good and to be motivated. That stimulation alleviates anxiety and frustration. There is evidence that laughter can send chemical signals that actively inhibit the firing of nerves in the amygdala, thereby dampening fear. Laughter, then, can help to temper negative emotions. In some ways, risk-taking is like a puzzle.[12]

Playfulness is one of the five Edgewalker Qualities of Being, and playfulness is essential to risk-taking. According to Gonzales, laughter and play help people in high-risk situations to stay in touch with reality and to stay calm in the face of life and death situations. "It sounds horrible," he says, "but survivors laugh and play, and even in the most horrible situations—perhaps especially in those situations—they continue to laugh and play."[13]

In the medical field, the patients who are more likely to survive a terminal diagnosis are the rebels and rule breakers. "Psychologists who study survival say that people who are rule followers don't do as well as those who are independent in mind and spirit."[14] The medical field refers to them as "bad patients," the ones who are unruly, troublesome, annoying. They ask questions. They challenge everything. They don't always follow instructions. And they are more likely to survive.

Chip Conley, the CEO of Joie de Vivre, the hospitality company in San Francisco mentioned in Chapter 3, says that starting a company begins with a "crescendo of emotion and instinct, and from that comes the 'conception' of an idea. . . . And rarely does a rebel's venture begin with a rational decision."[15] Rebels (Conley's term for Edgewalkers) take risks and often put their own survival at stake.

Entrepreneurs and successful business leaders are very much alike. They are playful, they know how to use laughter to short-circuit fear in challenging circumstances, and they break the rules. They are risk-takers, and they are survivors. The survivors in Gonzales's study were able to stay focused on the reality of the situation and to break large tasks into smaller, manageable tasks. They were able to stay aware in the moment and to even notice beauty around them, which helped them to notice more details in their environment. And they were committed to their goal of getting out alive. They didn't quit. There is a lot we can learn from these risk-takers.

If you are strong in risk-taking skills, you have an indefinable feeling that you pay attention to. You hunger for adventures that will stretch you and make you feel more alive. As you listen to what this indefinable feeling is calling you to do, you take some kind of step to actually respond to that call. Like Igor Sikorsky, it could be trying to build a prototype of what you envision. Like Jerry Wennstrom, it could be letting go of everything that is not "It." Like Carolyn, it could be simply delegating tasks that do not bring you joy and take you away from your mission.

I seldom feel any sense of adventure or playfulness in interactions with most of the organizational leaders I meet. Corporate leaders are always asking for the numbers before they take a risk. That is one of their biggest mistakes. When something new is emerging, when a new opportunity presents itself, when you are creating something that has never existed before, there are no numbers to justify taking a risk. Joel Barker, the former director of the Future Studies Department of the Science Museum of Minnesota and the popularizer of the concept of paradigm shifts, writes about people who take risks:

> Captivated by a set of rules that suggests they may be able to succeed where before they failed, these pioneers risk their reputations, their positions, even their economic situations, on a nonrational decision. It is the aesthetic appeal of the new paradigm, the beauty of which it appears to solve problems, rather than quantitative proof of problem solving that precipitates the decision to change.[16]

Risk-taking means letting go of your old image of yourself and stepping into new territory. There are no maps or compasses, except your internal compass. Like the young man in the Giacomondi painting (see the first page of each chapter), you are walking out into nothingness on a tightrope, but you hold the rope and let it out before you take one step at a time. It is a complete act of trust. Trust is the bottom line in risk-taking. It means trusting yourself far more than you ever have before. It means trusting others more than you are comfortable doing. And it means trusting the Universe completely, knowing that you are divinely guided and supported.

STAGE THREE: MANIFESTING: THE ABILITY TO TAKE A THOUGHT, IDEA, OR VISION AND TO TAKE CONCRETE, PRACTICAL STEPS TO BRING IT INTO BEING

For anything new to emerge there must first be a dream, an imaginative view of what might be. For something great to happen, there must be a great dream. Then venturesome persons with faith in that dream will persevere to bring it to reality.
—Robert Greenleaf

As an Edgewalker, you have enhanced your ability to know the future, and because of your vision you are willing to take risks to do something that has never been done or to create something that has never existed. That means that you now need to develop the skills of manifesting.

There are two ways to look at manifesting: the macro approach and the micro approach. Both are essential to creating what has never been created before.

The macro approach is based on the principle that you create your own reality. A friend of mine, Joe Spellman, has a magnet on his refrigerator that reads, "If you don't like the way your life is going, change your mind." The macro approach is based on your attitude toward life and is very much connected to Stage 5 of Edgewalker development, Appreciation. Julia Cameron, author of *The Artist's Way*,[17] and Oprah Winfrey both advise people that if they begin to keep a daily gratitude journal, their lives will improve. Making a list of the things you are grateful for is a wonderful way to change your reality. You begin to see all the good that is in your life, and your positive attitude attracts more good.

The micro approach to manifesting is based on the practices of intention, visualization and affirmation, and footwork. The word "manifestation" comes from the Latin *manifestus,* which literally means "struck by the hand." The dictionary defines the verb "manifest" as "apparent to the senses or the mind; obvious, to show plainly; reveal."[18] I define manifestation as "the ability to take a thought, idea, or vision and to take concrete, practical steps to bring it into being." Or, to say it more simply, "to take something that is invisible and make it visible."

The Macro Approach to Manifesting: You Create Your Own Reality

The skill of manifestation begins on the macro level. In order to be able to manifest anything worthwhile, you must believe that you create your own reality.

The opposite belief is the belief that you are powerless and that you are a victim of circumstances. People who have victim consciousness are incapable of creating what has never been created before. They use their powerlessness and their victimhood to keep themselves stuck in the rut they have always been in. When they say "Things will never change," they are right—but only because that is the reality that they have created. Gonzales says that one of the things that separates who lives and who dies in survival situations is whether or not the person can rise above victim consciousness. Survivors identify themselves as survivors, not victims. And, often, in group settings, survivors identify themselves as rescuers as they set about finding ways to save the others with them.[19]

One of my most important and beloved mentors was Jack Gibb, creator of Trust Theory.[20] Jack taught that we all have a theory of life, whether we know it or not, and that theory becomes our perception of life. For instance, we can have a theory that says that the world is a dangerous and unsafe place, and so we decide that we need to defend and protect ourselves constantly. We don't trust other people, and we find that people live up to (or down to) our expectations. Or we can have a theory that says that the Universe is a friendly and trusting place and that we can be open and interdependent with other people. If this is our theory, we are more likely to attract people and circumstances that support our view.

Research is beginning to show that not only do we create our own reality by our attitudes and theories about life, but also our emotions may have a direct impact on our longevity. Martin Seligman, father of the field of Positive Psychology, reports on a study of nuns and longevity. When a novice takes her vows to become a nun, she is asked to write a short sketch of her life on this occasion. Researchers studied the number of positive statements in 180 of these sketches and compared them to the nuns' longevity.

When the amount of positive feeling was quantified by raters who did not know how long the nuns lived, it was discovered that 90 percent of the most cheerful quarter were alive at age 85, whereas only 34 percent of the least cheerful quarter were. Similarly, 54 percent of the most cheerful quarter were alive at age 94, as opposed to 11 percent of the least cheerful quarter.[21]

According to Seligman, optimists and pessimists experience a big difference in life and work outcomes. "Optimistic people tend to interpret their troubles as transient, controllable, and specific to one situation. Pessimistic people, in contrast, believe that their troubles last forever, undermine everything they do, and are uncontrollable."[22] "Pessimists are up to eight times more likely to become depressed when bad events happen; they do worse at school sports, and most jobs than their talents augur; they have worse physical health and shorter lives; they have rockier interpersonal relations."[23] In a study that measured the positive emotion of 272 employees over an 18-month period, it was found that happier people received better evaluations from their supervisors and higher pay.[24] In his earlier work, Seligman was able to show strong correlations between optimism and higher sales in salespeople, between optimism and promotions, and between optimism and salary.[25]

Chip Conley is a wonderful example of someone who understands that he creates his own reality. He is a consummate manifester, and a dyed-in-the-wool optimist. At the age of 25, he began creating his business plan for what would eventually become a unique and successful hospitality company. He describes this early beginning: "There was nothing rational about it. I had never worked in a hotel. My entrepreneurial experience was limited to selling calf-nursing bottles full of booze at Stanford football games. I had no money."[26]

Even before Chip knew what business he was going to be in, he named his company Joie de Vivre ("joy of life" in French). Talk about creating your own reality! It doesn't get much better than that. In his initial business plan, he boldly projected that he would have 10 hotels by the company's tenth anniversary. He was wrong. He had 13!

He got the idea for a unique type of hotel because, as he says, "visiting friends would lament the lack of fun hotels in town. My goal was to create a company with hip hotel concepts that appealed to a younger customer base—people like me. And I was going to do this without a necktie strangling me."[27] And, as with most Edgewalkers, everyone thought he was crazy. But he had a vision and passion, and he didn't let that stop him.

Chip focused on attracting the entertainment market to his first hotel, the Phoenix, a renovated "pay-by-the-hour" hotel with a pool. As "luck" would have it, two days after the grand opening, a 60-foot pink tour bus pulled into the motel parking lot and out popped Brenda Lee, a pop star from the fifties. Her group was driving through San Francisco and had not booked a hotel. Chip seized the opportunity to sit down with her and with the folk icon Arlo Guthrie, whom Brenda had run into, and asked them what they looked for in hotel. His vision was to become the world's greatest rock-and-roll hotelier.

One of the key lessons in Chip's experience is that if you are going to manifest something that has never been created before, the best way you can compete with the big guys is through niche marketing and by getting involved with something you are passionate about. He learned that most hotels look on rock-and-roll musicians with disdain, and he wanted to create a place where they would feel respected. One of the innovative ways he was able to create this kind of respect was to hire staff not from traditional hotel schools or training programs but from recording studios and concert venues—the people who admire rock musicians and who would give anything to be around them.

The Phoenix has been very successful and has consistently had occupancy rates above average for San Francisco.[28] And what is the lesson learned?

> A rebel business leader needs to be a visionary, able to imagine what doesn't exist today. I dreamed about the great parties I could throw and the sense of community

celebration we could create around the pool, paying no attention initially to the potential hotel market. I ran no focus groups or feasibility studies. I simply knew I was creating a niche product that my competitors could never imagine copying.[29]

Chip Conley practices what I call the "Field of Dreams" theory of manifestation. The movie *Field of Dreams* is about an Iowa farmer, Ray Kinsella, who hears a voice from his cornfield say to him, "If you build it, he will come." Ray interprets this message as an instruction to build a baseball field on his farm, believing that if he does, Shoeless Joe Jackson will be able to come and play baseball again. Shoeless Joe was a member of the infamous Black Sox team, the team believed to have thrown the World Series in 1919. The team was banned for life from the game. Ray has support from his family, but the townsfolk think he's crazy and shun him. But he believes in his dream and digs up his cornfield to build the baseball diamond. I won't spoil the end of the movie for you, but more than one dream gets fulfilled because Ray "builds it" or manifests the Field of Dreams.

Chip Conley believed in his dream. He built a hotel for rock-and-roll musicians, and they came. Believing in yourself and believing in your vision are key elements of the "macro" part of manifesting. Now let's look at the micro aspect of manifesting.

There are three skills in the micro aspect of manifesting: (1) intention, (2) affirmation and visualization, and (3) footwork.

Intention

Wayne Dyer, the best-selling author of *The Power of Intention: Learning to Co-create Your World Your Way*,[30] says that he has moved from a more traditional way of defining intention to a more spiritual view of the power of intention in our lives. For years, he saw intention as "a strong purpose or aim, accompanied by a determination to produce a desired result. People driven by intention are described as having a strong will that won't permit anything to interfere with achieving their inner desire."[31] For years, Dyer spoke about intention this way and lived it. This all changed while he was waiting for a cardiac procedure to open one clogged artery that had led to a mild heart attack. He was reading *The Active Side of Infinity*, by Carlos Castaneda, and found these two lines that changed his life. Castaneda's words were: "Intent is a force that exists in the universe. When sorcerers (those who live of the Source) beckon intent, it comes to them and sets up the path for attainment, which means that sorcerers always accomplish what they set out to do."[32]

For Dyer, the implication of these two sentences is that intention is not about something you *do* "but rather as a force that exists in the universe as an invisible field of energy!"[33] Intention, then, is getting clear about what it is that you want to manifest and then tapping into what Lynne McTaggart calls "The Field." McTaggart is an investigative journalist who was studying the medical field when she found that she kept coming up against scientifically valid studies of healing methods that flew in the face of the current paradigms of medicine. These studies would talk about an underlying energy field, and she began a personal quest to find out what leading-edge scientists were doing that suggested an alternative view of the world. She writes:

> For a number of decades respected scientists in a variety of disciplines all over the world have been carrying out well-designed experiments whose results fly in the face of current biology and physics. Together, these studies offer us copious information about the central organizing force governing our bodies and the rest of the cosmos.
>
> What they have discovered is nothing less than astonishing. At our most elemental, we are not a chemical reaction, but an energetic charge. Human beings and all living things are a coalescence of energy in a field of energy connected to every other thing in the world. This pulsating energy field is the central engine of our being and our consciousness, the alpha and the omega of our existence.[34]

McTaggart reviews the leading-edge research in disciplines such as physics, biology, medicine, psychology, and chemistry and reports on the conclusion of scientists that there is a "Zero Point Field." It is this "seething maelstrom of subatomic particles fleetingly popping in and out of existence"[35] that is the creative energy that Castaneda talks about when he says, "Intent is a force that exists in the universe." Scientists use the concept of Zero Point Field to explain the results of the many studies on remote viewing, ESP, nonlocal synchronicity, and distance healing. The Zero Point Field hypothesizes that we are all interconnected energy particles and that what affects one affects all. Therefore, our thoughts and our intentions are much more powerful than we might have ever thought possible.

In the 1970s, a Princeton University engineering student became interested in some of the parapsychology studies taking place at Duke University and proposed a study on the power of intention to alter random number generators. Her dean, Robert Jahn, was skeptical at first, but she was a bright student, so he supported her research, and after she graduated and left her intriguing results behind, Jahn continued to pursue this area of study. The computer revolution was just beginning, and he knew that microprocessor technology was becoming increasingly sensitive and vulnerable. McTaggart reports that "if it were true that living consciousness could influence such sensitive equipment, this in itself would have a major impact on how the equipment operated. The tiniest disturbances in a quantum process could create significant deviations from established behavior, the slightest movement send it soaring in a completely different direction."[36]

Jahn created the Princeton Engineering Anomalies Research (PEAR) program. The studies all followed the same design. In earlier parapsychology studies, participants were chosen on the basis of their abnormally strong ability to intuitively sense information at a distance. In this study, Jahn wanted to find out if the power of conscious intention was more generally distributed throughout the population. So participants were representative of the general population. The random event generators, as they came to be called, would produce a series of 1's and 0's.

Each participant sitting in front of the machine and would undergo three tests of equal length. In the first, they would will the machine to produce more 1s than 0s (or "HI"s, as PEAR researchers put it). In the second, they would mentally direct the machine to produce more 0s than 1s (more "LO"s). In the third, they would attempt not to influence the machine in any way. This three-stage process was to guard against any bias in the equipment. The machine would then record the operator's decisions virtually simultaneously.[37]

After 12 years of studies, with nearly 2.5 million trials, Jahn and his research partner, Brenda Dunne, found that "52 percent of all the trials were in the intended direction and nearly two-thirds of the ninety-one operators had overall success in influencing the machines the way they'd intended. . . . So long as the participant willed the machine to register heads or tails, he or she had some influence on it a significant percentage of the time."[38] Although this may not sound like a large number, when the expected outcome by chance would be 50-50, the statistical chances of something like this happening are about a trillion to one.

Elisabeth Targ spent months designing a scientific protocol for a research study on the power of intention on healing. She measured the effects of healing energy sent by 40 different healers to AIDS patients. "The results were unequivocal. The long distance healers contributed enormously to the physical and mental health of the patients. Targ discovered that it didn't matter which method the healers used as long as the *intention* [italics in original] was to heal the patients. Whether it was Jesus, Spiderman or grandmother that was summoned for help, the outcome was the same. What all the healers did have in common was their ability to 'not get in the way.' They surrendered themselves to the healing power as if they were opening a door and letting in something greater than themselves."[39]

If intention can influence a random event generator, and if prayer and healing energy can help AIDS patients, just imagine what they can do in our lives and our work. What intentions are you currently setting for yourself and for your organization? Or another question might be this—if Castaneda is right about intention: what does Source (or the Zero Point Field) intend to have emerge for you? I was once called to consult to a small group of people that wanted to create a new organization that would develop products and services that supported spirituality in the workplace. Marlow Hotchkiss, the group's facilitator, began the meeting by asking each of us to meditate on this question "What wants to emerge here?" The underlying intention of the group was to tap into that energy field that connects us all in order to get inspiration for the creation of an organization that would be meaningful and successful.

Intention can work in large and small ways in our daily life. I was reviewing Wayne Dyer's book *Intention* to prepare for this section. He mentioned Lynn McTaggart's book *The Field,* which I had purchased just a couple of weeks ago. So I was perusing that when I came across the concept of "Zero Point Field." As I read those words, I thought to myself, "I think I have a book with that title."

So I went downstairs to my library but could not find a book with that title. So I gave up and came back up to my office and began to straighten up some piles of papers that had fallen behind a filing cabinet before I settled back down to work. I had almost everything back in order, but it looked like there was a thin book still caught behind the cabinet, so I stretched a little harder to pull this book up. It wasn't a book at all but a copy of *Ode* magazine, with the words "Zero Point Field" written in large blue letters across the cover!

Affirmation and Visualization

Once your intention is clear, the next skills of manifesting are the skills of affirmation and visualization. I first learned about affirmation and visualization when I was in human resources at Honeywell. Our boss brought in someone to train our organizational development team in a program called "Investment in Excellence." This was in the early 1980s, and the course was unlike any corporate program I had ever taken. It really was a course about the power of the mind, and it taught us about the importance of setting clear intentions and then writing positive affirmation statements about those intentions. Once we had written our affirmations, we were encouraged to repeat them daily and to visualize our goal as if it were successfully accomplished.

I decided to experiment with this process and to see how it might work. I wrote my affirmations as we were taught and then wrote them on 3 by 5 index cards. Every morning and every night I would get in a relaxed, meditative state of mind and would read them to myself slowly as I visualized success. One of my affirmations was about gaining greater visibility in the company and receiving more opportunities. I visualized "opportunity" actually knocking on my door. Within about a week, invitations to speak, to be on committees, to travel, and to join high visibility projects started rolling in. It freaked me out! I got scared and overwhelmed, and so I stopped. And life went back to normal. But I was thoroughly convinced that the process worked. I just had some lessons to learn about being careful what you ask for!

Shakti Gawain popularized the process of affirmations and visualization in her book *Creative Visualization*. She describes creative visualization as "the technique of using your imagination to create what you want in your life."[40] We actually do this every minute of every day, but we are not usually conscious of it. Imagination, according to Gawain, is the ability to create an idea or mental picture in your mind.

An affirmation is a very clear, positive statement of something we desire as if it were already so. According to Gawain, "The practice of doing affirmations allows us to begin replacing some of our stale, worn out, or negative mind chatter with more positive ideas and concepts. It is a powerful technique, one which can in a short time completely transform our attitudes and expectations about life, and thereby totally change what we create for ourselves."[41]

In a business context, we might state a goal such as "To increase sales by 10 percent by the end of the year." If we want to turn that into an affirmation, instead of wording it in the future tense, we word it as if it has already occurred: "Sales increased this year by 10 percent." However, that is a fairly sterile affirmation. It is helpful to be clear about why you want to increase sales by 10 percent and what the benefits will be to you and to your organization. This is where visualization comes in.

Imagine what it will feel like when you have attained the goal. Perhaps you can see yourself receiving praise or an award or a bonus. Feel the feelings of satisfaction, excitement, or pride. Make the image and the experience as real as you can in your mind. After creating this image and these feelings in your imagination, you might want to rewrite your affirmation so that it includes more energy, more feelings, and more concrete images. For example, "I take great pride in the 10 percent increase in sales I achieved this year, and I enjoy the stronger relationships I have with customers."

If you spend as little as three to five minutes a day reviewing this affirmation and refining your visualization of your increased sales productivity, you will soon notice evidence that your manifesting process is working.

The Kripalu Gift Shop staff at the Kripalu Center, a spiritual retreat center in the Berkshires, practice affirmations and visualizations every day as a group before the store opens. They do what they call "Abundance Meditations," in which they visualize satisfied customers taking great delight in purchasing what they have for sale. I was told by one of their staff members that their average sales for each person who walks in the door is $80. I had to laugh, because I had just spent $84 myself, and I had only intended to window shop!

Prayer can also be a form of affirmation and visualization. Gregg Braden, a former earth science expert and computer systems designer, writes about how science and spirituality converge in a nondenominational form of prayer left to us by the Old Testament prophet Isaiah. He suggests that prayer is the union of thought, feeling, and emotion, and that it "represents our opportunity to speak the language of change in our world as well as in our bodies."[42] He describes a shift in consciousness that needs to take place if prayer is to be successful. "Rather than *asking* [italics in original] that the outcome of our prayer come to pass, we acknowledge our role as an active part of creation and give thanks for what we are certain that we have created. Whether we see immediate results or not, our thanks acknowledge that somewhere in creation our prayer has already been fulfilled. Now our prayer becomes an affirmative prayer of thanks, fueling our creation, allowing it to blossom into its greatest potential."[43]

Robert Ouimet, the Chairman of O.C.B. Holding, mentioned in Chapter 3, believes that prayer should never ask God for anything; we should just thank Him. He says, "That embarrasses the Lord!" In Ouimet-Tomasso, the leaders have created a Spiritual Support Group that meets once a month for the sole purpose of making contact with the Transcendent. They do not pray for guidance or for specific needs for themselves or the organization; they simply make contact. That's all. One of their key values is humility, and this is a beautiful example of that.

Most of us are not that humble, or that trusting, and prefer to use approaches that are more proactive. Perhaps someday more organizations will reach that level of enlightenment.

The key to successful affirmation and visualization is to be really clear about what you want. It's not enough to say that you want a promotion or that you want a project to be successful. You need to visualize work that you love doing in the job you have been promoted to. Picture the surroundings. Feel the positive emotions that go with this new work. Or visualize the positive outcomes of your project for your customers. See their smiling faces. Picture money flowing in, or your bank account numbers increasing. Again, feel the positive emotions that go with the successful completion of the project. Gawain and others also suggest that when you are working with your affirmations, always end with a phrase something like this: "This or something better is now manifest in the world for the good of all." Since we are all powerful creators, it is our responsibility to create those things that make the world a better place.

Footwork

I seldom see this step in any of the writings on manifesting, yet I think it is one of the most important steps. Doing your footwork means taking some concrete action to make your intention, affirmation, and visualization visible in the material world. I first got this concept from a description of the way the Senoi Indians, in Malaysia, work with dreams. The most important question in Senoi life was "What did you dream last night?" Every morning at the breakfast table, each family member would share his or her dream, the family would talk about it, and the parents and elders would provide advice on how the dreamer could have responded better in the dream. Finally, they would recommend social actions based on the events or the messages in the dream.

Since life was simple and abundant for the Senoi people, they did not need to spend a lot of time gathering or preparing food, clothing or lodging. So their days were based on creating something material based on their dream. It might be artwork, or something mechanical, a song, or a dance. If there was a conflict with another member of the tribe in the dream, the dreamer was instructed by the elders to make something and take it to the person with whom they had the conflict. Even the governance and collective action of the tribe was based on dreams.

The Senoi people determine most activities of daily life from the interpretations and decisions that arise out of their council discussions: Friendships are formed; tribe members organize dream-depicted projects; tribe members even agree on when to move the compound based on dream discussions. . . . The day is largely spent in these dream-inspired activities; at night, all the people retire to dream, to live another dream-directed day.[44]

"So what?" you might ask. "They're just a primitive tribe and have nothing better to do with their time." Dr. Garfield agrees that they are what we would normally refer to as "uncivilized." Their grasp of numbers is simple, with only four quantities: one, two, three, and "many." They are aboriginal people who live in the jungle. Garfield says, "Although we are far beyond the Senoi in every material sense, they are more advanced than we are in other ways. They have achieved things we have vainly struggled for. The Senoi are a peaceful culture; violence of any sort is extremely rare. . . . The Senoi maintain this peacefulness despite war-like tribes near them; the other tribes are fearful of what they regard as the magic power of the Senoi."[45]

What struck me most when reading about the Senoi is Garfield's description of their extraordinary psychological adjustment. For me, this is the answer to the "so what?" question about the Senoi. According to researchers who visited the Senoi, mental health problems were almost nonexistent. They tended to be very nonpossessive of people and things, perhaps as a result of their advanced psychological development, according to Garfield.[46] Other anthropologists disagree with her findings, but this conflict of opinion may be a result of the fact that this peaceful culture may have been lost during the counterinsurgency activities in the 1950s, where many Senoi were rounded up and kept in camps to keep them from helping the communists. Many died, and when they were released a couple of years later to return the jungle, their culture was probably severely affected.[47]

We do not have scientific proof that spending time on manifesting messages from dreams (or the invisible world) leads to positive outcomes, but I do believe that doing the footwork is an extremely important element of manifesting. In 12-Step programs, recovering alcoholics, addicts, and codependents are encouraged to "do the footwork and leave the results to God." The Serenity Prayer is a wonderful guide to support this: "Grant me the serenity to accept the things I cannot change, the courage to change the things I can, and the wisdom to know the difference." It is not enough to sit around navel-gazing and imagining that your work or life is improved. It is essential to take some concrete action to help make your goal or vision more real.

My first experience doing this came when I decided to go into coaching. I was not a certified coach and had not had any training, but I felt that, with all my years of experience doing organizational development work, as well as my experience advising students, I would be a good coach, and I knew I would enjoy the work. I decided to put this "footwork" principle into action, trusting that if I created something tangible that represented this new service, I would be tapping into the "Field," and would draw the perfect clients. So I created a brochure on my computer for this new service, which I called "Right Livelihood Coaching." I printed several copies and put them in a brochure display holder in my living room. That night, I had a meeting of my local Spirit at Work chapter group at my house and did not mention the brochures or the coaching, but three people approached me at that meeting and asked to have coaching sessions with me. Coaching is now an integral part of any of the work that I do with corporate clients, and I always build a coaching offering into any workshops that I run.

I do much the same thing when I have an idea for a book. I gather all the material I have on a particular topic, organize it to some degree, find a graphic for the title page, and print and bind it so that it looks like the beginning of a book. It is the footwork for manifesting an actual book in the future.

It doesn't matter how simple or small the action is. It just matters that you take some symbolic action that demonstrates your intention to take an idea or vision from the invisible world to the visible world. "A brilliant idea without action is like Mark McGwire playing baseball without a bat!"[48]

STAGE FOUR: FOCUSING: THE ABILITY TO BE VERY CENTERED AND TO GIVE ALL YOUR ATTENTION TO AN ACTION, PERSON, OR PROJECT THAT HAS SIGNIFICANCE AND IMPORTANCE

I never could have done without the habits of punctuality, order and diligence. . . . The determination to concentrate myself on one subject at a time.

—*Charles Dickens*

Multitasking is a highly valued skill in today's fast-paced world, but it's not all its cracked up to be. It works when we have several mundane things that need to be accomplished. If these tasks do not require much thought or quality, it may be more efficient to do several of them at once. However, multitasking can become an addiction. We get an adrenaline rush from handling many things at once, and we convince ourselves that we are being highly productive. Yet the truth is that great work comes from being focused, not from multitasking.

I doubt that any major new products, important business strategies, creative marketing campaigns, or innovative business processes came from someone who was juggling several tasks at once. Instead, most creative breakthroughs occur when people immerse themselves in a problem, challenge, or opportunity. As they live and breathe this situation, their minds are primed to see relevant information and important resources wherever they look. Their unconscious minds work when they are asleep or relaxing. It's the Archimedes "Eureka" phenomenon in the bathtub.[49] It's Robert Louis Stevenson's "brownie" phenomenon in his dreams.

In 2001, I attended a course called "Leadership Development Intensive (LDI)," facilitated by John Scherer, Lynnea Brinkerhoff, and Patricia Varley. It was a profound five-day course, and one of the key learnings I took away from the course was the concept of giving 110 percent attention to what you are doing. This concept was applied to interpersonal relationships, but it is applicable to anything we do. Most of us continue to multitask when someone drops into our office to talk to us. One of the people I am coaching at one of my client companies told me that whenever he walks into his boss's office, his boss is sitting with his back to the door and does not even acknowledge that this man has entered, even though he knocks and says hello. My coachee sits down and waits, and his boss never turns around and talks to him. So he uses the time to sit, think, and get centered and then gets up and walks out, with no interaction. Not a terribly motivating experience! In this case, the boss is 110 percent focused on his work, but not on his employee. There may be times when, as a leader, we need to say to someone, "I can't give you all of my attention right now because of this project. Can we talk after lunch?" People will respect that.

One of the women in our LDI course was the executive director of a nursing home. She brought her whole staff to the program. When the concept of 110 percent attention came up, she realized that she probably gives about 50 percent of her attention to anyone who comes to her office. She continues to go through her papers, she doesn't make eye contact in the hope that the visitor will leave so that she can get her work done, and she acts disengaged in other ways. Her staff gave her the feedback that she seemed unapproachable and disinterested and that it was hard to tell her about potential problems or to offer creative suggestions for improvement. She made a commitment to focus 110 percent on anyone she was talking to, and her staff later reported significant increases in morale, sense of team, employee commitment, and problem solving.

We have a bundle of cells in the back of the brain that serve as the filter for what enters the conscious and unconscious mind. It is called the "reticular activating system," and it sorts out the urgent and important information from the less important. Remember the last time you bought a new car? Most likely you immediately began to notice the number of cars like yours on the road. Your reticular activating system was paying attention to something that had become important to you. Edgewalkers know how to utilize the power of the reticular activating system by consciously choosing to focus on that which they are creating. They find that when they focus all of their attention on one thing, they begin to notice subtle signs, cues, and synchronicities. It's like a puzzle, where more and more of the pieces seem to fall into place.

Affirmations and visualizations are actually a very effective way of consciously utilizing the reticular activating system. By repeating words and images of what you intend to create, you begin to notice people, books, programs, and other resources that can help you actualize your vision. Most people find that when they really commit to the process of manifestation, unusual and valuable synchronicities occur.

The authors of the *Chicken Soup for the Soul* series say that focus is the key factor in entrepreneurial success. They advise business owners to focus on what they do best and to let others do what they do best—exactly what Buckingham and

Clifton say when they tell people to build on their strengths. Canfield, Hansen, and Hewitt write about the Rolling Stones, one of the most successful bands in history, whose 1994 world tour earned more than $80 million in profits. It took more than 200 people to build the mammoth stage structure, and more than 20 semitrailers to haul it from city to city. The Stones don't get involved in the logistics or in the setup of the stage. They pull up in their limo, walk onstage, and pick up their instruments. They play for two hours, putting on a show as they do what they do best, and then, after the final encore, they leave the stage and step into the waiting limousine. They are focused on what they do best.[50]

One tool that helps you to focus is a notebook. You could call it your Vision Notebook, your Manifesting Notebook, your Creativity Notebook, or your Ideas Notebook. It should be a size that is easy to carry around in a pocket, briefcase, or purse. Every time you have a thought, an inspiration, or a piece of information that is relevant to whatever it is that you are bringing from the invisible world to the material world, write it down in your notebook. This is telling your reticular activating system that any thoughts, ideas, or information are important, so that part of your brain begins to pay more attention to anything in your environment that is relevant.

Every summer, I go to Summer Acoustic Music Week in New Hampshire to immerse myself in music and songwriting. One of my instructors, Pete Kennedy, advised us to create a songwriting notebook. He has a whole structure laid out with sections for favorite words, interesting phrases, unique images, unusual names for song characters, potential song titles, interesting rhymes, and so on. I get a lot of songwriting ideas at concerts and when driving in my car. My book fits in my purse so that I can take it with me and jot down ideas when they occur. This seems to open the door to more of those kinds of ideas coming in.

Canfield, Hansen, and Hewitt make the point that the brain thinks in pictures, so they suggest creating a Picture Goals Book as another tool. You can buy a large photo album and then collect any pictures, brochures, or other material that help create an image of your desired outcome.[51] Gawain has a similar tool called a Treasure Map; the idea is that you create a collage of photos related to your goals or vision and post it somewhere where you will see it daily.[52] These tools help you to continue to focus on what you want to create and help eliminate a focus on barriers or feelings of cynicism.

Joseph Jaworski and Otto Sharmer interviewed entrepreneurs and asked them to describe the deeper aspects of their creation journeys. The especially wanted to know why the entrepreneurs, in spite of all the adversities, kept going. How did they stay focused? "They all answered that they felt compelled to continue, that they couldn't 'not do it.'"[53] The authors call this kind of response "Surrendering into Commitment," which is described as "the gateway to operating from one's deepest purpose, in concert with a larger whole."[54]

Csikszentmihalyi calls this "flow," which he defines as "the state in which people are so involved in an activity that nothing else seems to matter; the experience itself is so enjoyable that people will do it even at great cost, for the sheer sake of doing it."[55] In his research on optimal experiences, he found that every flow activity had this in common: "It provided a sense of discovery, a creative feeling of transporting the person into a new reality. It pushed the person to higher levels of performance, and led to previously undreamed-of states of consciousness. In short, it transformed the self by making it more complex. In this growth of the self lies the key to flow activities."[56]

There is both an exhilaration and growth that comes from giving your total focus to something you are manifesting.

STAGE FIVE: APPRECIATING: THE ABILITY TO VALUE THE UNIQUENESS OF SELF, OTHERS, AND THE SITUATION

The fifth stage of Edgewalker development is Appreciating. In this stage, Edgewalkers have developed their ability to value their own uniqueness, to celebrate the uniqueness of others, and to accept the gifts that are inherent in every situation. They have an aura of openness and acceptance about them that naturally attracts people. There are four primary skills that can be developed in this stage: (1) Multicultural skills, (2) Connecting skills, (3) Appreciative Inquiry skills, and (4) Blessing skills.

Multicultural Skills

Edgewalkers by nature have strong multicultural skills. Because they have walked between different worlds, they have learned to be multilingual. They are multilingual in the sense that they can understand the nuances of different worlds or cultures. Edgewalkers know how to pick up on subtle body cues and language cues that are different from their own. They pay minute attention to people different from themselves and have an open, warm curiosity about people from other cultures. They are boundary spanners and translators. They look for the commonalities more than the differences, and they want to know more about the worldview of that other person.

For most of her career, my dear friend Sharon has been in the information technology field. She works for a large utility in Connecticut and is very good at what she does. But Sharon is an Edgewalker, and she felt hemmed in by being able to work only in this discipline. She enjoys technology, but she also has a deep interest in people, and she found herself wanting to change careers to human resources. So she went back to school to get an M.B.A. with a concentration in human resources.

The organization really wasn't interested in having her move to another function because she would have been very hard to replace in her original position. Fortunately, just about the time that she graduated, the utility decided to spin off the natural gas business and created a subsidiary. The company was looking for people to move over to work in the subsidiary, and Sharon saw this as her opportunity to take a position in human resources. One of the job openings was for a director of knowledge management, and it was a job custom-made for an Edgewalker like Sharon. She knew how to set up information systems that would help the organization take advantage of the knowledge of employees. She also knew what kinds of training, leadership development, organizational development, and reward systems needed to be in place to help increase the knowledge within the company.

Sharon could explain human resources issues and needs to the information technology people, and she could explain technology to the human resources people. She knew the language and mindsets of both functions and could serve as a bridge builder between the groups. Because of her years of managerial experience, she could also serve as a bridge builder between upper management and lower levels in the organization.

How did Sharon learn these multicultural skills? As a teenager, she came to realize that she was gay, and she pretty easily accepted this about herself. However, her family and her friends at high school would not have been so accepting if they had known about her sexual orientation. So she learned to hide parts of herself and to pay close attention to her environment so that she would know when it was safe to be herself and when it was not. She had to learn to fit into the dominant heterosexual culture and to speak its language. It wasn't easy, and she ended up developing a very creative inner life that in later years would express itself through wonderful poetry and incredibly creative photography.

In her outer life, Sharron got involved in sports, and to this day she is still a huge sports fan. She learned how to be a woman in a man's world, and that also served her well in corporate life. Her childhood had been difficult, but she has come to appreciate the gifts in her early experience. Because she knew what it was like to be marginalized, she has developed a great deal of compassion for anyone who may be perceived as "different" in some way. This makes her a wonderful bridge builder.

As mentioned earlier, most Edgewalkers come from backgrounds that were quite challenging. They learn to become hypervigilant regarding possible threats to their self-esteem and/or physical well-being. They develop the skill of reading between the lines and of listening as deeply to what's not said as to what is said. They learn to read very subtle shifts in facial expressions. Knowing whom to trust becomes essential.

When Edgewalkers are young, this is a survival skill. Many people who experience difficult upbringings build walls of defensiveness around them and retreat within themselves. Only a few become Edgewalkers, and it's hard to say why. Sometimes there is one person who makes a difference in their lives and brings them out of their shells. Sometimes it's a part of their own healing process as they recover from early trauma and become committed to helping others with similar issues. Sometimes it is the result of moments of grace or mystical experiences. But something about their experience moves them beyond their concern with their own survival and toward a commitment to something larger than themselves.

Recently, while doing some training work for Unilever, in Arkansas, I met a very talented young lady named Tai Boen. She and Josh Northrup were the organizers of the program, and it was delightful to spend time with these energetic, creative, and hard-working young people. Tai told me that her full name is Tairica. Tai's mother is from Thailand, and she fell in love with an American serviceman there. They got married and moved to the United States, where Tai was born. Her name comes from the first part of the word "Thailand" and the last part of the word "America." It is the quintessential Edgewalker name.

Actually, Tai's mother is the real Edgewalker. She is the one who had the courage to leave her home country and to move to a foreign land, not knowing anyone but her husband. I told Tai about how Edgewalkers live in two worlds, spanning both of them but never really quite fitting into either. Tai said she never really thought about what that must be like for her mother and that our conversation gave her new insight into and compassion for her mother's experience.

Tai is the child of an Edgewalker, and so she has the advantage of knowing both cultures more fully and actually feeling that she does fit in both—more than her mother probably feels. Tai is what I call the "New Global Human." She is a child of the world and is likely to feel comfortable in whatever environment she finds herself in. This gives her an edge over people who have lived more homogenous lives. Tai will naturally be a bridge builder and translator for people in different worlds. Chances are that she may not even be aware of doing this because she's been doing it all her life.

My new grandson, Nicholas Max Neal, is half-Chinese. His mother, Cathy, my daughter-in-law, was born in the United States, but her parents immigrated from China to the United States, and, even though they have been here for decades, they do not speak much English. Cathy, on the other hand, does not speak much Chinese and is thoroughly American. She has a high-powered job at Merrill Lynch, right in the center of capitalism. Nicholas Max, like Tai Boen, has the opportunity to develop into an Edgewalker because of his multicultural background. My son, Shaun, is a computer wizard, an entrepreneur, and a rock and roll musician. Their children are growing up in a rich, complex, and multicultural world. The future rests on the shoulders of these young people.

Connecting Skills

Malcolm Gladwell, in his best-selling book *The Tipping Point*,[57] has coined a term, "The Law of the Few," to describe the influence of a small number of people in creating a social epidemic. It's like the famous quotation from Margaret Mead: "Never doubt that a small group of thoughtful citizens can change the world. Indeed, it is the only thing that ever has." Gladwell calls these influential people Connectors, Mavens, and Salesmen. It's the Connectors we're interested in here.

The Connectors are people who know lots of people and who seem to be at the center of networks. They have an extraordinary knack for making friends and acquaintances, and they connect people to each other. Gladwell created a test he called his "acquaintance survey" to quantify just how connected people are, and one of his high scorers was a successful Dallas businessman named Roger Horchow. Gladwell describes how Horchow seemed to know everyone:

> Horchow has an instinctive and natural gift for making social connections. He's not aggressive about it. He's not one of those overly social, backslapping types for whom the process of acquiring acquaintances is obvious and self-serving. He's more an observer, with the dry, knowing manner of *someone who likes to remain a bit on the outside* [emphasis added]. He simply likes people, in a genuine and powerful way, and he finds the patterns of acquaintanceship and interaction in which people arrange themselves to be endlessly fascinating.[58]

Connectors seem to have the knack of staying loosely connected with acquaintances, when, according to Gladwell, most of us would shy away from that kind of connection. Connectors walk in several worlds but also *remain a bit on the outside.* This is what allows them to reach across networks and to be involved to some degree in all of them.

The purpose of making an acquaintance, for most of us, is to evaluate whether we want to turn that person into a friend; we don't feel we have the time or the energy to maintain meaningful contact with everyone. Horchow is quite different. The people he puts in his diary or on his computer are acquaintances—people he might run into only once a year or once every few years—but he doesn't shy away from the obligation that that connection requires.[59]

Gladwell also writes about the actor Rod Steiger as an example of a Connector in the film industry and describes all the different kinds of films he was in. John Wayne was actually in more films, but they were usually Westerns, so he didn't have as many varied connections as Rod Steiger.

Rod Steiger was the best-connected actor in history because he managed to move up and down and back and forth among all the different worlds and subcultures and niches and levels that the acting profession has to offer.

This is what Connectors are like. They are the Rod Steigers of everyday life. They are people whom all of us can reach in only a few steps because, for one reason or another, they manage to occupy many different worlds and subcultures and niches. In Steiger's case, of course, his high level of connectedness was a function of his versatility as an actor and, in all likelihood, some degree of good luck. But, for most Connectors, their ability to span many different worlds is a function of something intrinsic to their personality, some combination of curiosity, self-confidence, sociability, and energy.[60]

I disagree with Gladwell when he says that being a Connector is intrinsic to one's personality. I do think it is more natural for some than others, but I also think it is a skill—or, more likely, an attitude or level of consciousness—that can be cultivated. Edgewalkers who have strong Connector skills see everyone as intrinsically interesting, and they are curious to learn as much as they can about someone new. They ask lots of questions, and they look for the connections between this new acquaintance and themselves, and for connections between the person and other people that the Connector knows.

If you want to strengthen your Connector skills, first, work on your own sense of connectedness to the world. Cultivate the attitude of Oneness. Take time for contemplative practices that focus on our connectedness to each other and to the planet. Read books like *ONE*, by Lance Secretan[61] and *The Global Brain Awakens*, by Peter Russell.[62] If you truly see yourself as interconnected, you will more naturally want to reach out and strengthen your connections. Then, ask questions. Be curious about people. Look for the links. And, most of all, find ways to help other people connect to each other. As an Edgewalker, you already have the skill of seeing underlying patterns and themes in what is emerging in the world. You can use this skill to look at patterns and interconnections in your relationships and with the people you meet.

Being a Connector is different from being a networker. People who network are doing it for instrumental purposes. I have a friend who calls me only when he is out of work and wants to know if I have heard of any job openings. He is networking, not connecting. Today I received a call from another person who calls only when he wants help in promoting his work. He is networking, not connecting. When I receive these kinds of calls, I can see a picture in my mind of this kind of person in his home office with his list of people to call. Once he has spent his allotted 15 minutes with me, he ends the call and goes on to the next person, checking my name off the list.

If you are a Connector, on the other hand, you are always thinking about how you can be of service to others. Who do you know that might help them? How might they help someone else that you know? You are always offering to introduce new acquaintances to other people or to call a group of like-minded people together so that people can feel more linked. It's a different level of consciousness. Barrett talks about seven levels of consciousness and that powerful place of transformation where we shift from a focus on ourselves and our ego-needs to a "focus on the common good—meeting the needs of the soul."[63] A Networker focuses on ego-needs. A Connector focuses on the common good.

Appreciative Inquiry

The third Appreciative Skill is a process called Appreciative Inquiry (AI). This process teaches people how to shift to a more appreciative mindset. In my book

Creating Enlightened Organizations,[64] I describe the Appreciative Inquiry process as one of a small handful of explicitly spiritual approaches to organizational or systems change. Even though you don't see it described that way in the Appreciative Inquiry literature, this process is based on the spiritual Law of Attraction. This law basically states, "What you give energy to grows."

Typically, in life and at work, we give energy to problems. We look at what's not working and try to make it better. I first learned about how problem-focused we are as a culture when I took an empowerment workshop from David Gershon and Gail Straub. They said in the beginning of the workshop that the more we focus on problems and on what's not working, the more we will see problems and see what's not working. It's a mindset—a problem orientation. They describe this problem orientation as the pathology of our culture and teach people how to make the shift "from pathology to vision."[65] That was a radical idea to me—that we actually attract more problems into our lives when we focus on problems. But if we focus on what's working and appreciate what we have, then we attract more of that into our lives. I talked about this earlier in this chapter when I discussed the process of manifestation.

There are eight basic assumptions of Appreciative Inquiry:

1. In every society, organization, or group, something works.
2. What we focus on becomes our reality.
3. Reality is created in the moment, and there are multiple realities.
4. The act of asking questions of an organization or group influences the group in some way.
5. People have more confidence and comfort to journey to the future (the unknown) when they carry forward parts of the past (the known).
6. If we carry parts of the past forward, they should be what is best about the past.
7. It is important to value differences.
8. The language we use creates our reality.[66]

This model moves away from problem solving and creates a path to the future that is based on strengths of the past and on future possibilities. Edgewalkers can develop the skill of asking appreciative kinds of questions instead of problem-oriented ones. The Appreciative Inquiry model has four basic phases: (1) Appreciating and valuing the best of "what is," (2) Envisioning "what might be," (3) Dialoguing "what should be," and (4) Innovating "what will be."[67] In each situation, unique AI questions can be formed for each of these phases.

My first experiment with Appreciative Inquiry came at a monthly Spirit at Work group that I held when I was a faculty member at the University of New Haven. Each month we would have a different topic, and on one particular month I suggested we experiment with the AI process. We broke up into pairs, and people interviewed each other with these two questions: "Tell me about a time when you felt really proud to be working for the University of New Haven" and "What brings you joy in your work?" Person A would ask Person B these questions and take notes. Then the partners switched roles. After both interviews were complete, they would look for any common themes in their answers. We discussed their results in the group, and you could feel a powerful shift happen in the group. This tended to be a fairly positive group, by its nature, but overall morale was fairly low in the University, and this group was a kind of refuge for many people. But, after this discussion, people felt inspired by remembering what really matters to them about this organization and had several ideas about how the culture could move forward in ways that would build on the strengths of the past.

More recently, one of my associates, Thad Henry, and I have been working with a marketing and distribution firm that is experiencing fairly high turnover and low levels of trust and satisfaction. We are working with the top two levels of management, and about a month ago we met with the top executive team to talk about how it can be more supportive of the second-level managers in helping to bring about cultural change. Unfortunately, even though our commitment was to taking an Appreciative Inquiry approach to our work with this organization, we fell into the trap of talking about what was wrong with the team, instead of focusing on its strengths. We pointed out that the top-management team seemed to be divided in its basic management philosophy, with about half the group being very people oriented and the other half of the group being strictly bottom-line oriented. We told the team members that they needed to become more cohesive as a team, to reach out to their direct reports, and to be more supportive. We were looking at what wasn't working, and it's no surprise that some people got uncomfortable and defensive. Several people left the meeting before it was over to go to another meeting, and things did not end very well.

When we met with this top-management team the next time, we took a more Appreciative Inquiry approach and asked the members to talk about what their strengths were as a team and what they did well in supporting the cultural change they want to see in this organization. Although one person clearly was cynical about these kinds of "touchy-feely" questions, everyone was able to say something positive, and the energy in this meeting was noticeably different. A few days after this meeting, the executives went offsite for a day to talk more deeply about their values and about how they can support people development in the organization, and it was a very successful meeting. One of the vice presidents told me that it was the first time that they had ever worked so well together, and they came to see that they had a greater sense of shared values than they thought.

Blessing Skills

The fourth Appreciative Skill is the skill of Blessing. I learned something very important about the power of blessing from reading *The Hidden Journey*, by Andrew Harvey.[68] Andrew was born in India and educated in the United Kingdom, the perfect background for an Edgewalker. "He spent his childhood in a household which, though Christian, was actually a crossroads of many faiths, filled with Moslem and Hindus, holy men and woman saints who laid the foundations of wonder and sacredness in the child's imagination."[69] At the age of nine, he left this wonderful Edgewalker incubator environment to attend school at Oxford. At age 25, he was desperate to escape what he called the "concentration camp of reason" to return to India. There he met Mother Meera, on Christmas Day, and she became his spiritual teacher.

In his book, *Hidden Journey,* he recounts a mystical experience he had in the early stages of his spiritual development. He felt his body fill with soft light and then began to hear a voice. He knew it to be the voice of Mother Meera, his teacher. She said:

> You cannot transform what you have not blessed. You can never transform what first you have not accepted and blessed.

I wonder how many of us are trying to transform our lives, our work, and our organizations without first blessing them. What does it mean to "bless" something? One definition is to "make holy."[70] In your work, do you see yourself as holy, as connected to the Divine? Do you see the Divine in others? Do you see the Divine working through the organization?

I believe that an organization has a soul, one that is made up of the collective souls of the people who have worked there and who are currently working there. The Organizational Soul is particularly influenced by the dreams, visions, wounds, and shadows of the founding members and of the current leaders. To bless your organization means to see the Organizational Soul as holy, even if you are not completely happy with the way things may be manifesting in the moment.

Another definition of blessing is "to ask Divine favor for." In our Edgewalker work with organizations, we can pray for our organizations and can visualize the best possible outcomes.

When I was a manager at Honeywell, we had a network of people throughout different divisions of the organization who prayed for organizational healing. We met once a month by teleconference and talked about what needed healing in each of our divisions. We then chose a time when we would all commit to prayer or meditation on behalf of the organization. This was not an officially sanctioned group, and there is no way of knowing whether or not our prayers made a difference, but we all felt that it was worth doing.

A third definition of the word "bless" is "to protect from evil or harm." Mary Ann Vlahac is a bank manager for a large credit union in Connecticut and is a practitioner of Wicca. It is part of her regular practice to visualize her son, her house, her car, and her company surrounded in protective white light. She says prayers of protection for all of them. In these days of corporate corruption and greed, I imagine that many people are praying for their workplaces to be protected from evil or harm. One other very important way to protect your organization from evil or harm is to tell the truth when you see evil or harm taking place. It is extremely important to take a stand for truth and to not turn your head the other way when you see wrongdoing taking place.

Those of us in the consciousness movement are committed to transforming ourselves and our organizations and to supporting business as an agent of social and spiritual change in the world. Let's make sure that we are blessing ourselves and the institutions that we want to see change. It is all too easy, especially these days, to see business and organizations as evil, soulless, and full of harm. But, if Mother Meera is right, we will not be able to bring about the transformation we envision, unless we:

1. Make our workplaces holy.
2. Ask Divine favor for our organizations.
3. Protect our organizations from evil or harm.

ORGANIZATIONAL IMPLICATIONS

We are reaching the limits of the old paradigm of rationality and linearity in our institutions, what Harvey calls the "concentration camp" of reason. Traditional problem-solving approaches seem to breed more problems. Our organizations and our lives get more complex. This chapter has presented four stages of development that are not normally encouraged in the corporate world—the stages where we learn to create what has never existed before by moving from the spiritual or invisible world to the material or visible world.

Each of these stages has several skills that people can develop and strengthen. People can learn to increase their abilities to take risks and to endure when some risks end in failure. Organizations that learn to value and support risk-takers will be more innovative and agile. I once had the opportunity to visit a large Procter & Gamble factory in Mehoopany, Pennsylvania. It employed 4,000 people and was a company that encouraged risk-taking and learning. The company policy was that if you tried something and failed, you would not be punished. But you would be asked to create a one-page "Learning Document" that you would send to people who might benefit from what you learned from your experience. By the way, this plant would put 11 people on a team that needed only 10, because it always wanted someone to be free to attend classes or team meetings, and it paid its employees more than any other P&G plant and more than other factories in the area. But it was also 25 percent more profitable than any other P&G plant because of its innovativeness and creativity.

Organizations manifest all the time by producing goods and services, but they are only beginning to tap the power of manifestation, especially on a collective level. Other than the Kripalu Gift Shop, I have never heard of an organization that consciously uses skills such as intention, affirmations and visualization, and footwork. Lou Tice's *Investment in Excellence* program teaches people how to do this, so perhaps there are some case studies out there. Chances are that if there are organizations that are using these skills, they are keeping it a secret either for competitive advantage or, if they are publicly owned, so that stockholders don't think they have "gone over the edge"!

Organizations tend to be structured in ways that keep people from focusing, especially with expectations that email, phone calls, and other forms of communication will be answered in a timely manner. However, some organizations are experimenting with ways to help employees focus. I visited a plant that cleaned and distributed work uniforms to other companies. The CEO insisted that there be no meetings or phone calls during the first half hour of the day. He expected his managers to sit quietly in their offices and just think or meditate. He wanted them to have time to focus on bigger issues and important questions. Other organizations create a "meeting-free afternoon" so that people can focus and get individual work done during that time. But focus is also an inner way of being, and people who have contemplative practices are more likely to be able to take advantage of these focus times in organizations.

Thanks to the great work of David Coopperrider, Sue Annis Hammond, and others, we have a lot more organizational examples of the skills associated with appreciating, especially Appreciative Inquiry. The most difficult switch to make is the shift from problem-solving to appreciating, from what's wrong to "what's possible." Organizations that learn how to do this are able to unleash tremendous creativity, passion, and commitment.

GUIDANCE FOR EDGEWALKERS

As an Edgewalker, you most likely have progressed through many, if not all, of these stages. Now, having read this chapter, you can better assess your own level of development and can create your own personalized plan for further growth as an Edgewalker. Use the assessment form in Appendix C to rate yourself on your level of development within each of the five Edgewalker Stages.

One of the most important things to do for your own growth, and your own sanity, is to find other Edgewalkers to be around. We have created an Edgewalker Online Community at www.edgewalkers.org. Visit our Web site for inspiration, resources, and the opportunity to connect with fellow Edgewalkers.

Chapter Six

THRIVING AS AN EDGEWALKER IN A MAINSTREAM WORLD

There is a light in this world, a healing spirit more powerful than any darkness we may encounter. We sometimes lose sight of this force when there is suffering, too much pain. Then suddenly, the spirit will emerge through the lives of ordinary people who hear a call and answer in extraordinary ways.

—Mother Theresa

Kermit the Frog used to sing, "It's not easy being green." Edgewalkers understand the message of that song. It's not easy being an Edgewalker. You see things that other people don't see. You know things in your bones that other people adamantly disagree with. If people really knew what you were about, they would think you were crazy. Sometimes you think maybe they are right. Maybe you are crazy. Yet you have a strong commitment to being authentic and being true to your values and vision. Like Don Quixote, you are going to keep tilting at windmills. At least that's how it feels sometimes.

The first part of this chapter takes an individual perspective and addresses some of the issues that Edgewalkers typically face in organizational life and provides some suggestions on how to handle them. The second part of the chapter takes a managerial perspective and describes the roles that Edgewalkers and others play.

HOW INDIVIDUALS THRIVE AS EDGEWALKERS

Like a forest of alder and fir, two cultures now inhabit the same space.
One—focused on death—dying; another—focused on life—emerging.
Unseen, the dying of one purifies, prepares and enriches the soil for the other.
Amidst chaos and dissolution, celebrate the emerging new vitality!
                              —*Tom Bender (2004 Feng Shui Calendar)*

Fitting in Without Losing Your Soul

Edgewalkers are like the scout who goes ahead before the tribe to see if there are buffalo over the hill and to see if the way ahead is safe from hostile bands of marauding braves. When the scout returns with the a report on what's up ahead, the tribe must have some sense of trust and respect for the scout if it is to listen to what the scout has to say. So, as one of those scouts, how do you figure out how to be authentic, to share your view of the future, and to speak your truth, without being marginalized?

When I first began my corporate life, with a job in human resources at Honeywell, I had the good fortune to be sent to the Leadership Development Program at the Center for Creative Leadership, in North Carolina. In one of our exercises, we were each asked to create an imaginary person who had the qualifications of being a "world leader." We then met in a group and were tasked with trying to convince the rest of the group that our world leader was the best person for the job. I suppose it didn't help that I was the only woman in the group and the youngest person there, but my choice of world leaders didn't help me to fit in with this group or to be influential in any way at all. I was very quickly marginalized. You see, I chose a character, let's call him Moog, who was a chief from the Senoi Indian tribe, in Malaysia. The Senoi Indians are the tribe that has the dream culture and that is reputed to have no mental health problems and no crime. I thought, in my naïve and idealistic mind, that if we had someone like this as world leader, we could easily begin to create world peace.

In this situation, I was not an Edgewalker. I had gone over the edge. I was too far out there for the middle-aged, white, male managers who made up the group I was in. This exercise took place in a room with a one-way mirror, and a team of organizational psychologists observed our behavior in the group. Later, we each met with the person who had been assigned to observe us, and this person said to me that my ideas were just too way out in left field and too idealistic. He reviewed the large number of personality profile surveys that I had taken for this program and looked me in the eye and said, "You really might want to consider some other line of work besides corporate work." His message basically was, "You don't fit in."

The experience was devastating to me, but I really believed that I had some kind of mission to fulfill in organizational work, and so I learned that I needed to find a way to fit in without losing my soul. It wasn't easy. I came very close to feeling that I had lost my soul when I worked for Honeywell Defense Systems, in Joliet, Illinois. But I learned to tone down my more far-out creative ideas most of the time and to focus on presenting what my colleagues could accept and relate to. I had been spending so much time exploring alternative paradigms that I had forgotten about the mainstream paradigm that I was working in. So I needed to learn to build bridges between the current reality and other possible realities that I was exploring.

Dan Ruben is a person who knows very well about how to fit in without losing his soul. He worked for Harvard Pilgrim Healthcare, in Boston, as an administrator. Dan's spirituality is tied to a feeling of concern for the Earth, and his volunteer work was focused in environmental awareness work. He saw many opportunities at Harvard Pilgrim for improving environmental consciousness in his workplace, but people didn't seem interested. Dan realized that if you want to build a bridge between the world of corporate materialism and the world of environmental sustainability, you need to appeal to people's heads, hearts, and pocketbooks. He saw that the organization wasted a tremendous amount of paper each year, and so he put together a new position description for himself.

> Seeing an opportunity to make a positive impact on the environment by changing behaviors and attitudes at Harvard Pilgrim, and inspired by the organization's programs and mission, I drafted a proposal for a position to develop and implement environmental programs. I tied the proposal to Harvard Pilgrim's mission, and I linked it to other goals of the organization: reducing administrative costs (by reducing the use of energy, water, paper, and other materials and by reducing waste disposal costs); improving the satisfaction of staff who desire a more environmentally responsible workplace; and satisfying many of our members and employer customers who are pleased when resources were used more efficiently.[1]

Dan's approach to fitting in without losing his soul was to make proposals about things that mattered to him deeply, but to do it in a language that addressed issues that mattered to others. His proposal was to create a systemwide paper-reduction program that would save money, streamline processes, and be good to the environment. He wrote, in an article:

> Harvard Pilgrim uses roughly 500,000,000 sheets of paper per year, which is made from approximately 50,000 trees. I have found that our paper use is not only degrading to the earth, but also needlessly expensive and inefficient. I influence managers

and staff to participate in the paper conservation program by appealing to their heads (reduce organizational costs, improve efficiency), hearts (save trees, prevent climate change, reduce pollution), and pocketbooks (help achieve the staff bonus). Whenever possible, I make the connection between our lifestyle choice (how much paper we use) and the consequences for the earth, and its present and future inhabitants.[2]

This program was very successful, and Dan estimated that it saved the organization more than $6 million per year.

The key is to find projects that are an expression of your values and that also line up with the values and goals of the organization. In most organizations, the more you can talk the language of the bottom line, the better bridge builder you will be. But don't forget to constantly keep in touch with your values and your personal sense of mission while doing this. Sometimes it may mean making career tradeoffs instead of selling out. Trust me, it's worth it in the long run.

> When I dare to be powerful, to use my strength in the service of my vision, then it becomes less and less important whether I am afraid.
>
> —*Audre Lord*

Necessary Costs of Being a Maverick and Risk-Taker

Edgewalkers often feel lonely, disconnected, and not valued by their organizations. The typical organization has built-in mechanisms to keep behavior fairly predictable, and, while leaders say they support innovation, watch how often they tend to squash it. It may help to know that these feelings of loneliness and disconnectedness are part and parcel of the role of being an Edgewalker. Like the scouts mentioned earlier, you find yourself called to be out in front of the tribe, discovering new territory. It's lonely out there, but there is a beauty in the aloneness. And a freedom.

Although there are ways, like those already described, that can help you learn to fit in better, in your heart of hearts you know you will never completely fit in. And the truth is that you don't want to. As an Edgewalker, you find yourself gravitating to the sidelines a lot in order to better observe the patterns and rhythms of what is going on in the organization. It's not unusual to feel the paradox of passion and detachment. You are passionate about your vision of the future and what is possible, but you have some level of detachment from the organization.

When I first went to work at the University of New Haven, I was passionate about living in alignment with my spiritual values, particularly the values of authenticity and integrity. I worked hard on designing and teaching courses that would be meaningful, I joined every committee I was asked to be on, and I got involved in projects that mattered to me, particularly those focusing on diversity.

Because spirituality is so important to me, I needed to be authentic about that. So I applied for a university grant to do summer research on spirituality in the workplace, back in 1992, when there was very little written about this topic. The committee that approved grant applications was the same committee that approved tenure and promotion. I said to myself, "Well, let's see if this is a place where I can be who I am. If the grant doesn't get approved, I will know that this is not the place for me, and I will find (with help from the Universe) some other place that will accept me for who I am." Fortunately, the grant got approved, and I continued to be supported in my research and interests while I was a faculty member there.

One of the teachings of Buddhism is nonattachment. Twelve-step programs suggest that you "let go and let God." It helps to accept that your career path and your role in the organization are likely to be nontraditional, simply because you wouldn't have it any other way. Edgewalkers chafe at being put into standardized boxes. Chances are that if you are in a traditional organization, and if you are true to your Edgewalker nature, you are not likely to get promoted into one of the top positions in the organization. On the other hand, if you are working in an organization that understands the value of Edgewalkers, the sky is the limit.

If you are working for a very traditional boss, it can be extremely difficult to communicate your sense of the future and to get your creative ideas accepted. You may often be told, "You're not being paid to think. Just do your job." One of the ways to deal with a boss like this is to stress your competency and your performance.

Richard Hackman was one of my favorite professors in the doctoral program at Yale. His work was brilliant and cutting edge. It was creative and interesting. He would do things like fly with cockpit crews when he studied the culture of People Express Airlines so that he could get a firsthand view of their team dynamics. He would go out drinking with the crew after its New York-to-London flight and would continue to observe the team dynamics. He developed a theory about the role of alcohol in team building (I don't think he ever published these results!). In class, he would always walk around in his socks and often resorted to various kinds of theatrics and playfulness. We quickly learned that he was a sucker for chocolate chip cookies, so we would bring stacks of them and put them on our desks so that he could help himself to cookies as he walked around the room.

He taught us the concept of "idiosyncratic credits." People earn idiosyncratic credits by building trusting relationships and through competence. The more idiosyncratic credits you have, the more you will be forgiven if your behaviors or ideas deviate from the norm. Edgewalkers need to learn how to pay attention to this balance. If you are new to an organization or team, it helps to realize that it takes time to build up these idiosyncratic credits. In the beginning, you may have to make an extra effort to figure out what it takes to build that trust before you start to express more of that which makes you unique.

There is always the risk that Edgewalkers will be marginalized or even forced out of the organization. Some organizations are so risk-averse, and structured so tightly to prevent what they might consider uncontrolled innovation, that they send out the equivalent of organizational antibodies to attack what is perceived as a foreign invader. If this happens to you, bless the organization for sending you a strong message that you are more needed somewhere else, and then go find yourself an Edgewalker organization like Joie de Vivre, Ouimet-Tomasso, or RMG Search. Better yet, become an Edgewalker entrepreneur and create an innovative organization that will attract other Edgewalkers!

Balancing Competing Demands from Different Worlds

Sharon, the woman mentioned in Chapter 5 who bridges the worlds of information technology and human resources, always finds herself performing a balancing act. She works in an organization that values technology more than people, so she is constantly finding herself pulled back to work full-time on information technology projects when she wants to be in human resources. These projects are always of limited duration, but they are frustrating for her.

To keep her sanity, she finds ways to integrate her human resources values and skills into the information technology projects. For instance, the primary reasons that implementation of new technology fails are that (1) users are not involved in the implementation, (2) users don't receive adequate training, and (3) the HR rewards, recognition, and promotion systems are not set up to support the use of the new technology. Sharon is able to bring her human resources skills into the information technology projects to help implementation go more smoothly. During the times when her work is primarily focused on information technology, she will take the time to go to Society for Human Resource Management meetings, to human resources conferences, and to workshops that support her interests in personal growth and transformation. Even though she might not be able to use her human resources skills all the time, at least she feels she is growing professionally.

Sometimes being a bridge builder who links different functions, departments, or parts of the organization means that you end up having to go to more meetings, having more deliverables, and spending more time integrating work from different areas. You feel like you are juggling more balls than you can handle. If this is the case, it's important to take the time to assess your priorities and your activities. It's very tempting to get into the detail work of multiple functions when you are an Edgewalker. You love learning about new areas. But if you find yourself too caught up in the details of cross-functional work, you may need to step back and take an eagle's-eye view of the project. Your role is not to micromanage; it's to build bridges between people who see the world differently and who may speak different languages. Remind yourself that you are a facilitator and a translator but that you don't have to work out all the details for those involved. You can help them to do it for themselves.

Here's one last piece of advice about balancing competing demands from different worlds. At times, it may seem to you that the material world and the spiritual world are competing for your time and energy, but that is only an illusion. All work is spiritual work, and all action is spiritual action. Each moment of the day provides an opportunity to be walking in both worlds at once, because they overlap. According to Ken Wilber, the more you spend time in nonordinary or meditative states, the more quickly your consciousness evolves and the faster you move to an ongoing stage of unity consciousness.[3] I strongly encourage you to take on or to deepen your contemplative or meditative practice because, among many other things, it helps you to be more centered in the midst of competing demands and to tap into your highest levels of intelligence.

Andre Delbecq and I were both instructors in a doctoral program in Mexico several years ago, and I got the opportunity to sit in on his course with international leaders. He explained the importance of having an inner life and taking the time for contemplation. I sat next to Andre during lunch, and we talked about the importance of spirituality in our lives and work. I mentioned to him that I was working so hard on projects, courses, and writings related to spirituality in the workplace that I found it hard to find the time for my own meditation. He told me, "Then double the amount of time you spend on meditation." I looked at him in surprise because this didn't make sense at all. But he told me that his spiritual director had once said the same thing when he felt too busy for prayer and contemplation. He had found that by doubling the amount of time that he was currently dedicating to his inner life, he became more centered, more inspired, and more effective. Think of it as an experiment, and try it for yourself!

Dealing with Rules

Edgewalkers tend to drive too fast, roll through stop signs, and walk across the road at red lights if there is no car coming. They trust their own judgment more than they trust some "Big Brother" who is making up rules for an ordered society. I'm not talking about criminals here, because Edgewalkers have very strong value systems and are not prone to breaking the law. However, they do have trouble with rules, and they enjoy finding ways to create exceptions to the rules. And sometimes they bend the rules out of frustration with a system that seems to put rules in the way of quality work.

I used to live on the Branford River, in Connecticut, and one day while I was out walking on the riverbank with a neighbor, I noticed that the water was all muddy and brown instead of its usual clear color. My neighbor told me that the Army Corps of Engineers was dredging the river to make it easier for boats to get further upriver to some of the new docks that were being built. She said that there was quite a furor about it at the Branford town meeting because the Army Corps had not asked for a permit to do this work. So, with 75 percent of the work done, a representative of the Army Corps of Engineers went to the Town Hall and put in the required applications for permits to do the work. The town had no choice but to approve the work. My neighbor said that one of the Corps' basic operating principles was, "It is more effective to ask for forgiveness than permission."

I call this the Army Corps of Engineers Principle and advise Edgewalkers to use it judiciously. You need to be able to pick your battles and be discerning about when you act first and ask permission later. This works best in areas where you are doing something that has never been done before, so no rules exist yet. My first boss at Honeywell, Bill van Horn, was a genius at this principle. For example, he would set up a meeting with the V.P. of human resources and, without asking, would bring our whole team to make a presentation. Or he would invite a plant manager to say a few words of welcome before the beginning of a training program. After the plant manager was finished, he would say, "Stay up there for a few more minutes. Does anyone have any questions?" And he would turn the prepared speech into an open exchange. Another time, he held an offsite for our team at Arcosanti, an unusual community in the desert north of Phoenix. He invited the staff to sit in on part of our team meeting, which hadn't been on our agenda, and out of that session emerged several innovative ideas for possible collaboration between Honeywell software engineers and Arcosanti.

Another way to deal with rules is to propose to pilot-test something. If you believe that some rules are getting in the way of creativity, flexibility, or customer service, you can propose to pilot-test an alternative system. The rules stay in place for the majority of the organization, but you have requested an exception for your unit or project. If it goes well, then you have a strong argument for changing the rules throughout the organization.

Finally, it helps to be clear about your values. If there is a conflict between your values and the rules, or between your values and "the way things are done here," stay true to your values, regardless of the cost.

Several years ago, I was invited to be a guest on Oprah Winfrey's show. She was doing a program on whistleblowers, and she invited four different whistleblowers to come to her studio. The primary guests were John and Colleen Swanson. They were invited to be on the show because of John Byrne's book *Informed Consent*,[4] about their experience as whistleblowers. Colleen Swanson had had breast implants, and she believed that they were the cause of her debilitating illness. Her symptoms included severe migraines, debilitating joint and back pain, numbness in her arms and hands, and extreme fatigue. The breast implants were leaking silicone into her system, and she had them removed. Her husband was John Swanson, creator and overseer of Dow Corning's ethics program, considered to be one of the best programs in the country. The breast implants were sold by Dow Chemical, and this created a powerful moral dilemma for John Swanson. He began to do some internal investigation on the breast implants, and he came to believe that Dow was covering up information about the dangers that existed. His role as ethics officer had been to fight the complaints and lawsuits that were coming in about the implants, but, after his wife's experience, he no longer could follow the corporate rules laid down for him.

When I met them, in 1994, in the green room of the Oprah Winfrey show, Colleen was still very ill, and John was suffering from depression. When he refused to continue fighting the implant cases for Dow, the company took away his job duties and put him in a room with boxes, a small desk, and no windows. He was eligible for early retirement soon thereafter, and he took it.

He paid a huge price for taking a stand for what was right. He had been a rising star, and his career came to a screeching halt. But he did the right thing, and he brought Dow's unethical behavior into the public eye. His actions also helped to publicize the dangers of breast implants and may have helped to prevent untold numbers of women from having to go through what his wife went through. When Oprah asked him if he would do it all over again, he said with conviction, "Absolutely."

> Almost all great art has a strong charge of the negative in it, and conversely, bland popular culture has little power for survival. Popular culture is a smoothing of the collective ego. In order to break that smoothness, the significant artist must step in and give it a one-two punch. Almost always the great artist straight-arms the reader at the beginning of his work; it is both a grabbing action and a statement of intent. This is done in many ways, but it stems from a primary disposition of restlessness. The great artist has a divine impatience with the way things are.
>
> —*William Everson*

LIFE IN THE CUBICLES

Cubicle farms are one of the most difficult physical environments for Edgewalkers. In fact, I don't know any normal human being who likes being in a cubicle. They are like impersonal cages with no privacy. One of my clients has a facility with several floors of cubicles, and their inhabitants are not allowed to bring in family photos or any expressions of their individuality. Only approved company propaganda is allowed on the fabric-covered cubicle walls. When you walk through the facility, there is very little sense of energy or life happening there. And it's hard to find your way around because everything looks the same. It's like being on the inside of some kind of machine. The company is proud that things run like clockwork, but I don't sense much room for innovation.

Deborah Cox, who is the president of IgniteSpirit!,[5] used to work for Pitney Bowes as the Manager of Change Management. I met Deborah when she took an online M.B.A. course that I offered on Spirituality in the Workplace for the University of New Haven. She has since become one of my closest friends and is often a spiritual guide for me. She is also my Reiki Master. In our online course, Deborah gave many examples of ways that she practiced spirituality in the workplace at Pitney Bowes.

In one example, she told the class members a story about a time when there was a lot of conflict in her department. Everyone was in cubicles, so if someone had sharp words with someone else, the discussion was audible to everyone, and it affected the working environment. During one such incident, Deborah went into a meditative state to ask for guidance about how to reduce the tension and stress, and she was given the inspiration to play a soothing music CD on her computer. The sound traveled gently through the cubicles, and the two people who were having angry words with each other suddenly stopped their argument and went back to work. Deborah would also send Reiki energy throughout the office when she felt that the people in her team needed clarity and inspiration.[6]

Pat Sullivan spent several years researching how people personalized their workplaces in order to provide a sense of meaning and purpose. She called this project "Workplace Altars,"[7] and she believes that almost all of us create sacred space in our work, whether we realize this or not. Photographs of loved ones, sacred objects from nature, religious objects, and inspirational sayings on our computers—all these are examples of how we create our workplace altars. Even people in cubicles can find ways to create a sense of sacred space. They might have to keep certain objects or photos in their drawers, if company policy is extremely rigid, but it is worthwhile to take the effort to remind yourself of the bigger picture of why you do what you do at work.

In 1992, I had the opportunity to visit AT&T Universal Card Systems, right after it had won the Malcolm Baldrige Award for Quality. This was a values-driven organization, and its values were visible everywhere—on banners, posters, coffee mugs, laminated cards, bookmarks, and t-shirts. Lots of companies do that, but what was more impressive is that anytime I asked an employee about the company values, the person could rattle them off immediately. Everyone had memorized all seven values and could explain what they meant. The employees' cubicles really caught my attention.

Each cubicle was unique and expressed the personality of the person who worked there. Many of the staff had collections of small construction-paper circles of several different colors displayed in creative designs on their cubicle walls. When I asked about them, I learned that each employee had been given seven of these circles, and they stood for the seven values of the organization. If you saw someone else doing something that exemplified one of the seven values, you could hand the person one of your circles and express how you admired the way that the person lived the value of trust, open communication, fairness, service, or whatever it might have been. People were very proud of these values circles, and you could feel the energy and creativity in this maze of cubicles.

So, if you are an Edgewalker and find yourself in the psychic prison of cubicle life, there are both invisible and visible things you can do to make the environment more conducive to creativity and innovation. And, if you are a manager in this kind of environment, I encourage you to do everything in your power to allow people to express their individuality. If they can't do it in their cubicle, how in the world do you expect them to do it in their work?

INTERVIEWING FOR A NEW JOB

The opportunity to apply for a new job, either in your current organization or in a new organization, presents interesting dilemmas for an Edgewalker. The key question for both you and the interviewer is "Is there a fit?" But you and the interviewer probably mean different things by that question. Most likely, the interviewer will just be looking at your skills and experience. You, on the other hand, will be looking to find out if this job fits into your larger sense of mission and purpose in life and whether or not it is aligned with your values. You are less concerned about your skills and experience, because you have an inherent trust in your ability to learn whatever you have to learn in order to be successful and to make a contribution. Your potential employer is likely to be focused on what you have done in the past, while you are focused on what you could do in the future.

The best way to handle an interview opportunity like this is to remember your strengths as a bridge builder. You are someone who is capable of understanding the practical business needs required by this new position. You are also able to see all kinds of potential and possibility. Use your intuition and ability to read subtle cues to assess just how much creativity and risk-taking your interviewer is interested in. The best policy is to be your authentic self and to be professional. Build bridges between yourself and the interviewer. Show the person that you understand the business needs met by this position and that you have thought about some ways to address them. In addition, you should make sure to find ways to have the interviewer understand your values and what matters to you.

Mary Ann Vlahac, the banker mentioned in Chapter 5, faced this challenge when she decided to leave Peoples Bank, in Connecticut. She applied for a job as the marketing director at a local credit union. It might help to know a little bit about Mary Ann's unusual background.[8]

Mary Ann's grandmother came from Eastern Europe, and Mary Ann is proud of her gypsy heritage and of the unusual Edgewalker abilities that her grandmother passed on to her through the practice of Wicca, an ancient nature-based religion. As a child, Mary Ann learned to see into the future from the older women in her family.

Mary Ann feels that she was born with this ability and that her family helped her to hone it to a fine skill. "My mother was against the 'ways of our family' and was a strict Catholic. But her sister and my grandmother had ceremonies and taught me from the very beginning. There were gatherings of women on certain days, and it usually involved taking something from the earth and doing something with it. I learned dream interpretation and palm reading."

Mary Ann is highly successful in her profession. She has a doctoral degree and is well respected in her field. I met Mary Ann when she was one of my doctoral students, and we used to have very interesting conversations about spirituality in the workplace. About that time, *Personnel Journal* contacted me for an article it was doing on spirituality in the workplace,[9] and I suggested that the writer contact Mary Ann to interview her. She agreed to be interviewed on the condition that the magazine not use her name or place of work, but, unfortunately, it did not respect her request. This caused a great deal of discomfort for Mary Ann. She says, "People shunned me in the ladies' room. They were afraid of me. There was a bias towards me. I had been there 18 years, and I felt I deserved promotions, but I didn't get them. People would say, 'You are different.'"

However, when she interviewed for her new job at the credit union, she decided that it was important that the organization accept her for who she is, and she told the interviewer to check her out and to read the *Personnel Journal* article. Her new boss is very accepting of Mary Ann's "walking between the worlds," and Mary Ann feels that she can be herself there. "In my office you'll see elements of my religious beliefs, although I try to be subtle about it. There are pentagrams and a small altar. I have a Buddha and crystals in my car, and tarot cards in my bookcase." In this environment, Mary Ann feels creative and whole and is excited about finding ways to create relationships between the credit union and the community in a way that makes a significant difference in people's lives.

She loves her job and feels it is a great place that supports her in her uniqueness. One of her favorite projects is creating financial literacy for young people between the ages of 15 and 18. Her credit union is partnering with the Rotary Club and is funding accounts of $25 per student. She says that her job is to help kids understand what money means to them. "They pay me to do this! I did it on my own time before, when I was the VP of Marketing Research for a much larger bank." Mary Ann's authenticity and integrity, as well as her skills and experience, helped her to find a job that was just perfect for her.

Some people actually walk between the worlds when they want to find a new job and spend time making their intentions clear. They create affirmations and visualizations. And then they do the footwork. The book *Noble Purpose,* by Barry Heermann,[10] is a wonderful workbook that helps people to get clear about what kind of work would express their "Noble Purpose" and is filled with all kinds of exercises that include affirmations, visualizations, and ways to make your intentions manifest in the material world through journaling, artwork, and music.

Work in the invisible world at least as hard as you do in the visible.

—*Jalaluddin Rumi*

WHAT IF YOU GET FIRED?

Chances are that if you are any kind of a decent Edgewalker, you will get fired at least once in your career. And I'm not talking about getting laid off because your job has been eliminated. I'm talking about the most painful kind of firing, where you are rejected because the organization does not want you anymore. You may get subtly pushed out the way John Swanson got pushed out of his job at Dow Corning and the way I got pushed out of my job at Honeywell. This is what commonly happens to whistleblowers. The company takes your job duties away and hides you in a little office in Siberia. Or you may be told to leave because of disagreements with your boss, or because of personality clashes, or because you are getting in the way of someone else's political agenda. It never feels fair, and it almost always hurts and makes you angry.

If this happens to you, it is helpful to take time to remember your basic beliefs about the way life works. All of us have philosophies and inspirational things we tell ourselves when times get tough. When I was forced out of my job at Honeywell after I blew the whistle, a strange sort of calm came over me, even in the midst of anger, fear, and pain. There was this calm place in my center where I knew that all of this was happening for a reason and that I just needed to trust that there was some bigger force operating behind the scenes. I now look back at that event and truly believe that it was one of the biggest gifts in my life. It helped me to discover an inner strength that I never knew I had, and it led my on my path to the work that I do now.

Steve Jobs, creator of the Apple computer and the CEO of Apple and Pixar, is one of the most eminent Edgewalkers in Silicon Valley. He had a very similar reaction to being fired from Apple when he was 30 years old. He spoke about this in his commencement address at Stanford University, in 2005. For the full text of this commencement address (which is really worth reading), see Appendix D.

I really didn't know what to do for a few months. I felt that I had let the previous generation of entrepreneurs down—that I had dropped the baton as it was being passed to me. I met with David Packard and Bob Noyce and tried to apologize for screwing up so badly. I was a very public failure, and I even thought about running away from the valley.

But something slowly began to dawn on me—I still loved what I did. The turn of events at Apple had not changed that one bit. I had been rejected, but I was still in love. And so I decided to start over.

I didn't see it then, but it turned out that getting fired from Apple was the best thing that could have ever happened to me. The heaviness of being successful was replaced by the lightness of being a beginner again, less sure about everything. It freed me to enter one of the most creative periods of my life.

During the next five years, I started a company named NeXT, another company named Pixar, and fell in love with an amazing woman who would become my wife. Pixar went on to create the world's first computer-animated feature film, *Toy Story,* and is now the most successful animation studio in the world. In a remarkable turn of events, Apple bought NeXT, I returned to Apple, and the technology we developed at NeXT is at the heart of Apple's current renaissance. And Laurene and I have a wonderful family together.

I'm pretty sure none of this would have happened if I hadn't been fired from Apple. It was awful-tasting medicine, but I guess the patient needed it. Sometimes life hits you in the head with a brick. Don't lose faith. I'm convinced that the only thing that kept me going was that I loved what I did. You've got to find what you love. And that is as true for your work as it is for your lovers. Your work is going to fill a large part of your life, and the only way to be truly satisfied is to do what you believe is great work. And the only way to do great work is to love what you do. If you haven't found it yet, keep looking. Don't settle. As with all matters of the heart, you'll know when you find it. And, like any great relationship, it just gets better and better as the years roll on. So keep looking until you find it. Don't settle.[11]

BASIC GUIDELINES FOR EDGEWALKERS

In summary, here are some basic guidelines on things you can do to thrive as an Edgewalker:

1. Write a mission statement and a values statement for the work you want to do in the world.
2. Read professional material in fields that are unfamiliar to you.
3. Listen deeply to what people and the world have to say to you.
4. Trust your inner instincts about ways you can make a difference.
5. Remember to take time to nurture your inner being and to pay attention to the signs you receive.
6. Being an Edgewalker can feel very lonely. Connect with other Edgewalkers for support and inspiration.
7. Commit to a daily spiritual or contemplative practice.
8. Review your values on a daily or weekly basis.
9. Work with intention, affirmation, and visualization to create positive outcomes for yourself and others.
10. Do the footwork to manifest ideas into the material world.
11. Value your unique background and/or cultural differences; see them as a gift.
12. When you find yourself in a difficult situation, don't sell your soul.
13. Know your environment and the values and norms of your organizational culture. Learn where the edges are.
14. If the environment you are in is too much like a psychic prison for you, first challenge the restrictive rules and find ways to change things. If that doesn't work, find or create new work that will allow you to fully use your gifts.
15. Always remember that you are a bridge builder, and find ways to strengthen connections between you and people who see the world differently.

FIVE ORGANIZATIONAL ORIENTATIONS

Throughout this book we have focused on Edgewalkers as individuals. Let's now expand this concept to the organizational level of analysis and explore the idea of an Edgewalker organization. An Edgewalker organization is an organization that seeks to be on the leading edge, is curious about what is emerging just over the horizon, supports creativity and innovation, and nurtures the human spirit. The organization develops collective methods of knowing the future. It encourages risk-taking. The leaders understand how to use vision, imagery, and inspiration to paint a picture of a desired future. Employees are taught the skills of manifestation so that they can create what has never been created before. And the culture is based on appreciative inquiry and the importance of putting energy into strengths and what works.

The Edgewalker organization, like all organizations, has great diversity in its leaders and employees. Differences are valued to a much greater degree than in a traditional organization, simply because Edgewalkers are curious and always want to learn about other people's worldviews.

The CEO of the organization must have strong Edgewalker Qualities of Being if he or she is to lead an organization that is going to be on the leading edge. And he or she should be relatively advanced through the stages of Edgewalker development. The CEO should know how to read the future and how to work with others to create something from the invisible world and bring it into the material world.

But not everyone in the top leadership team needs to be an Edgewalker. And, as I said in earlier chapters, you wouldn't want an organization that was populated only with Edgewalkers. It would be like having a whole tribe of scouts. Everyone would be out exploring the wilderness, and no one would be home to tend the hearth and plant the corn.

There are five different orientations that people can take in an organization, and these affect the extent to which the organization can truly be on the leading edge. These five orientations are:

1. Edgewalkers
2. Flamekeepers
3. Hearthtenders
4. Placeholders
5. Doomsayers

Each of these will be defined, and then we will look at the implications for organizational culture and performance.

These orientations are based on two factors: (1) relationship to time, and (2) relationship to change. The "relationship to time" factor is a continuum between focus on the past and focus on the future. The "relationship to change" factor is a continuum between being closed to change and being open to change. (See Figure 6.1.)

Do not follow where the path may lead.
Go instead where there is no path and leave a trail.

—*Harold R. McAlindon*

Edgewalkers

Edgewalkers are people who walk between worlds and have the ability to build bridges between different worldviews. They have a strong spiritual life and are also very grounded and effective in the everyday material world. They have five qualities of being: self-awareness, passion, integrity, vision, and playfulness. As they grow and develop, they increase their skills in these five stages of development: knowing the future, risk-taking, manifesting, focusing, and appreciating. Edgewalkers are much more oriented toward the future than toward the past,

Organizational Orientation

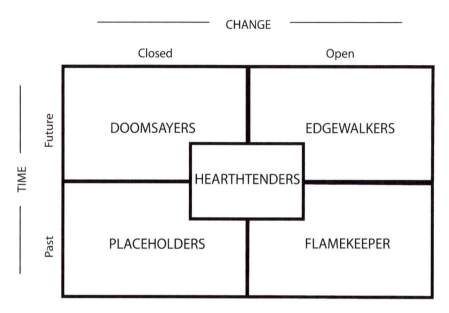

Figure 6.1 Organizational Orientation.

so much so that they can sometimes run roughshod over tradition and can close their ears to what has worked in the past. They are also high on the change continuum, with a basic philosophy of "If it ain't broke, fix it anyway."

They are restless and always seeking newness and change. For this reason, they can sometimes be difficult to manage, especially for a traditional manager. The Edgewalker may be more focused on his or her creative ideas than on what is most needed in the organization.

> Will you teach your children what we have taught our children? That the earth is our mother? What befalls the earth befalls all the sons of the earth. This we know: the earth does not belong to man, man belongs to the earth. All things are connected like the blood that unites us all. Man did not weave the web of life, he is merely a strand in it. Whatever he does to the web, he does to himself.
>
> —*Chief Seattle*

Flamekeepers

Flamekeepers are those people who keep the original vision and values of the organization alive. They are like the Olympic torchbearer, keeping the flame lit at all costs, or like the keeper of the flame in a temple, the one who keeps the sacred candles lit morning, noon, and night.

Collins and Porras, in their breakthrough *Built to Last* study, concluded that one of the successful habits of visionary companies is what they call "Preserve the Core/Stimulate Progress."[12] They give the example of how Don Petersen, CEO of the Ford Motor Company in the 1980s, and his top management team turned Ford around when it was bleeding profits. Petersen is quoted as saying:

> There was a great deal of talk about the sequence of the three P's—people, products, and profits. It was decided that people should absolutely come first [products second and profits third].[13]

This top-management team was serving in the role of Flamekeepers by breathing life back into the values of the founder, Henry Ford, who said, in 1916:

> I don't believe we should make such an awful profit on our cars. A reasonable profit is right, but not too much. I hold that it is better to sell a large number of cars at a reasonably small profit. . . . I hold this because it enables a larger number of people to buy and enjoy the use of a car and because it gives a larger number of men employment at good wages. Those are the two aims I have in life.[14]

I know of only two organizations that have institutionalized the concept of Flamekeepers. The first is a nonprofit group called the Kripalu Consultant Collaborative (KCC).[15] This is a group of consultants, trainers, coaches, and others that meets two to three times a year. Members share an interest in spirituality in the workplace and meet to support each other's spiritual and professional growth. The group has designated the founders of the group, Ron and Randy Nelson, and a few others who have been in the group a long time as "Flamekeepers." Their job is to keep the original vision of the organization alive and to continually explore how the organization can more fully live that vision.

The second organization was the Strategic Programs Division of Xerox, in Rochester, New York, which created the first truly green, "zero to landfill" copying machine, the Document Center 265DC. The organization went through a massive six-year cultural change to support the development of a whole new series of products. In order to support its larger vision of a culture that focused on people first, it created what was originally called the Council of Elders, later renamed the Council of Wisdom Keepers. A nominating committee selected 16 people, 2 from each of the eight functional groups. In the beginning, the people chosen had to be 55 years or older and have at least 20 years' service with the organization. Later Xerox decided that it would be better to have more diversity on the team, since most of the employees 55 years or older were white males. The Council members were given the freedom to create their own charter:

Charter:

COUNCIL MEMBERS shall act from an altruistic place, larger than their personal self, to ensure that wisdom borne within Strategic Programs is lived and carried forward from generation to generation of both people and products.

While the Council is honorary and has no official organizational power, it embodies and represents the natural authority of people who have gained true wisdom and earned deep respect.

Service is voluntary, by nomination and election.[16]

The role of the Wisdom Keepers was to walk around taking the temperature of the cultural change program, to serve as ombudsmen, to cut red tape when necessary, and to catch anything significant that might be falling through the cracks. Some of their official responsibilities included:

1. To support the Company with wisdom previously gained, in both engineering and human dimensions.
2. To hold both people and the vision of the products to the highest ideals and standards.
3. To advocate the well-being and quality of life of all Company employees.
4. To convene from time to time as they see fit to bring issues of importance to the attention of the appropriate people.[17]

Many of the longer-term employees at Sikorsky Aircraft serve an informal role as Flamekeepers. Even though they may have never met Igor Sikorsky, they keep his image alive by telling stories about him. Unfortunately, most people end their stories with sentiments such as "Igor would be rolling over in his grave if he could see what his organization is doing now." When I interviewed Igor's son, Sergei Sikorsky, it was obvious that he was just as much a mystic and an Edgewalker as his father, from the kinds of stories he told and the way he obviously felt about his father. Sergei had risen through the ranks to become the vice president of international marketing and had the deepest respect and appreciation for the kind of values his father had stood for and the way he had created an organization that lived these values.

After his father died and after Sergei retired, he still served on the Board and as a consultant to the organization, but over time he saw Sikorksy Aircraft drift further and further away from the founding values. It broke his heart to see this happen, and he did everything he could to influence things differently, to no avail. I spoke to the vice president of human resources about the morale issues I observed among employees at the company and suggested that he consider bringing Sergei back in to help the top management team get back in touch with the original core values and vision. He brushed me off and said that there would be no interest in that.

Not long ago, the unions at Sikorsky ended an acrimonious strike that lasted six weeks and put 4,300 people out of work.[18] Perhaps things would have been different if the Sikorsky leaders valued their Flamekeepers more.

Flamekeepers are focused on what is best about the past and on preserving the core values of the organization. At the same time, they are open to change and are willing to look at how the organization can build on what has been developed in the past. They may not be your biggest innovators, but once they see how a new product, service, or strategy fits with the core values and is in alignment with the vision of the founders, they will be the biggest supporters of change.

Take a moment to think about who the Flamekeepers are in your organization. Do you have any? How are they treated? Is there some way that your organization could build on the strengths and wisdom that they have to offer?

> To know is to comprehend.
> Do you know, do you comprehend,
> In this moment, who or what you serve?
> We must all be serving someone or something.
> Whom or what are you choosing
> to serve right now?
> It takes courage to ask this question of yourself.
> But without courage, you can't practice
> any other value consistently.
>
> —*Maya Angelou*

Hearthtenders

Hearthtenders are the people who get the day-to-day work of the organization done. They are the ones who keep the home fires burning when the Edgewalkers are out scouting new territory. They keep things running smoothly and are committed to a sense of family in the organization and to creating a "home away from home" atmosphere in the organization. Hearthtenders are the ones who remember people's birthdays and who enjoy the organizational milestone celebrations. They are the ones who think of creative ways to celebrate accomplishments and to bring people together.

They enjoy working on continuous improvement and, if given half the chance, will have creative ideas about how to improve the workflow in their area or how to better serve customers.

Hearthtenders are in the middle of the model in Figure 6.1. In time orientation, they tend to be focused on the present, and they are moderately open to change. These people are generally satisfied with their jobs and with the organization and are happy to keep things the way they are unless someone has an idea on how to make their work more streamlined and less stressful.

Mario Sousa and Janice Tarasevich are two managers that I am currently coaching at Sennheiser, a high-end audio-equipment company. They both are deeply committed to taking care of their team members and doing what they can to improve the work environment that their teams work in. They get their individual teams together on a regular basis to review work processes and to provide encouragement and support. Mario's department provides customer service to customers who may be having a problem with equipment they have purchased, and he and his team are streamlining processes so that there is a quicker turnaround when someone sends something in for repair.

Janice's department takes orders and works with the sales department to make sure that customers get what they have ordered in a timely manner. She wants her team members to better understand the whole sales process, so she is going to be sending her staff members out in the field with sales reps and to trade shows. This will allow them to develop better relationships with people that they normally interact with only on the phone.

When Sennheiser was near the end of a pilot phase of a program we conducted with the company, we asked for volunteers to join the Celebration Team to create the program for our Celebration Dinner. One of the enthusiastic volunteers for this Celebration Team was a young man named Chris Currier. Chris is the credit manager for the organization, and, like Mario and Janice, he was deeply involved in creating more positive energy in his team. But he was also excited about creating an event that would bring top and middle managers together to celebrate the cultural change that was beginning to happen at Sennheiser. Chris is quite talented with creating video programs and so interviewed all the program participants and the two consultants (Thad Henry and myself). He also taped portions of the program and pulled all this together into a 10-minute video that celebrated the highlights of what was accomplished.

Mario, Janice, and Chris are all examples of Hearthtenders. They all also, by the way, have many qualities of Edgewalkers, but their current roles in the organization make it difficult for them to express these qualities and skills. So, like many others in Hearthtending kinds of roles, they often express their Edgewalker side in their personal lives, through other creative interests.

I first learned about the amazing untapped creativity in employees when I worked for Honeywell in the 1980s, helping to implement employee-involvement teams. I did my dissertation research on the employee-involvement process and interviewed a large number of people in management and on the front lines.I discovered that almost every single factory employee had a small business on the side. These businesses ranged from a part-time roofing business, to a tax-preparation service, to even a stock-investing service! There was no lack of entrepreneurship in these employees, but Honeywell had not figured out how to tap into that kind of energy.

Hearthtenders serve a very important function in the organization by providing stability and by keeping systems running smoothly. Depending on the climate and culture of the organization, Hearthtenders could move into any of the other quadrants. If you are trying to create an organization that is more values-driven and more innovative, you will want to actively find ways to help Hearthtenders to be either more future-oriented, thus moving into the Edgewalker orientation, or more past-oriented, thus moving them into the Flamekeeper orientation. Often Hearthtenders are Edgewalkers or Flamekeepers in disguise and can be encouraged to be more change-oriented if they are listened to, supported, encouraged, and rewarded.

Failure in truly creative work is not some mechanical breakdown but the prospect of a failure in our very essence, a kind of living death. Little wonder we often choose the less vulnerable, more familiar approach, that places work mostly in terms of provision. If I can reduce my image of work to just a job I have to do, then I keep myself safely away from the losses to be endured in putting my heart's desires at stake.

—David Whyte, Crossing the Unknown Sea

Placeholders

In contrast to Edgewalkers, who tend to be rare, just about every organization has Placeholders. Tom Brown[19] defines Placeholders as the people who are holding back organizational progress and innovation. There are the people who see boundaries instead of possibilities, who are focused on the past instead of the future, who use up resources instead of looking at renewal, and who value doing over dreaming. They are the ones who want to employ as few people as possible, in contrast to the leaders who engage all of humankind and look for ways to grow the enterprise. Placeholders are a drag on organizational energy and are usually the ones who clog the organization's arteries with bureaucratic processes. They will tell you why something can't be done and will resist change because "we've always done it that way."

Placeholders are motivated primarily by fear and ego. They are risk-averse because they are afraid of losing whatever they have. They feel that they can't afford to fail, and so they get frozen in place, fighting mightily to keep things the way they are. Oh, they will give lip service to change, but they will follow any words of support with statements such as these:

- You have to show me where the money will come from.
- Let's put a committee together, and I want a report in three months.
- Where else has this been done?
- How can you prove that we'll be successful?
- Corporate will never go for it (or human resources, or management, or the union, or someone else who can be the bad guy).

If you really want to see Placeholders in action, go to any university Faculty Senate meeting. When I first came from the corporate world to academic life, I was absolutely horrified at what I saw in these meetings. Anytime someone would propose a new course or program, the system would immediately go into gear to make implementation as difficult as possible. You had to prove that there was a market for this course that wouldn't cannibalize other existing courses. You had to show that there were at least three people who could teach this course (even though it didn't exist yet!). You had to provide textbook recommendations, which would be impossible if the course was truly leading edge and innovative. Textbooks take two to three years to create and publish, so if a course was really current and relevant, a textbook wouldn't exist. You were also required to meet with any department that might possibly think that this course was in some way related to its field of expertise, and you had to get its approval to bring the proposal to the Faculty Senate.

There were about five or six levels of committee approval that you had to go through before the proposal could come to the Senate, and since some of those committees meet once a month or less, it could take up to a whole year to go through the process. Even after you had jumped through all these hoops, you knew that when you got to the Faculty Senate meeting, the Placeholders would attack your proposal like vultures on a dead rabbit. A favorite tactic of the Placeholders was to get visibly upset about some nitpicky thing and then request that the proposal be tabled until the next faculty meeting while you addressed whatever issue they had raised. When you came back the next time, they would find something else and repeat the same scenario all over again. It is like death by a thousand cuts.

When some of the Edgewalkers in our university began to explore online courses, in the 1990s, it was even worse! The Placeholders circled round and insisted that if a current course was to be taught online, the department had to treat it like a brand-new course and go through this whole circus again. In addition, for every single course, you had to explain how you would evaluate students in an online environment, how you would know that it was your student taking the exam instead of her best friend, and jump through about four or five other hoops to get the course approved.

When I expressed my amazement at this blocking behavior to one of my colleagues, he explained that faculty are basically powerless when it comes to most organizational decisions. So they find whatever small bastion of power they can control, and they defend it for all it's worth.

Admittedly, universities are often much more bureaucratic than most corporations, but I'm sure that you have seen similar Placeholder behaviors in corporate environments. Placeholders are the self-proclaimed "stability police." They are extremely uncomfortable with change, and they want to keep things as they are, or, even better, as they were in the past, when life was simpler.

Unfortunately, in universities, Placeholders are almost always tenured professors, and there's not much you can do about them except perhaps shut down their departments. This is usually not a desirable thing to do and often leads to lawsuits. In the corporate world, a typical way of reducing the number of Placeholders is to offer early-retirement programs. However, the ironic thing is that you are just as likely to lose your Flamekeepers as your Placeholders to such programs. Flamekeepers will see the early-retirement offer as an opportunity to start their own businesses in a way that is more in alignment with their values.

Placeholders do have a tremendous amount of organizational memory, and perhaps even some wisdom. Placeholders are, in many ways, like pessimistic, angry, cynical Flamekeepers. Probably at one time they deeply believed in the vision and values of the organization and then had their faith and ideals trampled on one too many times. So they retreat into their protective shells and long for the past. And they try to block any new initiatives that move them even further from what they perceive as their idealized past.

It takes a tremendous amount of work, a high level of interpersonal skills, and maybe even spiritual intelligence to deal with Placeholders. If you are trying to create more of an Edgewalker culture in your organization, you are likely to create even more fear in Placeholders unless you find a way to deal directly with their motives for being naysayers. From a spiritual perspective, it's important to remember that there is good in every person; if you are in a change-agent role, you want to find a way to unleash that goodness in your Placeholders.

Programs that increase self-awareness, that focus on values, and that help people to rediscover their inherent sense of service and higher purpose can be very successful with Placeholders at lower levels in the organization. One-on-one coaching, whether it is with a professional coach or with a competent boss, can also help Placeholders to be more open to change, particularly if they can be shown that they will have some influence on the new direction.

But if your top leaders are Placeholders, your organization is essentially stuck in the mud. Edgewalkers and Flamekeepers will eventually leave out of frustration, and you will be left with people who keep the machinery running but who have forgotten the higher purpose and mission of the organization.

> We can easily forgive a child who is afraid of the dark;
> the real tragedy of life is when adults are afraid of the light.
>
> —*Plato (ca. 400 B.C.)*

Doomsayers

The Merriam-Webster Dictionary defines a Doomsayer as "one given to forebodings and predictions of impending calamity."[20] Even more than Placeholders, they can be a tremendous drag on organizational energy. These folks are not just "the glass is half empty" folks; they are the "glass is broken, the water is going to stain everything, and I'm probably going to bleed to death" folks. They are very concerned about the future, but they always predict the worst possible calamity and then spend their time preparing for doomsday. Or else, in their fear, they just get paralyzed and helpless.

Typically, Doomsayers get pretty marginalized in organizations because they are such an energy drain. They tend to gravitate toward jobs like safety, environmental engineering, cost accounting, auditing, and other jobs that by their nature require them to look for what is wrong. The goal of these kinds of jobs is to prevent serious problems from happening and to quickly handle a crisis if it does. Many people in these professions handle the prevention work and the crisis work in a calm and professional manner. Doomsayers, on the other hand, turn everything into a drama.

They get themselves into a vicious cycle. When they see a potential problem emerging, they do whatever they can to get the attention of people who can do something about it. Often this includes using strong emotion to express their concern. Doomsayers also use exaggeration to get their point across. Because so many things seem like a crisis to them and because they tend to exaggerate and blow things out of proportion, they become like the little boy who cried, "Wolf." People become immune to their cries of alarm, and then, when there is a real emergency, no one believes them.

Like Placeholders, Doomsayers are change averse. But their resistance to change is based on a belief that the future holds danger. Their theory about the world is that it is not a safe place, and you have to protect yourself at all costs from bad things happening. And, as Jack Gibb said, our theories create our reality.[21] So, if the least little thing goes wrong, they are able to say, "See, I told you." They tend to ignore all the things that go right most of the time, and if you point that out to them, they say, "Well, we've been lucky so far, but just you wait."

When Dee Hock first came up with the idea for the VISA card, he ran into his fair share of Placeholders and Doomsayers in the banking industry. Over time he was able to convince them to buy into this new "Chaordic" form of organizing, and the credit card system was successful—that is, until, it became time to create an international credit card system. An international committee was set up to design the new system in a way that would work for all, but, after working for two years on the system, people found that their differences had hardened, rather than softened. There was no logical compromise that would be accepted by everyone, especially the Doomsayers.

A meeting to either finalize the plan or abandon the effort was held in San Francisco. Without calling it that, Dee took an appreciative inquiry approach to dealing with the fears and resistance.

> I gave up efforts to find a compromise and began to reflect on the exceptional effort of the past two years and the progress that had been made. I began to peel the mental onion; to get at the essential nature of that which had lifted such a complex, diverse group over seemingly insurmountable obstacles. It was hard to get at, but simple when it emerged. At critical moments, all participants had felt compelled to succeed. And at those same moments, all had been willing to compromise. They had not thought of winning or losing, but of a larger sense of purpose and concept of community that had transcended and enfolded them all.
>
> Several members of the staff joined in and within the hour we had a plan. We reduced our thoughts to the simplest possible expression: *The will to succeed, the grace to compromise* [italics in original].[22]

This phrase was translated into Latin: *Studium ad prosperandum, voluntas in conveniendum.* Gold cufflinks were created with one of the set as a half round of the Earth encircled by raised letters that read "*Studium ad prosperandum.*" The other part of the set was the other half of the Earth encircled with the words "*Voluntas in conveniendum.*" A set was made for every member of the committee.

As the committee met throughout the day, the disagreements got more and more entrenched, and Dee suggested that they adjourn the meeting for the evening and plan to meet in the morning to disband the effort. He had hired a private boat at Fisherman's Wharf for a trip across the bay to a fine French restaurant in Sausalito.

After several bottles of wine and a splendid dinner, Dee was asked to say a few words before the evening ended. He thanked the attendees for all their efforts and reminisced about all the obstacles they had overcome. A small gift was placed in front of each person. He then said:

> It is no failure to fall short of realizing such a dream. From the beginning, it was apparent that forming such a complex, global organization was unlikely. We now know it is impossible, notwithstanding two years of exceptional effort. Not knowing with certainty how today's meeting might end, we felt compelled to do something that would be appropriate no matter what happened.[23]

He then asked them to open the small, beautifully wrapped box in front of them. He told them that he wanted to give them something that they could keep for the remainder of their lives as a reminder of this day. He described the cufflink with half the world surrounded by the Latin phrase for "the will to succeed" and the other cufflink with the Latin phrase for "the grace to compromise." He continued:

> We meet tomorrow for the final time to disband the effort after an arduous two years. There is no possibility of agreement. As organizing agent, we have one last request. Will you please bring your cufflinks to the meeting in the morning? When it ends, each of us will take them with us as a reminder for the remainder of our lives that the world can never be united through us because we lacked the will to succeed and the grace to compromise. But if, by some miracle, our differences dissolve before morning, this gift will remind us to the day we die that the world *was* united because we *had* the will to succeed and the grace to compromise.[24]

The next morning, all members were wearing their cufflinks, and the chairman began the meeting by asking, "Is there anyone who wishes to speak of disbanding the effort?" The people who had acted like Doomsayers originally had been up all night calling officials of their bank or constituency, demanding authority to reach agreement. Within an hour, agreement was reached on every issue, and "The will to succeed, the grace to compromise" became the corporate motto of VISA International.

Dee had used a combination of inspiration and embarrassment to move the Doomsayers out of their fearful, entrenched positions. He appealed to their future orientation with images of two different scenarios. In one, they would remember with shame that they had failed to create an organization that would unite banks and customers worldwide. In the other, they could remember with pride that they had created a system that would serve humanity.

Doomsayers are very difficult to change. However, if you are creating an Edgewalker organization, you will have to find a way to deal with them because their negative and fearful energy can be so contagious. Do anything you can do to help them develop a more positive relationship with the future. They are already future-oriented, but it is a fear-based orientation. If you can help the Doomsayer to understand how he or she creates his or her own reality, you have gone a long way toward transformation. Once they can begin to accept that there may be other ways to think about the future, you are on your way toward moving the Doomsayers to either the Hearthtender quadrant or even the Edgewalker quadrant.

Appreciative inquiry is a wonderful process for beginning to open up the consciousness of the Doomsayer. They often find it very difficult to shift their thinking in this way, but it is possible. When I offer workshops, I often build in a one-hour or two-hour vision quest in nature as part of the process. This kind of experience can also be very helpful to Doomsayers. Other programs, like the Noble Purpose program or the ONE program, also have the potential for helping Doomsayers to see that they could choose a more positive future for themselves. Once they see this on a personal level, they naturally begin to see it on an organizational level, as well.

BASIC GUIDELINES FOR ORGANIZATIONS

Here are some actions you can take to begin to create more of an Edgewalker Culture in your organization:

1. Assess your organization in comparison to others in your industry. Are you on the leading edge, in the middle of the pack, or a laggard in terms of innovation, creativity, and risk-taking?
2. Decide as a management team if you would like to be more on the leading edge than you currently are.
3. Evaluate your current mix of Edgewalkers, Flamekeepers, Hearthtenders, Placeholders, and Doomsayers. Does this need to change in order to meet your strategic and cultural objectives? There is more on this in Chapter 7.
4. Benchmark Edgewalker organizations, such as those mentioned in this book. Visit them and talk to leaders and frontline workers. Find out what makes the organization tick. Discuss what you learned with your management team, and make decisions about actions you can implement.
5. Hold Edgewalker discussion groups. Use this book as a resource. Other resources include *Fast Company Magazine* and books like *The Translucent Organization,*[25] *Noble Purpose,*[26] *Are You Ready to Succeed,*[27] *Building a Values Driven Organization,*[28] and *ONE: The Art and Practice of Conscious Leadership.*[29] For other recommended reading, see Appendix C.
6. Study the organizations that have received the International Spirit at Work Award. Attend the annual International Spirit at Work Awards conference to learn from the CEOs and executives of the organizations that have received the award.[30]
7. Explore training programs, hiring practices, reward practices, and other human resources systems to see what can be done to shift people with Placeholder or Doomsayer orientations to Hearthtender, Flamekeeper, or Edgewalker orientations.
8. Don't forget that nature is our best teacher. Plan a vision quest for your top team. Then schedule a quest for everyone else in the organization.

LOOK FOR THE GIFTS

I remember a cartoon from years ago that pictured a little boy delightedly shoveling out a stall full of manure. When someone asked him why he was so happy about his shoveling, he replied, "With all this dung in here, there's got to be a pony somewhere!"

Sometimes being an Edgewalker can feel like you are up to your neck in horse manure. Being an Edgewalker is a hard path to walk, but it has many rewards. It is always exciting to break new ground and explore new frontiers. And you meet so many interesting people on the way! You are never bored, and no one would ever accuse you of being boring. But, more than anything else, you have the opportunity to make a positive difference in the world.

If you are trying to create an Edgewalker organization, it is helpful to understand the different orientations that people have toward time and towards change. And, like the little boy in the stall, it is valuable to look for the gift in each of these orientations, even among the Doomsayers. When you focus on people's strengths and what they bring to the organization, what you focus on will grow.

What the caterpillar calls the end of the world, the master calls a butterfly.

—*Richard Bach*

Chapter Seven

THE EDGEWALKER ORGANIZATION

We look forward to the time when the power to love will replace the love of power. Then will our world know the blessings of peace.

—William E. Gladstone

The following profile describes what an Edgewalker organization might look and feel like. Imagine that your company has just contracted with another company to help your business unit with new product design. . . .

The drive up to the corporate headquarters of Genesis Systems[1] is breathtaking. You ride along tree-lined roads that follow the twists and turns of the brook that feeds Lake Astron. Beautiful sculptures and gardens are nestled here and there among the trees, and tame deer lift their heads from their feeding as you pass by. The winding road takes you part way up the mountain, and then you see this simple but beautiful building in front of you. It is mostly glass, stone, and wood, and there are solar panels on the top of the building. The shape of the building from the front seems to conform to the round contours of the mountain. You also notice a windmill higher up on the mountain and a charming waterwheel next to the waterfall. In the distance, you can see other large buildings dotting the hills, and you notice how tastefully they seem to fit into the environment.

You park your car in the lower parking lot, and a solar-powered cart picks you up and drives you up to the main entrance. On the lawn in front of the building, several people are playing with some kind of large circular toy that flies between them, although you can't make out exactly what it is. You just notice that it seems to float almost effortlessly for a while when someone throws it. A young man leaps gracefully in the air and grabs this flying disk and spins it off to someone else. A large golden retriever is joyfully barking and running between the players.[2]

There are seven steps leading up to the entrance, and, just below the Genesis Systems sign above the door, you read these words carved in marble: "The Universe pays us for being who we are and doing what we love doing." How odd, you think to yourself as you ponder what this might mean. As you walk up the last step, the two wooden doors gently open, and you hear soft music drifting out from the foyer. There are plants everywhere, and you almost feel as if you are in a greenhouse.

Your host, Gary Williams, walks in to meet you, and warmly shakes your hand. Gary is the account executive for your project. You have come here to begin your working relationship with Genesis Systems because your organization has contracted to use the company's product design services to help develop a new consumer product line for your food business. He guides you further into the building and invites you to sit with him in a café-type setting in the middle courtyard. You notice that the inside of the building is circular and is completely open in the center, with about four levels of balconies surrounding this courtyard. You can see offices on each level and realize that every single one of them must have a view of the outside, from the way the building is designed.[3]

Water from the brook outside has been diverted to a small stream that runs through the building, providing the soothing sound of trickling water in the background in the café area. There are beverage menus on the table, and Gary asks you if you would like anything from the coffee bar or juice bar. You ask for a cup of coffee, and Gary brings that back for you and gets himself a fruit smoothie.

As you begin to drink your beverages, Gary outlines the day for you. "First you will meet with Rob Rabbin, the vice president of corporate consciousness.[4] Gary says, "All clients meet with Rob so that he can explain the company's core values and also talk about some of our unusual ways of working. Rob is a mystic, and we rely on his intuition and his access to higher levels of consciousness to help us make sound business decisions that are good for our clients, good for the company, and good for life on the planet." Gary explains that we will begin our time with some shared moments of silence so that our work together comes from our highest source.

"Rob will introduce you to our concept of 'Spiritual Support Team,' to see if that is something your organization would like to take advantage of. We do not charge for this service, but we believe it makes a powerful difference. Basically, we ask that two people from our company and two people from your organization make an agreement to set aside a half hour every month to share meditation or prayer. It doesn't matter where each person is; they just commit to taking that time, say at 8 A.M. on the first Friday of every month, to connect with the Source or the Transcendent with no agenda. The only purpose is to connect.[5]

"Next you will meet the chief creative officer, Sonia Borysenkov, who will explain the way the company's engineers work with artists, high school and college students, and indigenous shamans. An integrative, multifunctional team will be assigned to your project," he explains. "She will introduce you to the team members, and we will begin doing some creative, mind-opening exercises that will get us into the kind of consciousness that will help us best serve you and your company."

He continues, "Finally, you will end the day with our learning liaison, Bill Kumar, who will ask you for feedback on your day, assess how we might better serve you in the future, and also ask you about what you learned that was of value to you. Bill helps us to see every interaction as a positive opportunity for learning and growth. This helps to support the kind of corporate culture that attracts the best and the brightest talent from all over the world." Gary then asks if you have any questions, and you feel like you have a million of them but don't know where to start. He laughs and says, "Well, you can begin with whatever comes up first, so why don't we get started? I'll take you on a brief tour as we head over to meet with Rob."

Your mind is buzzing. You want to ask questions about the design of the building. Your engineering mind has taken in a lot of details, and you suspect that the organization is energy self-sufficient. Why is the building round? Why were people outside playing in the middle of the workday? Are dogs allowed in this workplace? What did that phrase above the door mean? Where did they get the ideas to have a vice president of corporate consciousness and Spiritual Support Teams?

He takes you past the Meditation Center, where you see another circular room with plants, waterfalls, inspiring pictures, candles, cushions, chairs, and symbols from all of the world's great traditions.[6] Several people are in there sitting quietly, and one person is kneeling on his prayer rug. Next, you go by the corporate library, which includes all the latest technology. Gary explains that their library is actually better and more up-to-date than that of the nearby university.

As you walk by some offices, Gary suggests that you look in and notice the original artwork on the walls. "Genesis has a full-time art director that we hired away from a nationally recognized art museum," he tells you. "She is in charge of our art collection. We feel that our employees will be more inspired if they have access to original art, so they can select a Van Gogh or a Cezanne or Georgia O'Keeffe painting from a catalogue and can borrow it from our collection for three months. At the end of three months, they can select a new piece of art."[7]

Just before you get to Rob's office, Gary takes you to the Learning and Wisdom Center. He shows you the various types and sizes of training rooms and takes you outdoors briefly. He points to the woods and a pathway off to the left. "That's all state-protected land with old-growth forests and land that has been sacred to the First Peoples. We sponsor regular vision quests for people in the company who are interested in taking time to explore the next stages of their life and/or work. We feel that it is very important to be close to nature and living things and that this closeness energizes and inspires us and helps us to keep a holistic perspective on any of the product development work that we help to create."

You say to him, "I've always wanted to go on a vision quest."

He responds, "Let me take you back in to the Learning and Wisdom Center and give you one of our catalogues. We make all our programs available to our clients and vendors at no charge. We are committed to helping all the people we interact with reach their highest potential. That's really our main reason for being in business.[8] Product design services just happen to be the way we fulfill our mission."

As you are walking back in, Gary points out a separate circular building nearby connected by a covered walkway. He said, "That's our Family Care Center. It is a multigenerational care center where we have full-time child- and eldercare staff. Many of our employees are in the so-called Sandwich Generation, where they must care for their children and also for their elderly parents. We have found that the children and the elderly love being together. We have Internet cameras and communication systems so that our employees feel connected to their family members throughout the day. Many of them eat lunch with family members at the Family Care Center cafeteria. Our working hours are 8 A.M. to 5 P.M. We have a real commitment to the principle of "Family First," and we turn the lights out at 6 P.M. and insist that people go home and get renewal with their family."[9]

Gary takes you up to Level 3 in the building, and, as you are walking around to balcony to get to Rob's office, he points out all the small areas for group gatherings, with couches, tables, plants, electronic white boards, and coffee nooks. He tells you that the company had an architect design the building so that it was ecological, energy self-sufficient, aesthetically pleasing, and supportive of chance meetings of individuals and groups. "Our research tells us that all these things contribute to creativity, innovation, and job satisfaction," he informs you.

You have now reached Rob's office, and it is unlike any office you have ever seen before. There is a candle burning and very relaxing music playing in the background. On his walls are masks from Africa, hand-carved flutes from South America, and bowls of natural items such as driftwood, stones, and feathers. Rob himself is a tall, elegant man dressed in loose clothing and sandals—decidedly uncorporate! He reaches out to shake your hand, and you wonder if it is your imagination as you feel a warm energy surround you.[10]

You think to yourself, "This is going to be unlike any other business experience I have ever had!"

CREATING THE EDGEWALKER ORGANIZATION

Organizations are communities of people, and the culture and the effectiveness of the organization is based on the shared values and collective consciousness of the members of the organization. An Edgewalker culture is one that values innovation, creativity, risk-taking, the unleashing of the human spirit, and living in alignment with values of sustainability, justice, compassion, and joy.

The leader in any organization is the primary creator of the culture, and this is especially true in Edgewalker organizations. Edgewalkers within the organization cannot go out to the creative edge of things any further than the CEO herself is willing to go. An Edgewalker organization must have a leader who is an Edgewalker. This person creates the mindset or overall consciousness of the rest of the organization.

In this section, we will revisit the Orientation Model and explore the idea of getting the right mix of people to create an Edgewalker culture. Some suggestions for how to diagnose your organization are offered. We will also look at what happens when individuals or organizations get too far out on the edge.

GETTING THE RIGHT MIX

Every large organization has a mix of people who see the world through one of the five orientations mentioned in Chapter 6: Edgewalker, Flamekeeper, Hearthtender, Placeholder, or Doomsayer. If we were to draw a bell curve of the distribution of the typical organization, it might look something like this:

This particular mix portrays an organization that has equal amounts of Edgewalkers and Doomsayers (5% each). They basically cancel each other out and prevent the organization from moving toward a more innovative culture. This hypothetical organization also has equal numbers of Flamekeepers and Placeholders (10% each), and, without strong direction from the Edgewalkers, the Flamekeepers and Placeholders keep the organization oriented to the past. The Hearthtenders make up the large majority of the organization's orientation (70%), and their focus is on the present, keeping the day-to-day work of the organization going.

This traditional organization mix works fine when the organization is in a relatively stable environment with few competitive challenges. However, it will be a pretty frustrating place for Edgewalkers to work, and if their creativity and values are not respected and nurtured, they will go to work for an organization that is more dynamic.

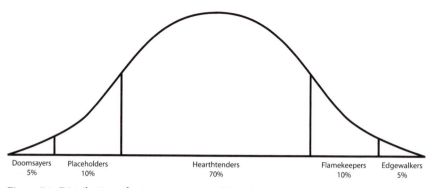

Figure 7.1 Distribution of orientation in a traditional organization.

If, on the other hand, your organization is in a rapidly changing, turbulent environment, the kind of environment that Peter Vaill calls "permanent white water,"[11] then it is essential to have a very different mix. You have a highly competitive environment where technology is changing constantly, your customers change their values and requirements almost overnight, and your old models of predicting the future just don't work anymore. In this kind of environment, you need to have an Edgewalker organization so that the organization is focused on the future and quick to adapt to changes in the internal and external environment.

An organization's ability to be successfully is directly related to the proportion of Placeholders and Doomsayers to Edgewalkers. Having too many Placeholders and Doomsayers can suck the life and inspiration out of a few lone Edgewalkers. And, since Edgewalkers are risk-takers, they will take all their good ideas and go play in somebody else's sandbox. They won't just sit there quietly and turn into deadwood.

In Figure 7.2, there is a very different distribution of people. You will notice that this organization does not have any Doomsayers or Placeholders at all. People who are uncomfortable with change will not be happy in an Edgewalker organization because this kind of organization not only responds to change—it creates change. It creates new rules for the game and sets the pace for other organizations. Both Doomsayers and Placeholders tend to hold a more fearful and negative view of the world, and their energy would only be a drag on the Edgewalker organization.

As I described in Chapter 6, there are ways to help Doomsayers and Placeholders move out of their mindsets, and, if possible, you want to provide them every opportunity to begin to see the world differently and to join the emerging creative energy of the organization. Several of the methods of Edgewalker development mentioned in this book could be helpful, particularly appreciative inquiry and personal coaching. If none of these approaches work, the most humane thing to do

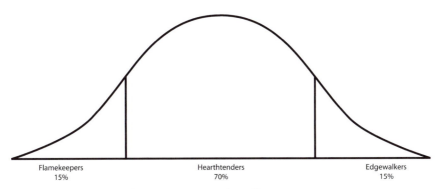

| Flamekeepers | Hearthtenders | Edgewalkers |
| 15% | 70% | 15% |

Figure 7.2 Distribution of orientation in an Edgewalker organization.

is to help the person find an environment that feels more comfortable to him. This should be done in the most supportive way possible, using outplacement services, personal development programs, and reasonable severance pay.

In the company distribution curve presented in Figure 7.2, there are only three orientations: Edgewalkers (15%), Hearthtenders (70%), and Flamekeepers (15%). In this model, there are three times as many Edgewalkers as in the traditional organizational model. Although 15 percent is not a large portion of the overall employee base, it is at the level of critical mass and is significant enough to keep the organization moving in creative and inspired new directions. The actual percentages that are the right mix for each organization vary, depending on the kind of business (for example, advertising versus auto manufacturing), the organization's past cultural history, the current stage of development, and the organization's vision of the future.

It is always easier to create a new organization than to change an existing company. You can hire the right mix of people to help you fulfill your vision, and you can establish the kinds of values and practices that will keep you on the leading edge. In fact, most innovation and job growth in U.S. companies comes from small, entrepreneurial firms. The large organizations that have been the titans of the corporate world are now the biggest contributors to the unemployment numbers. These dinosaurs are not known for innovative breakthroughs in their products, services, or management processes. Most positive change comes from the edges of the business world, not the center.

If you do not have the luxury of creating a new start-up, then how do you help your organization to be more of an Edgewalker organization? As mentioned in Chapter 6, one of the things you will want to do is to evaluate your current mix of Edgewalkers, Flamekeepers, Hearthtenders, Placeholders, and Doomsayers. A simple way to do this is to hold focus groups in your organization, explain the definitions of the five orientations, and then ask people to individually create their own distribution curve for the five orientations in your company. Ask each individual to share his or her chart and explain the reasoning behind that particular distribution. Once everyone has shared, the group can create a collective chart based on a consensus on where the organization is. Depending on the size of your organization, you may want to do this with several groups, making sure that there is representation of all the levels and functions at each meeting.

If you prefer a more quantitative approach, visit our Web site, www.edgewalkers. org, to learn about our organizational survey process.

CREATING CHANGE

The Edgewalker approach to change is that transformation does not happen in a gradual, linear way. Land and Jarman studied transformation processes in nature as well as in human systems and found that there is a three-stage process to what they call "Breakpoint Change":

> Breakpoint change abruptly and powerfully breaks the critical links that connect anyone or anything with the past. . . . The entire notion of change turns out to be amazingly different from what we have long thought it to be. Change actually follows a pattern that results in momentous and seemingly unpredictable shifts. Long periods of great disorder can shift abruptly to regularity, stability, and predictability. Equally long periods of incremental, continuous, and logical advancement shift to an entirely different kind of change—one in which unrelated things combine in creative ways that produce unexpected and powerful results. At Breakpoint, the rule change is so sharp that continuing to use the old rules not only doesn't work, it erects great, sometimes insurmountable, barriers to success.[12]

The first phase of breakpoint change is "Exploring and inventing the pattern," which means searching for the underlying patterns, connections, and order when things around you seem tumultuous or chaotic. You may randomly experiment with different ways to respond. In phase two, "Extending and improving," you have discovered the pattern or created a prototype and you begin to focus on replicating your success. At some point, you reach the limits of success and you hit a breakpoint. At this point, you either transform and change the rules of the game or you die, because the old ways no longer work. Phase 3 is called "Integrating the new and different," and it demands new behavior. This could include "innovating, partnering with customers and suppliers, adding new value to products and services, opening up the system to involve women and minorities, and taking on community and environmental responsibility."[13] I would also add that it could include seeing the world from a perspective that suggests that there are both material and spiritual realities.

Malcolm Gladwell describes a similar phenomenon when changes that happen quickly. He says that rapid, discontinuous change has three characteristics:

> one, contagiousness; two, the fact that little causes can have big effects; and three that change happens not gradually but at one dramatic moment—are the same three

principles that define how measles moves through a grade-school classroom or the flu attacks every winter. Of the three, the third trait—the idea that epidemics can rise or fall in one dramatic moment—is the most important, because it is the principle that makes sense of the first two and that permits the greatest insight into why modern change happens the way it does. The name given to the one dramatic moment in an epidemic when everything can change all at once is the Tipping Point.[14]

The transformation of the butterfly into the caterpillar is a wonderful example of this process. The blueprint of the butterfly is in the DNA of the caterpillar as the caterpillar matures and follows its destiny to create a cocoon. Once inside the cocoon, it goes into a quiescent state, and something called imaginal disks start to form. At first the caterpillar's immune system attacks these pre-cellular forms as if they were invaders. But they begin to multiply and link up. As they begin to develop faster and faster and form clusters, the immune system breaks down and these new cells consume the body of the caterpillar. These cells eventually transmute into the body of the butterfly.[15]

A similar process happens in organizations when they become truly committed to valuing diversity. In the early phases of embracing diversity, an organization or group hires one person who is different from the mainstream. This person might be an African American in an all-white organization or a woman in an all-male organization. According to Rosabeth Moss Kanter,[16] this tokenism sets up an uncomfortable dynamic for both the token and the dominant group. It's as if the dominant group has to insulate itself from the one who is different, much as the caterpillar's immune system attacks the first imaginal pre-cells that are produced. Kanter says that change is a matter of numbers. When the pattern moves from an organization that has just a token to one that has a minority group, the dynamic shifts, as people from the minority group link up and begin to legitimize their needs. The final stage in Kanter's model comes when there is a plurality, when no one group can be defined as dominant. As this stage, she says, each person is seen as a unique person, and people no longer act in response to stereotypes or bias. Therefore, everyone is able to bring his or her best talents and skills to the table and to feel valued as a member of the organization.

It's the same in organizations that have decided to create an Edgewalker culture. If the Edgewalkers are just a small minority and are marginalized, it is impossible to have a vibrant, energized, and leading edge culture. However, if the organization begins to encourage more Edgewalking behaviors and finds ways to move Placeholders and Doomsayers into the other three categories, it can reach a level of critical mass, and the culture of the organization can shift suddenly.

This may seem like an impossible task, but people who have the potential to be Edgewalkers are a much larger segment of the population than you might think. In Chapter 1, I mentioned the research by Ray and Anderson that says that 26 percent of the population shares values related to spirituality, personal development, organizational transformation, ecology, and social justice. They call this group the Cultural Creatives and present evidence that it is the fastest-growing group in the United States and Europe, with the greatest impact on national cultures. Cultural Creatives have more than reached critical mass in terms of numbers, but they are still like the individual imaginal cells: most of them have not yet linked up. Ray and Anderson predict that when the Cultural Creatives begin to identify themselves as a collective group with shared values and a common vision for the future, a powerful shift will occur in the United States and Europe.[17]

If we extrapolate from Ray and Anderson's numbers to organizational life, then we can estimate that around 26 percent of the employee population of any organization are Cultural Creatives. They are the people who already are Edgewalkers or who have the potential to become Edgewalkers. If your organization currently has about 5 percent Edgewalkers and you are hoping to change the mix so that Edgewalkers account for 10 to 15 percent of the employees instead, you might find that within this small group of people are the ones who will create the tipping point that will change the culture of the organization fairly quickly.[18]

SUPPORT SYSTEMS IN THE EDGEWALKER ORGANIZATION

In order to create an Edgewalker organization, you need to have several kinds of support systems in place. Each organization is unique, but you will want to look at the way that you attract and retain people, the way you reward people, and the way that you train and develop them. Here's an example of an Edgewalker CEO who has figured out creative and energizing ways to reward his employees.

Cognex Case Study—Innovative Reward Systems

Robert Shillman is the chairman and CEO of Cognex Corporation, in Natick, Massachusetts. Cognex is the world's largest maker of industrial vision systems. Like many Edgewalkers, he has lived in two very different worlds and has found a way to build a bridge between them.

> Dr. Shillman, a ruddy-complexioned man with swept-back hair, aspired to be an actor until his father insisted he finish his MIT doctorate in computer science. But he remains a showman—wrestling an alligator at a Cognex picnic, designing an annual report that resembled Mad magazine and declaring his gubernatorial candidacy as an April Fool's joke.[19]

Cognex has a strong company culture and uses unconventional pay and reward systems to attract and retain the best employees. Most organizations believe that you have to have the highest pay and benefits to attract talent, but Shillman eschews that. And he is probably the best model of someone who focuses on more than money. In April 2001, he stopped taking a salary, and he stopped taking a bonus in 2004. The *Wall Street Journal* asked him, "When did you decide that you had enough money?" He replied:

> In 2001, the Internet bubble burst. Most high-tech companies suffered—as we did. To try to save jobs, I decided senior people should take a 4% salary cut. I set a better example by taking zero salary. At that time, the board decided to give me extra stock options.[20]

The *Wall Street Journal* then asked, "Did you expect to resume your salary once business improved?"

> In a capitalistic society, you should get paid for your efforts. But after 2001, I didn't miss the money. I said, "Well, if I don't miss it, then why should I keep taking it? Let's just give it to charity." [Cognex donated Mr. Shillman's 2004 and 2005 bonuses, totaling $517,000, to a public charity but hasn't donated his forgone salary since April 2001. At his request, the company will donate his 2006 salary and bonus.][21]

One of the unique things that Cognex did to reward people was the "rich for the night" event, where each person in the U.S. organization was treated to dinner for two and a limousine ride. Shillman estimates that the cost was about $500 per employee. He believes that it is better to create a reward that is a memorable experience than to give people the cash. If you give them cash, people put the money in the bank and forget about it. If you create a unique experience, they never forget. At his annual meeting, he said, "We are all getting a bonus, but the bonus isn't going to make you rich. I can make you feel rich. You are going on a night on the town in a chauffeur-driven limousine."[22]

Shillman does crazy things; once, he drove up in an ice-cream truck while wearing a hat that said "Cognex Good Humor Man" and gave ice cream away to everybody. Each year he sends a cake to all employees at their homes to recognize both their birthdays and Thanksgiving. Employees who have been with the company for 15 years receive a trip for themselves and their spouse to one of the wonders of the world, like the Great Wall of China. He says, "All you do is show up. You get $1,000 in spending money and an extra week vacation. After 20 years, it's the same thing with eight of your best friends plus your spouse and $1,500 in spending money."[23]

Bonuses are offered to every employee, full- and part-time, but the company does not offer executive perks. When one of his executives joined the company and asked what kind of company car he could buy, Shillman responded, "The company's U.S. policy is that you can buy whatever car you want out of your own money." He doesn't want the kind of executive who wants perks.

OTHER EXAMPLES OF REWARD SYSTEMS

When I worked for Honeywell's Large Computer Products Division, in Phoenix, Arizona, our crown jewel was a circuit-board plant in nearby Chandler, Arizona.

The plant manager, Chet Kendricks, had attended a leadership development program presented by our organizational development team and had had a personal awakening during that course. He came to see that he had one set of behavioral rules for the workplace and a separate, more loving set of rules for his family. He was uncomfortable with this inconsistency and realized that his true nature was more compassionate, caring, and fun loving, and he began to express that at work. Chet became more trusting of his employees and saw them as members of his extended family.

This plant tended to pay less for factory jobs than the other 10 plants in the Phoenix area, but because of the kind of culture that Chet was able to create, the best and the brightest wanted to come to work in Chandler. He attracted people with new and creative ideas because people knew they would be listened to and would most likely have the chance to implement their suggestions.

If you want to attract and retain Edgewalkers, don't focus on pay. Certainly, you want to pay people fairly, but, for Edgewalkers, it's not about the money. Focus on creating opportunities to be involved in something leading edge that is meaningful. Focus on helping them to grow through challenges and experiences that will expand them beyond their current boundaries. Edgewalkers are attracted to cultures that value diversity and that provide work that allows people to work across functions, across cultures, or outside their areas of specialty.

In the early 1990s, Yankee Gas found itself in a rapidly changing environment. It was facing deregulation, and the organizational culture was stodgy and rigid. Employees had a sense of entitlement and were not interested in changing. There was a strong union, and the average age of the workforce was mid- to late forties. Many of the employees had 20 to 25 years with the company and were just looking to hold on until retirement. Yankee Gas was a Placeholder organization. Fortunately, there was an Edgewalker CEO, an Edgewalker VP of human resources, and my Edgewalker friend Sharron Emmons, who was in charge of knowledge management at the time. These three people knew that the only way to wake this organization up to the new realities was to find the people that they called the "Cowboys and Rebels," bring them together, and give them a voice in the organization. As in so many Placeholder organizations, these people had been marginalized, and many were cynical and disgruntled. Some might even have called them troublemakers. But the leadership of the organization saw that they had a valuable perspective that was not usually listened to, and so they made them a team, elevated their status in the eyes of the organization, provided them developmental opportunities, and gave them access to the top of the organization.

I wish I could tell you that there was a happy ending to the Yankee Gas story and that the "Cowboys and Rebels" team did make a difference in the culture. But the parent organization, Northeast Utilities, decided that it no longer made strategic sense to have Yankee Gas as a subsidiary and folded it back into the larger organization. The dominant culture of the utility swallowed up any creative impact that had been created. Maybe there is a happy ending after all. This particular "Cowboys and Rebels" experiment got written about in human resources magazines and perhaps has inspired other organizations to try something similar.

TRAINING AND DEVELOPMENT

Training and development programs are an extremely important support system in creating an Edgewalker organization. The ideal programs are focused on the whole person—body, mind, emotion, and spirit. Like Times of India, mentioned earlier, Edgewalker organizations value the development of human potential and see that as an inherent part of their mission and purpose.

This is done through helping employees to (1) increase their physical well-being through exercise and nutrition, (2) enhance their mental abilities through traditional learning and by increasing their awareness of how the mind works, (3) nourish their emotional well-being by increasing their understanding of the importance of emotional intelligence and their own emotional patterns, and (4) develop their spiritual well-being by developing their understanding of their core values and their sense of purpose and meaning in life.

Development programs that appeal to Edgewalkers will include such things as time in nature, outdoor challenges, vision quests, focus on inner work, and opportunities to explore how their lives and work fit in the bigger world picture. An outline of a sample program based on workshops I have offered is in Appendix C.

SOUNDS TRUE CASE STUDY—DEVELOPING HUMAN POTENTIAL[24]

The paradox of Edgewalking is that to truly walk the edge between two worlds, you do not see the edges. You see only oneness. You see wholeness and interconnectedness.

Tami Simon, CEO of Sounds True, mentioned in Chapter 3, taught me this when I interviewed her. I gave her my definition of Edgewalker as "someone who walks between the worlds; the material world and the spiritual world."

She said to me, "Then I may not be a good person to talk to, because I only see one world. There is only *one* world," she asserts. "Nirvana (the spiritual world) and Samsara (the material world) are the same thing. To think that they are different and separate is an illusion."

This is not your typical statement from a CEO, and Tami Simon is not your typical business leader. She is a profound example of the new type of leader that is emerging in the business world today.

Sounds True, a $9 million company, publishes spoken-word audio programs, videos, and music for the inner life. The company has been listed twice on *Inc.*

magazine's list of the nation's 500 fastest-growing privately owned businesses. "Sounds True came out of the vision and inspiration I received when I was 20 years old and went to India and Nepal," Tami relates. "I remember when I meditated for the first time, and I wanted to share it with others."

Before she dropped out of college, she had gotten involved with the Swarthmore College radio station, and upon her return from India and Nepal she moved to Boulder, Colorado, and began hosting a program on the local public radio station, KGNU. She interviewed well-known experts in psychology, religion, and personal development. These interviews were taped and archived because Tami has a strong sense of vision and believed that it was important to save the knowledge of the wisdom teachers and to make it widely available.

In 1985, a $50,000 inheritance enabled Tami to take the material she had recorded and to launch Sounds True. The mission of the company is simple and clear: "To disseminate spiritual wisdom."

Every inch a spiritual seeker, Tami sees her work as a place for spiritual development for herself and her employees. As they learn from the wisdom teachers that they record, Sounds True employees strive to live and work in congruence with these teachings. One of the Core Aspirations of the company reads, "We aspire to honor and include a contemplative dimension in the workplace." (The complete list of Core Aspirations is presented in Appendix E.) There are many examples of how the company lives up to this particular aspiration. For instance, it offers ongoing training in the practice of mindfulness in the workplace. Sounds True begins its all-company meetings with a minute of silence. There is a meditation room on site. The company has used feng shui in the corporate headquarters. It has responded to employees' requests for spiritual rituals. And it allows well-behaved pets to come to work with their owners.

NATURE AS TEACHER

The best teacher of oneness is nature, and bringing pets to work is one simple way that some organizations subtly create an environment that is connect to nature.

An important component of Edgewalking programs is a vision quest, which allows people to spend time alone in nature as they contemplate a powerful question. Years ago, I conducted a series of interviews with people who were consciously integrating their spirituality and their work, and I asked them what they did to nourish their spirits at work. I expected to hear meditation, prayer, or yoga, and I did hear those things, but time in nature was the most frequently mentioned activity.

Sleeping Giant Mountain is not far from where I live, and it is filled with wonderful hiking trails. Some are low and meandering along the lowlands at the base of the mountain, some wander along the crystal clear creek, and some are more challenging, leading up to the top of the mountain and along the ridge.

One bright summer day, I decided to walk up to the top of the mountain. I took my time and enjoyed my hike up the broad path, meeting families with kids, couples with dogs, and other lone hikers along the way. It's not that long a hike to the top, and I was feeling energized, so I set out along one of the ridge trails.

After a few minutes, I began to notice the quiet of the woods and the peacefulness of the day. There were no other hikers on my part of the trail, and I began to feel myself relax into a kind of dance with the mountain. I danced the twists and turns and ups and downs of the trail, thoroughly enjoying the sense of flow.

I came to a small clearing where there was a large, flat rock outcropping that overlooked one whole side of the mountain and the valley below. It seemed a wonderful place to rest. I lay on the rock and was surprised at how comfortable it was. My back absorbed the coolness of the rock while my face absorbed the warmth of the sun, and my skin was brushed with the gentle breeze of the day. I meditated while laying on that rock, feeling totally peaceful and fulfilled. I felt gently held by that rock, as if I were being cradled. Sitting up, I gazed out over the valley and watched a hawk gliding on the wind currents below me. His graceful flight was like his own dance with that mountain.

I began to listen to the sound of the breeze in the trees below me and watched the way the wind moved through the trees in slow waves. As I felt my own breath ebb and flow, I felt a oneness with Mother Earth's wind breath as it ebbed and flowed through the trees. I experienced Earth as a living being and was moved to tears by the wonder of it all.

In the moment, I realized how disconnected from nature business has become and wondered how different business decisions would be if leaders had the opportunity to experience Mother Earth as a living being. What if they had the opportunity to breathe with her like this? What if they had the opportunity to nurture their spirits on a regular basis?

I came down from that mountain that day knowing that spirituality, ecology, and the future of our planet are integrally connected to the consciousness of our business leaders.

Yet, how often is nature incorporated in leadership development programs or organizational development activities? Training programs are held in windowless hotel rooms or corporate training rooms. Strategy planning retreats are held on the twenty-first floor of a concrete and steel edifice, far removed from Mother Earth. John Cowan has a wonderful essay titled "Dirt" in his book *Small Decencies*.[25] In it he writes, "I wish all managers had their own plot of sacred dirt. One they could sit on regularly, getting grass stains on their shorts, stray ants on their backs, and a little bark from the tree in their hair. A spot where if they sit for an hour or two, they can remember who they are and see the world for what it is."

The Xerox facility mentioned in Chapter 6 is the best example I know of an organization that truly adopted the idea that nature is a teacher. Over the course of three years, every single employee went through a weeklong training program run by a consulting group called Living Systems. Most of the program was run in nature, and every participant went on an overnight solo vision quest to seek a vision for himself or herself and for the organization.

Cognex, Sounds True, and Xerox have many elements of Edgewalker organizations and show that it is possible to use unique and inspiring ways to attract, retain, and develop the talented people who will help your organization to be on the leading edge.

HOW NOT TO FALL OFF THE CLIFF

Edgewalkers, in their enthusiasm for the next new thing, can often get too far ahead of the pack. If this happens, they lose their credibility and the opportunity to influence others to do creative work. It's nice to have someone say "This person is ahead of his (her) time," but there are few rewards for being too far out there. The most successful Edgewalkers are the ones who can still keep a foot in the world that they came from and can remember the language and values of this world so that they can be a bridge to the new world of possibility that they see. They see themselves as integrators.

However, once in a while, someone goes over the edge and crashes and burns. We have seen far too much of that lately with leaders of companies like Enron, Global Crossing, Parmalat, and Tyco. Leaders of these organizations seemed like Edgewalkers at one time and were the darlings of their industries. They broke new ground, created new markets, and changed the rules of business. But, in each case, they went a little too far.

What follows is the profile one such Edgewalker, who met an untimely death. The French financier Edouard Stern was one of the richest men in Europe. He was the heir to a 19th-century banking dynasty—Bank Stern—and was considered brilliant (if ruthless) in the way he handled business deals. He amassed a $1 billion fortune in his career through the purchase and sale of a number of financial institutions. He seemed to be just as strategic in his choice of marriage partner.

In 1984, he sold the bank to a Lebanese investor for 300 million French francs, or the equivalent today of about $60 million, while retaining rights to the family name. That same year, he married Beatrice David-Weill, one of the daughters of Michel David-Weill, the patriarch and controlling shareholder of the venerable investment bank Lazard.

Mr. Stern quickly created a new bank, also called Bank Stern, and moved aggressively into the business of offering investment and deal-making advice, in competition with Lazard. He made waves in Paris by launching raids on companies, breaking the unwritten rules of France's cozy capitalism. At that time, hostile takeovers were largely unheard of, especially when conducted by blue-blooded family banks.[26]

Within a few years, he had built the new Bank Stern into a very large and successful business, and, rather than invest in continuing to grow it, he sold it to a Swiss financial institution that later became a part of UBS AG. He then went to work at Lazard with his father-in-law. Meanwhile, his marriage to Beatrice was floundering. They divorced in the late 1990s but did not tell her father for some time. Stern left Lazard and moved to Geneva, Switzerland, to start an investment fund.

One reason behind the change: Mr. Stern wanted to start anew, away from the stuffy world of French society, according to people familiar with his thinking. He often attended meetings with his lawyers unshaven, wearing casual clothes and sneakers. Most men in French business circles wear a suit and tie.[27]

This may have been one of the signs that he was starting to go over the edge. Edgewalkers may chafe at rules and social convention that don't make sense, but they know how to keep a foot in the mainstream world, even if they are not completely comfortable with it. Edgewalkers not only test the limits in business challenges but also are likely to be unconventional and to test the limits in personal relationships.

Stern met a woman named Cecile Brossard at a dinner party. She was an artist who was quite a bit younger than he.

She enjoyed sculpting, painting, and writing poetry. They became lovers, according to Pascal Maurer, Ms. Brossard's lawyer. Mr. Stern flew her on his Gulfstream jet to exotic vacation destinations, including to Africa for hunting trips. Mr. Stern and Ms. Brossard also frequented sadomasochistic nightclubs, the lawyer says.[28]

Stern made promises to marry Ms. Brossard and then reneged on them. At one point, he had $1 million transferred into her bank account and then froze the money. Throughout their tumultuous relationship, Stern was having significant troubles with investment partners and became convinced that they meant him harm, so he began carrying a gun.

One night, he asked Ms. Brossard to meet him at his apartment in Geneva, and they ended up arguing over the money he had transferred to her. The next morning, people who worked for him found him "lying dead in a pool of blood in the bedroom of his Geneva apartment, clad head-to-toe in a skin-colored, latex bodysuit. There were two bullets in his head and one in his chest."[29] Cecile Brossard confessed to the murder, and it is being called a "crime of passion." She is likely to get 1 to 10 years in prison.

This story, in all its lurid details, was on the front page of the *Wall Street Journal*. It is impossible to know what happened to Edouard Stern. Perhaps he became mentally ill. Or perhaps, like Ken Lay, Sanjay Kumar, Bernie Ebbers, and John Rigas, his ego got so large that he believed that he could break whatever rules he wanted and remain immune to consequences.

One of the major differences between successful Edgewalkers and those who go over the edge is that Edgewalkers are committed to something greater than themselves and are driven by humanistic and spiritual values. Those who go over the edge are committed to their own self-aggrandizement and are driven by power and greed.

Very few people ever flame out as dramatically as Edouard Stern. The more typical way that people go over the edge is to make suggestions or take actions that are just a little too far outside the norms of their organizations. The result is that they get marginalized or insulated in their roles. People stop taking them seriously and do not include them in important meetings. Career opportunities dry up, and they plateau.

Here are some suggestions to consider if you think you might be getting a little too close to the edge of the cliff:

1. Watch for signs that you may be getting too far out on the edge, and revisit your own professional roots if this seems to happen. If you have been marginalized in any way, or if someone makes a sarcastic comment about something you say or do, you may be getting too close to the edge. It may be worthwhile to examine what kinds of work or contributions have given you credibility in the past and to focus on those kinds of efforts for a while.

2. When you have a new idea that you want to implement, make sure to talk to people who are likely to disagree with you or try to block you. Run your idea by the Flame-keepers, the Placeholders, and the Doomsayers in your organization. They may actually be able to show you potential flaws in your proposal.

3. Create relationships with people who provide a good "reality check" for you. These can be people who are role models or who have more expertise than you. Or they can be people who have strong Edgewalker qualities and skills and who can serve as good sounding boards.

4. Have patience with people who do not want to move as fast as you do. Take time to build relationships with them, and specifically ask for their support. By nature, you like to be out on the leading edge, and most other people are not as comfortable in uncharted territory. Have some compassion for them.

5. Cultivate the skill of honoring people who disagree with you, and listen for any pearls of wisdom they may have to offer. This can be tough, because our egos get in the way, and we like being right. But, when someone disagrees with us, they may have something to teach us. And, even if they don't, just the act of listening to them with respect will help you to build bridges.

6. If you feel that you are blocked at every turn by Placeholders and Doomsayers, consider finding a different organization to work for, or even going out on your own. Like a seed in barren ground, your ideas may not flourish in your current company. Make sure that you have tried to do everything in your power to move the organization closer to the leading edge before you give up. But, in the end, if you feel that being there diminishes your spirit, it is time to find a place that is more supportive of your unique qualities.

If I had to assess where the greatest Edgewalker risk lies, I would say that most people are at risk for not expressing enough of their Edgewalker qualities and skills. Very few are at risk for going over the edge. Nonetheless, it is important to remember that there can be a shadow side to being an Edgewalker as much as there is light.

THE EDGEWALKER JOURNEY CONTINUES

Over the past several years, it has been my privilege to interview fascinating people for this book. They have been teachers for me, and it is an honor to be able to provide this forum for their collective wisdom. I have also found it a great joy to run workshops with titles like, "How to Walk the Bridge between the Worlds," "Walking on the Leading Edge," and "Teaching on the Leading Edge." Together, we have explored new territory and found new visions, power, and inspiration.

I have been inspired by the work of people like Jean Houston,[30] John Renesch,[31] Gary Zukav,[32] and Peter Russell.[33] They each provide sound evidence of the truth of Teilhard de Chardin's profound statement that the Universe is evolving and that we, as inhabitants of the Universe, are evolving, too. These new, evolved humans are global in their consciousness. They see themselves as planetary citizens. They are multisensory. They are spiritual. They are social activists for humanity.

These new global humans are the Edgewalkers who are waking up and finding one another within and across organizations. Often they find each other through outside work with NGOs, personal-growth programs, and spiritual groups. It is as if the workplace is the last place you would think to look for a person like this. But they are there, too, and in growing numbers. In fact, organizations have the potential to offer some of the best opportunities to nurture this evolution of consciousness. They have the resources and the structure. They have the ability to tackle the largest problems the world faces—particularly problems of hunger, health, inadequate education, population growth, social injustice, and environmental degradation.

The solutions will come from the Edgewalkers. John Renesch says, "I have no doubt in my mind that we can have a world that works for all. You have to think it is possible first."[34] He coined the term "Future Shapers" and says that the way you shape the future is to be fully in the present, with consciousness about what you are doing. That's what leads to a future that works for all.

In Hawaii, a conch shell is blown when it is time to gather the community together. People all over the village can hear the sound and know it is time to come together. The conch shell has sounded for the human race, and the Edgewalkers, the Future Shapers, the Global Humans, the Multisensory Humans, and the Cultural Creatives are hearing the call to come and celebrate who they are and to work together to make a difference.

Mankind is divided into two camps, according to de Chardin. He calls one camp the "immobilists," who believe that nothing on Earth ever changes or progresses, including "the Genius of man of even his goodness."[35]

> But the other half of mankind, startled by the lookout's cry, has left the huddle where the rest of the crew sit with their heads together telling time-honored tales. Gazing out over the dark sea they study for themselves the lapping of waters along the hull of the craft that bears them, breathe the scents borne to them on the breeze, gaze at

the shadows cast from pole to pole by a changeless eternity. And for all these things, while remaining separately the same—the ripple of water, the scent of the air, the lights in the sky—become linked together and acquire a new sense: the fixed and random Universe is seen to move. No one in the world who has seen this vision can be restrained from guarding it and proclaiming it.[36]

Edgewalkers, you have the gift of sensing what others do not know. You are the butterflies emerging from the chrysalis and seeing the world from a new perspective. You are the imaginal cells of the future. You are finding one another and creating the new reality. The time has come to be proud of your qualities and skills and to step out to the edge of all your potential, for the world needs your wisdom and guidance.

"Come to the edge."
"We can't. We will fall!"
"Come to the edge."
And they came.
And he pushed them.
And they flew.

—Guillaume Apollinaire

Appendix A
EDGEWALKER INTERVIEW QUESTIONS

1. Thinking back on your life, what are some examples of times when you have "lived in two different worlds at once"?
2. What attracts you to living in two different worlds?
3. What is difficult about living in two different worlds?
4. What personal characteristics help you to live in two different worlds?
5. What skills have you developed as a result of living in different worlds?
6. What gifts or benefits have you received from living in different worlds?
7. When do you think you first became an Edgewalker, and how did that happen?
8. Edgewalkers are typically good translators and bridge builders between two different worlds. Can you tell me about a time when you served as either a translator or a bridge builder? (Being a translator does not just mean helping people with different languages understand each other. Sometimes, different organizational functions, such as engineers and human resources people, might need a translator in order to solve an organizational issue.)
9. What role, if any, does spirituality play in your being an Edgewalker? By "spirituality" I mean your deepest essence, your highest self, and/or your core values.
10. If you work in an organization, what can that organization do to help you develop your Edgewalker abilities?
11. If you work in an organization, what are some things the organization should stop doing so that you can be more fully yourself as an Edgewalker?

Appendix B

An Interview with Tony Visconti

EDGEWALKER FORMATION

Tony Visconti is the Edgewalker mentioned in chapters 4 and 5. He is a music producer, musician, ta'i chi student, and spiritual seeker. He graciously agreed to answer my interview questions by email, provided here. I then followed up with an unstructured telephone interview in January 2006.

1. *Thinking back on your life, what are some early examples of when you have "lived in two (or more) different worlds at once"?*

I had dreams of unassisted flying when I was around five. They were as real as bumping my head on a bookcase. I was severely disappointed when I realized that I couldn't fly several years later. This didn't stop me from the belief that it was possible. My father, a devout Catholic, told me that priests had knowledge of secrets that lay people were not permitted to know. I asked a priest if this was so and he replied, "yes." In the sixth grade, my teacher, Mr. James Flanagan, told us about men in Asia who could break wooden boards with their bare hands—through mental concentration. To me, this was tantamount to flying. I had read the Bible from cover to cover when I was 15, and a conversation with my chiropractor led me to believe that Christianity didn't have the kind of spiritual answers I needed. I wanted answers about the supernatural. Oddly, I began to study evolution and found the time scale of the life of our planet and when we came in a very spiritual revelation. To me it was evidence that humans were capable of the supernatural and that set us apart from beasts. When I was 21, I read a book by a Lobsang Rampa, a person who claimed to be a reincarnated lama. Rampa was eventually exposed as a German journalist who simply rehashed what was known about Tibetan Buddhism, but in a first-person dialogue. I was hooked, however.

2. *When do you think you first became an Edgewalker, and how did that happen?*

Although I had years of music training, I always saw music as the most metaphysical art. It disappears when it stops, unlike a painting or a sculpture. I somehow knew that music had more power than just to entertain. I was very moved by symphonic music as a child, and I was always wondering how music made people cry and could trigger other emotions. I felt music viscerally at first, but there was a higher feeling, beyond emotions that I became aware of. So here is where the Edgewalking comes in. I was always searching for the divine in whatever music I was involved in, jazz and rock. It was there, and I was in tune with it. At the same time, I was a sought-after musician in New York City in my late teens, and I was earning a full-time living as a musician. When I first heard the Beatles' album *Revolver*, I knew that they had tapped into the divine through rock music. I never wanted to do anything else for a living. I moved to England from New York City in 1967, and got hooked up with any guru I could find, be it people my age who knew astrology and palmistry, to a genuine Tibetan lama with whom I eventually studied meditation. I also studied four martial arts in London, already aware of their link with spirituality.

EXPERIENCE OF BEING AN EDGEWALKER

3. *What attracts you to living in two (or more) different worlds?*

As a Buddhist, I would say that we all live in two or more different worlds; duality is recognized as the source of all suffering. I find it necessary to float between perceived realities and rely on a spiritual background to deal with the boredom and harshness of life. I think any situation can be analyzed better when you can detach and ask, "What is really going on here?" In other words, not getting involved in the drama of a conflict, but seeing what has led to this moment and what needs to be done to proceed in an agreeable manner. I guess you'd call this spiritual troubleshooting. I think daydreaming can be a useful tool. Where do you go when you dream? I think you are going to where the other "you" lives, the world of truth behind symbols.

4. *What is difficult about living in two (or more) different worlds?*

In school I'd be reprimanded many times for not concentrating. But I wasn't wasting my time. I was actually analyzing the problem through my intuition, and sometimes I was just plain bored with standard scholastic learning. I think I was probably ADD, but that term only started in the nineties. Sometimes I have problems communicating an idea, if it's a big one and a very innovative one. People need references and make comparisons when they communicate. I've had big ideas that I couldn't pull into this world. The older I get, the easier it has become to communicate. The main reason is I've given up trying to look and act cool.

I am not good at small talk. If I'm at a party I have to sway a conversation towards something interesting for me. Sports are boring to me.

5. *What personal characteristics help you to live in two (or more) different worlds?*

I'm a good listener. I can hear the messages behind stumbling speakers, flowery speakers, and people who don't speak English very well. As a record producer, I'm always listening to an artist desperately trying to describe the unreachable sound, to achieve the most classic performance. I work in a society of Edge-walkers. Gestures and dreamy stares communicate more than words in this world. For some reason, I understand what they want, and I get it for them. It's so exciting to make a great recording. Some incredibly great song like "Heroes" by David Bowie now exists and will live forever, whereas a week before it was created no one had a clue it would exist. ("Heroes" evolved in a recording studio over the period of a week. It wasn't prewritten.) I am fortunate to be involved in this type of creativity. I also have a strong ability to concentrate, and I have really good physical stamina.

I wouldn't say I could read people's minds, but I am constantly told how nurturing I am and come up with the best combination of sounds and advice as a producer.

6. *What skills have you developed as a result of living in different worlds?*

I feel that no door of knowledge is closed to me. I've proved it by becoming fairly adept at several systems not directly related to music. I acknowledge that there are great masters on this planet, past and present, but I also know that they were children once and they had to take their first step, learn to walk, talk, and then go on to become great adepts. I think it's within all of us to learn and do exactly what we want. Unfortunately, most people are put off by hard work and feel that it's their right to just have an easy life and a good time. I can't believe it when people are discouraged when I tell them they could play decent guitar if they practiced every day for six months. I say that if you want something, you have no choice but to take the first step. Otherwise, how could you live with yourself? In this way I became good at t'ai chi (practicing since 1980), I am a qualified Alexander Technique teacher (since 1996), and I taught myself to do throat singing, the art of singing two notes at once as practiced in Tuva and Mongolia. I refuse to believe that something is only available to a select few. My next project is to become fluent in Mandarin.

Through several episodes in my life, I have realized that complete spiritual awakening is not possible if you still drink, smoke, or use drugs. I am an insufferable teetotaler.

7. *What gifts or benefits have you received from living in different worlds?*

I am surrounded by wonderful friends and teachers. I am excited to get out of bed every day and reluctant to go to bed every night. I love the way t'ai chi helps me in big ways, like avoiding conflict head on, to small ways like being able to ride on a bus or train without holding on to a pole. I am constantly revising and examining everything I do, from producing records to cooking eggs. I have realized that I am part of evolution and that everything is in a state of change, nothing is static. I don't get very sentimental. If I do, I have the sadness completely and then let go. I make it a point never to become bitter because the past cannot be changed, and I was the orchestrator of my past, anyway.

8. *Edgewalkers are typically good translators and bridge builders between different worlds. Can you tell me about a time when you served as either a translator or a bridge builder? (Being a translator does not just mean helping people with different languages understand each other. Sometimes, different organizational functions, such as engineers and human resources people, might need a translator in order to solve an organizational issue.)*

I think I can describe any complex process in layman's terms. The definition of my occupation is a strange concept, but I can reduce it to one sentence. One thing I am good at in the studio is what David Bowie and I call "hybridism." I took a group of rock musicians and explained the basics of Arabic and reggae music to them and come up with an intriguing production that came out as "Yassassin," a song on *The Lodger,* an album by David Bowie. I'm always putting several things together that shouldn't be. But every form of music has universality at its core.

SPIRITUALITY

9. *What role, if any, does spirituality play in your being an Edgewalker? By "spirituality" I mean your deepest essence, your highest self, and/or your core values.*

I am constantly checking myself, to make sure that I am coming from a spiritual space and not too much of an egotistical space. I think I have learned through Buddhism that you can't negate the ego, but you can work with it, detach and look at this awesome machine within us, that is our identity, our personality. I think it's possible to do a selfless act when you can momentarily detach. Only death separates Mind, Spirit, and Ego, but you can make the elastic cord that holds them together more flexible. I find that life can be playful. Being too serious is being too positional, a hindrance to creativity. An idea is only an idea. The average person has about 17 ideas a minute. You can't stop having ideas; just try it!

I am having a struggle with the definition with the term "higher self." It implies schizophrenia. I think my "self" sometimes works for the good of the whole; other times it is just working for itself. I can be all these "selfs" at once. My core values are basically straight up Buddhism (Mahayana). Life is illusory; it comes and it goes. We are all going to die. If the ego dies with physical death, what gets reincarnated, what goes to heaven? I don't lose sleep over this, since there is nothing I can do to stop death. I am looking forward to dying with peace of mind, knowing that I have done my best and that one's work is never finished. I admire monks and nuns who live apart from the rest of humanity, but one can live in this illusory world and be mindful of their actions. That is meditation in action.

10. *What spiritual or inner practices are important to you?*

Being a pragmatic person, t'ai chi scratches all my itches. I keep fit, I meditate, and I learn to defend myself all in one system. One develops a "root" in constant t'ai chi practice. This root is mental, not physical. When you have a very strong root, you can do the most amazing things in the physical world, however. There is a spontaneity and strategy in "pushing hands," a two-person exercise. Everything you learn in t'ai chi can be used in business and art.

11. *What would you say are your core spiritual values?*

We're here for such a short time. Our purpose is to make a difference, to others, our home planet, and ourselves. People can talk up spirituality and salvation until the cows come home, but actions are the only proof that you have made a difference.

12. *Do you have a particular religious tradition or spiritual path?*

Just Tibetan Buddhism.

EDGEWALKERS AND ORGANIZATIONAL LIFE

13. *If you work in an organization, what can that organization do to help you develop your Edgewalker abilities?*

Encourage meditation, yoga, martial arts, music—to take some of the emphasis off the "bottom line" and goals. People who live only for business goals burn out quickly, have addiction problems, and are in denial 99 percent of the time. Ultimately, they are not productive. I admire the Christian-run businesses only because the "higher purpose" of the businesses supersedes the "bottom-line" style of thinking. But I could never work in such an organization. Still, it illustrates how much more productive and happier people within an organization can be with spiritual goals as well as monetary goals.

14. *If you work in an organization, what are some things the organization should stop doing so that you can be more fully yourself as an Edgewalker?*

I think an Edgewalker, if he or she is strong enough and intuitive enough, can change an organization from within.

E-mail answers 12/21/05

Appendix C

TOOLS: RESOURCES FOR EDGEWALKERS

I. EDGEWALKER DEVELOPMENT DIAGNOSTIC

Edgewalker Development

This approach to Edgewalker development is in alignment with Buckingham and Clifton's[1] approach, mentioned in Chapter 4—a focus on enhancing your strengths rather than on overcoming your weaknesses. Here is a list of questions you can use to assess your current Edgewalker skills and to figure out how you might enhance the strengths you already have.

1. Describe your current level of skill in Stage 1, Knowing the Future.

    a. What are your skills in traditional ways of knowing the future, such as forecasting, trend analysis, reading in many different fields, and networking?

    b. What are your skills in intuitive ways of knowing the future, such as prayer, meditation, journaling, asking spiritual guides for help, astrology, or other intuitive ways of knowing?

    c. What are your skills in co-creating ways of knowing the future, such as being clear about what you want and watching for synchronicities and opportunities, working with others to create a larger vision, or working with the Universe to help birth what wants to emerge?

2. Describe your current level of skill in Stage 2, Risk-Taking.

   a. How skillful are you at paying attention to what is calling you at the deepest level? How good are you at asking, "What wants to emerge here?"
   b. What are you willing to let go of in order to create what has never been created before? Security? Material possessions? Self-identity? Control over other people's work?
   c. Ask yourself, "What would my life be like if I were as trusting as I could be?"
   d. How do you handle it when you have taken a big risk and failed? What helps you to stay centered in these circumstances?

3. Describe your current level of skill in Stage 3, Manifesting.

   a. To what extent do you truly believe that you create your own reality?
   b. If you find yourself beginning to fall into victim consciousness, how do you get out of it?
   c. What unique niche are you feeling called to fill?
   d. What process do you go through to tap into the Zero Point Field with your power of intention?
   e. How skillful are you in creating affirmations that are clear, positive statements of what you desire and stating them as if this already exists?
   f. How skillful are you at visualizing and feeling your manifestation as if it were real now? How often do you do this?
   g. What steps work best for you in doing the "footwork," that is, taking concrete steps that symbolize making your desires or goals real?

4. Describe your current level of skill in Stage 4, Focusing.

   a. How easily are you able to switch from multitasking to giving someone or something 110 percent of your attention?
   b. To what extent are you able to focus your time and attention on what you do well, and how well do you delegate the things that are not your strengths to other people?
   c. Do you keep a notebook that helps you to focus on what's most important?
   d. What do you do that helps you to get into the flow?

5. Describe your current level of skill in Stage 5, Appreciating.

   a. What are your strengths in valuing diversity and being cross-cultural?
   b. How well are you able to translate different worldviews for people?
   c. Are you a "connector," and, if so, what are some of the things that you do naturally to help people connect with one another?
   d. How well do you practice Appreciative Inquiry skills, that is, the art of asking positive questions about what works or about the strengths of a person or system?
   e. How often do you bless that which you would like to change?

Building on Your Strengths

Now go through your responses to the questions in the first part of this assessment, and identify your top five Edgewalker skills. For each one of these skills, list two or three actions that you can take to enhance these skills even further. These might include reading a book, taking a course, working with a coach, going on a retreat, planning an adventure that challenges you, or any number of other things.

Ideally, you will want to create a schedule for when you will undertake these action items. It will help a lot if you are working with an Edgewalker support group or with a coach who will hold you accountable for your commitments.

II. PERSONAL VALUES REFLECTION

This Personal Values Reflection will take you through four important steps.

ONE: Identify your five most important values, the values that are at the core of who you are, and put them in a prioritized order (with one being the most important).

TWO: Define each core value in a sentence or two. In your definition process, it may help to think of an experience in your life when you fully lived out this value or an experience when you deeply felt the absence of this value.

THREE: Reflect on where you are in the process of incorporating or integrating this value in your life using the values integration scale that follows.

1. I live this value every day. It has become a seamless part of my consciousness and everyday life. I feel great about how deeply this value has become an integral part of my everyday life.
2. I live this value consistently. It is more present than absent in my daily life. I feel that I am making significant progress toward the full integration of this value in my thoughts, actions, balance of time, and priorities. However, I am still challenged to live it more fully, especially in times of tension or stress.
3. I live this value in an on-again, off-again way. Sometimes I am able to really bring it alive in my life, and other times it seems that I am far from making it a reality in how I live every day. I really want to incorporate it more fully into my life, but I need to explore its practical applications more closely.
4. I live this value only occasionally. Although I believe in my heart that it is really important, I have only begun to translate this belief into everyday action. When I do act on this value, I feel that I am on the right track and living out of my true character.
5. I have intellectually recognized this value as very important to my life but I haven't really begun to put it into practice. I know that living out this value would bring greater meaning and satisfaction to my life. Now I need to find the ways to begin to incorporate it.

FOUR: Focusing on one or two values, create a set of action steps that will enable you to more fully incorporate the chosen core value into your everyday life.

Value Priority ONE: _____

Definition:

Integration Scale:

1	2	3	4	5
Live it Everyday	Live it consistently	On again, off again	Occasionally live it	Desire to live it

Value Priority TWO: _____
Definition:
Integration Scale:

1	2	3	4	5
Live it Everyday	Live it consistently	On again, off again	Occasionally live it	Desire to live it

Value Priority THREE: _____
Definition:
Integration Scale:

1	2	3	4	5
Live it Everyday	Live it consistently	On again, off again	Occasionally live it	Desire to live it

Value Priority FOUR: _____
Definition:
Integration Scale:

1	2	3	4	5
Live it Everyday	Live it consistently	On again, off again	Occasionally live it	Desire to live it

Value Priority FIVE: _____
Definition:
Integration Scale:

1	2	3	4	5
Live it Everyday	Live it consistently	On again, off again	Occasionally live it	Desire to live it

Action Steps for Values Integration

Choose one or two of your core values that you would like to more fully integrate into your everyday life. Reflecting on the following questions, create three to five action steps to incorporate this value into your daily existence. Questions: What situations are most challenging for me in living out this value? What people in my life seem to draw me away from this value? What people help me to stay on track with this value? What are the implications of this value for my everyday schedule? What kind of reflective processes might help me to live this value more fully? What is the one thing that I could do to really move me along in putting this value into practice?

VALUE_____
Action Steps:

VALUE_____
Action Steps:

III. EDGEWALKER WORKSHOP OUTLINE

Purpose of the Workshop:

- To help business leaders embrace their identity as Edgewalkers.
- To understand and enhance your Edgewalker qualities.
- To leave with tools that will help you to see underlying trends, to tap into deeper wisdom, to better anticipate and prepare for the future, and to sense your highest purpose in your work.

Length of Workshop: One day

Description:

An Edgewalker is someone who walks between two worlds. In nature-based cultures, each community has one or more shamans or medicine persons who enter invisible worlds to retrieve information or guidance for the community. The skill of walking between the worlds is at least as relevant for us in these times, when the threats facing humanity are so great and the prevailing paradigms and answers so inadequate for meeting these challenges. In every sphere of life, communities and organizations that will thrive in the 21st century will embrace and nurture Edgewalkers. Because of their particular skills, including their ability to live firmly grounded in both worlds, they are the bridge builders between paradigms. This is a highly experiential program for leaders who feel called to serve as Edgewalkers.

Agenda:

Morning

- What is an Edgewalker?
- Examples of Edgewalkers from the business world.
- The Five Qualities of Edgewalkers:
  - Self-awareness
  - Passion
  - Integrity
  - Vision
  - Playfulness

- Edgewalker lifeline exercise—drawing a symbolic map of events where you "walked between worlds."
- Identification of leadership challenge—"What challenge are you facing as an Edgewalker that holds the seeds of taking your leadership to a whole new level?"

Afternoon

- Mini-Vision Quest—Two hours in nature to find your vision for your next step of growth as an Edgewalker.
- The power of manifestation—Exercise and discussion.
- Dialogue with wisdom figure exercise—Guided meditation.
- Edgewalker Council and dialogue—Sharing the learnings of the day and asking the deep questions.
- Initiation, commitment, celebration—Ceremonies for closure.

IV. EDGEWALKER RESOURCES

Web Sites

Association for Spirit at Work, www.spiritatwork.org. This site has numerous resources for people who "walk between the two worlds."

The Edge Web site, www.edge.org. Each year, the Edge Web site has an annual question to which leading-edge scientists and science thinkers contribute their responses. The question for 2006 was, "What is your dangerous idea?" You can visit The World Question Center at http://www.edge.org/q2006/q06_index.html.

Edgewalker Web site, www.edgewalkers.org. This site offers updated information about people and organizations that take risks, create the future, and walk on the leading edge. There are also online resources such as updated individual and organizational assessment tools, detailed profiles of individuals and organizations, and updated recommendations for books and articles.

Institute for Human Economics, www.humaneconomics.org. This site is dedicated to helping business owners and corporate executives engage the full power of human talent and spirit—for business success, individual development, and the common good.

Management General Web site, www.mgeneral.com Visit this site to read Tom Brown's *Anatomy of Fire,* a great guide for Edgewalkers.

Magazines

Fast Company
ODE

Spirituality and Health
What Is Enlightenment?
Worthwhile Magazine

Books

Aburdene, Patricia. *Megatrends 2010: The Rise of Conscious Capitalism.* Charlottesville, VA: Hampton Roads Publishing, 2005.

Ardagh, Arjuna. *The Translucent Organization: How People Just Like You Are Waking Up and Changing the World.* Novato, CA: New World Library, 2005.

Barker, Joel. *Paradigms: The Business of Discovering the Future.* New York: HarperCollins, 1992.

Barrett, Richard. *Building a Values Driven Organization: A Whole System Approach to Cultural Transformation.* Boston: Butterworth-Heinemann, 2006.

Beck, Don, and Christopher Cowan. *Spiral Dynamics: Mastering Values, Leadership and Change.* Malden, MA: Blackwell Publishing, 1996.

Canfield, Jack, Mark Victor Hansen, and Les Hewitt. *The Power of Focus: How to Hit Your Business, Personal and Financial Targets With Absolute Certainty.* Deerfield Beach, FL: Health Communications, 2000.

Conley, Chip. *The Rebel Rules: Daring to Be Yourself in Business.* New York: Simon & Schuster, 2001.

Dyer, Wayne. *The Power of Intention: Learning to Co-create Your World Your Way.* Carlsbad, CA: Hay House, 2004.

Emery, Marcia. *Intuition Workbook: An Expert's Guide to Unlocking the Wisdom of Your Subconscious Mind.* Englewood Cliffs, NJ: Prentice-Hall, 1994.

Finney, Martha. *In the Face of Uncertainty: 25 Top Leaders Speak Out on Challenge, Change, and the Future of American Business.* New York: AMACOM, 2002.

Gladwell, Malcolm. *Blink: The Power of Thinking without Thinking.* New York: Little, Brown, 2005.

Gladwell, Malcolm. *The Tipping Point: How Little Things Can Make a Big Difference.* New York: Back Bay Books, 2002.

Gunther, Marc. *Faith and Fortune: The Quiet Revolution to Reform American Business.* New York: Crown Business, 2004.

Hammond, Sue Annis, and Cathy Royal (eds.). *Lessons from the Field: Applying Appreciative Inquiry.* Plano, TX: Practical Press, 1998.

Harman, Willis. *Creative Work: The Constructive Role of Business in Transforming Society.* Indianapolis, IN: Knowledge Systems, 1990.

Heermann, Barry. *Noble Purpose: Igniting Extraordinary Passion for Life and Work.* Fairfax, VA: QSU Publishing, 2004.

Hock, Dee. *One from Many: VISA and the Rise of Chaordic Organization.* San Francisco: Berrett-Koehler, 2005.

Krebs, Nina Boyd. *Edgewalkers: Defusing Cultural Boundaries on the New Global Frontier.* Far Hills, NJ: New Horizon Press, 1999.

Land, George, and Beth Jarman. *Breakpoint and Beyond: Mastering the Future Today.* New York: HarperBusiness, 1992.

Manz, Charles. *Emotional Discipline: The Power to Choose How You Feel.* San Francisco: Berrett-Koehler, 2003.

Neal, Judi. *Creating Enlightened Organizations: A Practical Guide for Implementing Spirit at Work.* East Haven, CT: Spirit at Work Publishing, 2006.

Ray, Michael. *The Highest Goal: The Secret That Sustains You in Every Moment.* San Francisco: Berrett-Koehler, 2004.

Ray, Paul, and Sherry Anderson. *The Cultural Creatives: How 50 Million People Are Changing the World.* New York: Harmony Books, 2000.

Rao, Srikumar. *Are You Ready to Succeed? Unconventional Strategies for Achieving Personal Mastery In Business and Life.* New York: Hyperion, 2006.

Renesch, John. *Getting to the Better Future: How Business Can Lead the Way to New Possibilities.* San Francisco: New Business Books, 2000.

Secretan, Lance. *ONE: The Art and Practice of Conscious Leadership.* Caledon, Ontario, Canada: The Secretan Center, 2006.

Senge, Peter, C. Otto Sharmer, Joseph Jaworksi, and Betty Sue Flowers. *Presence: An Exploration of Profound Change in People, Organizations, and Society.* New York: Currency Doubleday, 2004.

Stephen, Michael. *Spirituality in Business: The Hidden Success Factor.* Scottsdale, AZ: Inspired Productions Press, 2002.

Wheatley, Margaret. *Finding Our Way: Leadership for an Uncertain Time.* San Francisco: Berrett-Koehler, 2005.

Whiteley, Richard. *The Corporate Shaman: A Business Fable.* New York: HarperCollins, 2002.

Appendix D

STEVE JOBS COMMENCEMENT ADDRESS AT STANFORD UNIVERSITY

"YOU'VE GOT TO FIND WHAT YOU LOVE," JOBS SAYS

This is the text of the commencement address by Steve Jobs, CEO of Apple Computer and of Pixar Animation Studios, delivered on June 12, 2005 at Stanford University. Accessed April 15, 2006 from http://news-service. stanford.edu/news/2005/june15/jobs-061505.html.

I am honored to be with you today at your commencement from one of the finest universities in the world. I never graduated from college. Truth be told, this is the closest I've ever gotten to a college graduation. Today I want to tell you three stories from my life. That's it. No big deal. Just three stories.

The first story is about connecting the dots.

I dropped out of Reed College after the first 6 months, but then stayed around as a drop-in for another 18 months or so before I really quit. So why did I drop out?

It started before I was born. My biological mother was a young, unwed college graduate student, and she decided to put me up for adoption. She felt very strongly that I should be adopted by college graduates, so everything was all set for me to be adopted at birth by a lawyer and his wife. Except that when I popped out they decided at the last minute that they really wanted a girl. So my parents, who were on a waiting list, got a call in the middle of the night asking, "We have an unexpected baby boy; do you want him?" They said, "Of course." My biological mother later found out that my mother had never graduated from college and that my father had never graduated from high school. She refused to sign the final adoption papers. She only relented a few months later when my parents promised that I would someday go to college.

And, 17 years later, I did go to college. But I naively chose a college that was almost as expensive as Stanford, and all of my working-class parents' savings were being spent on my college tuition. After six months, I couldn't see the value in it. I had no idea what I wanted to do with my life and no idea how college was going to help me figure it out. And here I was spending all of the money my parents had saved their entire life. So I decided to drop out and trust that it would all work out OK. It was pretty scary at the time, but, looking back, it was one of the best decisions I ever made. The minute I dropped out, I could stop taking the required classes that didn't interest me and begin dropping in on the ones that looked interesting.

It wasn't all romantic. I didn't have a dorm room, so I slept on the floor in friends' rooms, I returned Coke bottles for the five-cent deposits to buy food with, and I would walk the seven miles across town every Sunday night to get one good meal a week at the Hare Krishna temple. I loved it. And much of what I stumbled into by following my curiosity and intuition turned out to be priceless later on. Let me give you one example:

Reed College at that time offered perhaps the best calligraphy instruction in the country. Throughout the campus every poster, every label on every drawer, was beautifully hand calligraphed. Because I had dropped out and didn't have to take the normal classes, I decided to take a calligraphy class to learn how to do this. I learned about serif and san-serif typefaces, about varying the amount of space between different letter combinations, about what makes great typography great. It was beautiful, historical, artistically subtle in a way that science can't capture, and I found it fascinating.

None of this had even a hope of any practical application in my life. But 10 years later, when we were designing the first Macintosh computer, it all came back to me. And we designed it all into the Mac. It was the first computer with beautiful typography. If I had never dropped in on that single course in college, the Mac would have never had multiple typefaces or proportionally spaced fonts. And since Windows just copied the Mac, it's likely that no personal computer would have them. If I had never dropped out, I would have never dropped in on this calligraphy class, and personal computers might not have the wonderful typography that they do. Of course, it was impossible to connect the dots looking forward when I was in college. But it was very, very clear looking backwards 10 years later.

Again, you can't connect the dots looking forward; you can only connect them looking backwards. So you have to trust that the dots will somehow connect in your future. You have to trust in something—your gut, destiny, life, karma, whatever. This approach has never let me down, and it has made all the difference in my life.

My second story is about love and loss.

I was lucky—I found what I loved to do early in life. Woz and I started Apple in my parents' garage when I was 20. We worked hard, and in 10 years Apple had grown from just the two of us in a garage into a $2 billion company with over 4,000 employees. We had just released our finest creation—the Macintosh—a year earlier, and I had just turned 30. And then I got fired. How can you get fired from a company you started? Well, as Apple grew, we hired someone who I thought was very talented to run the company with me, and for the first year or so things went well. But then our visions of the future began to diverge, and eventually we had a falling out. When we did, our board of directors sided with him. So, at 30, I was out. And very publicly out. What had been the focus of my entire adult life was gone, and it was devastating.

I really didn't know what to do for a few months. I felt that I had let the previous generation of entrepreneurs down—that I had dropped the baton as it was being passed to me. I met with David Packard and Bob Noyce and tried to apologize for screwing up so badly. I was a very public failure, and I even thought about running away from the valley. But something slowly began to dawn on me—I still loved what I did. The turn of events at Apple had not changed that one bit. I had been rejected, but I was still in love. And so I decided to start over.

I didn't see it then, but it turned out that getting fired from Apple was the best thing that could have ever happened to me. The heaviness of being successful was replaced by the lightness of being a beginner again, less sure about everything. It freed me to enter one of the most creative periods of my life.

During the next five years, I started a company named NeXT, another company named Pixar, and fell in love with an amazing woman who would become my wife. Pixar went on to create the world's first computer-animated feature film, *Toy Story*, and is now the most successful animation studio in the world. In a remarkable turn of events, Apple bought NeXT, I returned to Apple, and the technology we developed at NeXT is at the heart of Apple's current renaissance. And Laurene and I have a wonderful family together.

I'm pretty sure none of this would have happened if I hadn't been fired from Apple. It was awful-tasting medicine, but I guess the patient needed it. Sometimes life hits you in the head with a brick. Don't lose faith. I'm convinced that the only thing that kept me going was that I loved what I did. You've got to find what you love. And that is as true for your work as it is for your lovers. Your work is going to fill a large part of your life, and the only way to be truly satisfied is to do what you believe is great work. And the only way to do great work is to love what you do. If you haven't found it yet, keep looking. Don't settle. As with all matters of the heart, you'll know when you find it. And, like any great relationship, it just gets better and better as the years roll on. So keep looking until you find it. Don't settle.

My third story is about death.

When I was 17, I read a quote that went something like: "If you live each day as if it was your last, someday you'll most certainly be right." It made an impression on me, and since then, for the past 33 years, I have looked in the mirror every morning and asked myself: "If today were the last day of my life, would I want to do what I am about to do today?" And whenever the answer has been "No" for too many days in a row, I know I need to change something.

Remembering that I'll be dead soon is the most important tool I've ever encountered to help me make the big choices in life. Because almost everything—all external expectations, all pride, all fear of embarrassment or failure—these things just fall away in the face of death, leaving only what is truly important. Remembering that you are going to die is the best way I know to avoid the trap of thinking you have something to lose. You are already naked. There is no reason not to follow your heart.

About a year ago, I was diagnosed with cancer. I had a scan at 7:30 in the morning, and it clearly showed a tumor on my pancreas. I didn't even know what a pancreas was. The doctors told me this was almost certainly a type of cancer that is incurable and that I should expect to live no longer than three to six months. My doctor advised me to go home and get my affairs in order, which is doctor's code for prepare to die. It means to try to tell your kids everything you thought you'd have the next 10 years to tell them in just a few months. It means to make sure everything is buttoned up so that it will be as easy as possible for your family. It means to say your goodbyes.

I lived with that diagnosis all day. Later that evening, I had a biopsy, where they stuck an endoscope down my throat, through my stomach, and into my intestines, put a needle into my pancreas, and got a few cells from the tumor. I was sedated, but my wife, who was there, told me that when they viewed the cells under a microscope, the doctors started crying because it turned out to be a very rare form of pancreatic cancer that is curable with surgery. I had the surgery, and I'm fine now.

This was the closest I've been to facing death, and I hope it's the closest I get for a few more decades. Having lived through it, I can now say this to you with a bit more certainty than when death was a useful but purely intellectual concept:

No one wants to die. Even people who want to go to heaven don't want to die to get there. And yet death is the destination we all share. No one has ever escaped it. And that is as it should be, because Death is very likely the single best invention of Life. It is Life's change agent. It clears out the old to make way for the new.

Right now the new is you, but someday, not too long from now, you will gradually become the old and be cleared away. Sorry to be so dramatic, but it is quite true.

Your time is limited, so don't waste it living someone else's life. Don't be trapped by dogma—which is living with the results of other people's thinking. Don't let the noise of others' opinions drown out your own inner voice. And, most important, have the courage to follow your heart and intuition. They somehow already know what you truly want to become. Everything else is secondary.

When I was young, there was an amazing publication called *The Whole Earth Catalog*, which was one of the bibles of my generation. It was created by a fellow named Stewart Brand, not far from here, in Menlo Park, and he brought it to life with his poetic touch. This was in the late 1960s, before personal computers and desktop publishing, so it was all made with typewriters, scissors, and Polaroid cameras. It was sort of like Google in paperback form, 35 years before Google came along: it was idealistic, and overflowing with neat tools and great notions.

Stewart and his team put out several issues of *The Whole Earth Catalog*, and then, when it had run its course, they put out a final issue. It was the mid-1970s, and I was your age. On the back cover of their final issue was a photograph of an early morning country road, the kind you might find yourself hitchhiking on if you were so adventurous. Beneath it were the words: "Stay hungry. Stay foolish." It was their farewell message as they signed off. Stay hungry. Stay foolish. And I have always wished that for myself. And now, as you graduate to begin anew, I wish that for you.

Stay hungry. Stay foolish.

Thank you all very much.

Appendix E

SOUNDS TRUE 17 PRINCIPLES

1. Sounds True aspires to be both mission-driven *and* profit-driven.
2. We aspire to build workplace community.
3. We encourage authenticity in the workplace.
4. We aspire to have open communication company-wide.
5. Animals are welcome.
6. We encourage creativity, innovation, new ideas.
7. We strive to be flexible about work schedules.
8. We encourage individual teams to determine the best way to reach their goals.
9. We aspire to honor and include a contemplative dimension in the workplace.
10. We aspire to reach out to a diverse community.
11. We strive to protect and preserve the Earth.
12. We aspire to have a relationship with our customers that is based on integrity.
13. We aspire to take time for kindness, have fun, and get a lot done.
14. We aspire to acknowledge that every person in the organization carries wisdom.
15. We encourage people to speak up and propose solutions.
16. We encourage people to listen deeply.
17. We aspire to honor individual differences and diversity.

Notes

INTRODUCTION

1. Judith Neal, "How to Walk on the Leading Edge without Falling off the Cliff," in *Business: The Ultimate Resource,* ed. Nick Philipson (London: Bloomsbury, 2002), 229–230.

CHAPTER 1

1. Judith Neal, "How to Walk on the Leading Edge without Falling off the Cliff," in *Business: The Ultimate Resource,* ed. Nick Philipson (London: Bloomsbury Publishing, 2002), 229–223.

2. Peter Frost and Carolyn Egri, "The Shamanic Perspective on Organizational Change and Development," *Journal of Organizational Change Management* 7, no.1 (1994): 7–23; Richard Whiteley, *The Corporate Shaman: A Business Fable* (New York: HarperCollins, 2002).

3. Nina Boyd Krebs, *Edgewalkers: Defusing Cultural Boundaries on the New Global Frontier* (Far Hills, NJ: New Horizon Press, 1999).

4. Philip Harris, Robert Moran, and Sarah Moran, *Managing Cultural Differences: Global Leadership Strategies for the 21st Century,* 6th ed. (New York: Elsevier, 2005).

5. Philip Harris, "Diversity in the Global Work Culture," *Equal Opportunities International* 15, no. 2 (1996): 37–38.

6. Michael Stephen, *Spirituality in Business: The Hidden Success Factor* (Scottsdale, AZ: Inspired Productions Press, 2002), 30.

7. Krebs, *Edgewalkers,* 38.

8. Lance Secretan, *ONE: The Art and Practice of Conscious Leadership* (Caledon, Ontario, Canada: The Secretan Center, 2006), xvii.

9. Krebs, *Edgewalkers,*13.

10. Christopher Locke, Rick Levine, Doc Searls, and David Weinberger, *The Cluetrain Manifesto: The End of Business as Usual* (Boston: Perseus, 2001).

11. Daniel H. Pink, *A Whole New Mind: Moving from the Information Age to the Conceptual Age* (New York: Riverhead Books, 2005).

12. Lance Secretan, *Inspire! What Great Leaders Do: The Path to Higher Ground Leadership* (Hoboken, NJ: Wiley, 2004).

13. Joseph Jaworski, *Synchronicity: The Inner Path of Leadership* (San Francisco: Berrett-Koehler, 1997), 149.

14. Douglas Schuit, "The PeopleSoft Spirit Lives On, Workforce Management," retrieved from http://www.workforce.com/section/10/feature/24/13/20/index.html.

15. Ibid.

16. Stefan Rechtschaffen, *Time Shifting: Creating More Time to Enjoy Your Life* (New York: Doubleday, 1996), 1.

17. Ibid., 1.

18. Richard Barrett is the author of three very significant books: *Spiritual Unfoldment: A Guide to Liberating Your Soul* (Alexandria, VA: Unfoldment Publications, 1995); *Liberating the Corporate Soul: Building a Visionary Organization* (Woburn, MA: Butterworth-Heinemann, 1998); and *Building a Values-Driven Organization: A Whole System Approach to Cultural Transformation* (Burlington, MA: Butterworth-Heineman, 2006).

19. Pink, *A Whole New Mind,* 35.

20. Paul Ray and Sherry Anderson, *The Cultural Creatives: How 50 Million People Are Changing the World* (New York: Harmony Books, 2000), 4.

21. Joshua Greene, *Here Comes the Sun: George Harrison's Spiritual and Musical Journey* (New York: Wiley, 2005).

22. David Tacey, "*Rising Waters of the Spirit:* The View from Secular Society," *Studies in Spirituality* 13 (2003): 11–30.

23. David Noer, *Healing the Wounds: Overcoming the Trauma of Layoffs and Revitalizing Downsized Organizations* (San Francisco: Jossey-Bass, 1993).

24. *Time* magazine (November 19, 2001), CNN Poll.

25. Willis Harman. *Global Mind Change,* 2nd ed. (San Francisco: Berrett-Koehler, 1998).

26. Larry Dossey. *Healing Beyond the Body: Medicine and the Infinite Reach of the Mind* (Boston: Shambhala Publications, 2001).

27. Patricia Aburdene, *Megatrends: The Rise of Conscious Capitalism* (Charlottesville, NC: Hampton Roads Publishing, 2005), 4.

28. Ibid., xxi–xxii.

29. Jerry Wennstrom, *The Inspired Heart: An Artist's Journey of Transformation* (Boulder, CO: Sentient Publications, 2002), 34.

CHAPTER 2

1. Lars Bogucki, Chorus from original unpublished song titled "Borderline."

2. Rupert Sheldrake, *The Presence of the Past: Morphic Resonance and the Habits of Nature* (Rochester, VT: Park Street Press, 1995).

3. Sergei Sikorsky, personal interview, November 18, 2002.

4. "Igor I. Sikorsky," retrieved from http://www.sikorskyarchives.com/siksky2.html

5. Ibid.

6. Retrieved   from   http://www.sikorsky.com/frames/external_links/page/1,3041, CLI1_DIV69,00.html?extlink = http://www.sikorskyarchives.com.

7. Sergei Sikorsky, personal interview.

8. Barry Heermann, *Noble Purpose: Igniting Extraordinary Passion in Life and Work* (Fairfax, VA: QSU Publishing, 2004).

CHAPTER 3

1. Let Davidson, *Wisdom at Work: The Awakening of Consciousness in the Workplace* (Burdett, NY: Larson Publications, 1998), 65.

2. Kevin Cashman, *Leadership from the Inside Out: Seven Pathways to Mastery* (Provo, UT: Executive Excellence Publishing, 1998), 187.

3. Judi Neal, "Spirituality in the Workplace: An Emerging Phenomenon," *Studies in Spirituality* 1 (2005): 267–282.

4. Patricia Aburdene, ASAW Authors Teleconference, December 12, 2005.

5. Peter Ressler and Monika Ressler, *Spiritual Capitalism: What the FDNY Taught Wall Street about Money* (New York: Chilmark Books, 2005).

6. Two organizations devoted to the study of near-death experiences and the psychological and spiritual effects of these experiences are the Near Death Experience Research Foundation, www.nderf.org, and the International Association for Near Death Studies, www.iands.org.

7. Lance Secretan, *Inspirational Leadership: Destiny, Calling and Cause* (Toronto, Canada: MacMillan Canada, 1999).

8. Dominic Mele and Alphonse Corrales, *Tomasso Corporation: Including Spirituality in the Organizational Culture* (Barcelona, Spain: IESE Publishing, University of Navarro, 2005), 4.

9. Ibid., 5.

10. Chip Conley, *The Rebel Rules: Daring to Be Yourself in Business* (New York: Simon & Schuster, 2001), 46.

11. Shakti Gawain, *Living in the Light: A Guide to Personal and Planetary Transformation* (Mill Valley, CA: Whatever Publishing, Inc., 1986).

12. Ibid., 27.

13. Charles Manz, Karen Manz, Robert Marx, and Christopher Neck, *The Wisdom of Solomon* (San Francisco: Berrett-Koehler, 2001).

14. Video of Aaron Feuerstein at Hillel, University of Massachusetts Amherst, available from Robert Marx, Management Department, University of Massachusetts-Amherst.

15. Miguel Ruiz, *The Four Agreements: A Toltec Wisdom Book* (San Raphael, CA: Amber-Allen Publishing, 1997).

16. Peter Senge, C. Otto Sharmer, Joseph Jaworski, and Betty Sue Flowers, *Presence: An Exploration of Profound Change in People, Organizations, and Society* (New York: Currency Doubleday, 2004).

17. Some excellent books on the application of the new sciences to organizations include *Life at the Edge of Chaos: Creating the Quantum Organization,* by Mark Youngblood (Dallas, TX: Quay Alliance, 1997); *Leadership and the New Science: Learning About Organizations from an Orderly Universe,* by Margaret Wheatley (San Francisco: Berrett-Koehler, 1992); *A Simpler Way,* by Margaret Wheatley and Myron Kellner-Rogers (San Francisco: Berrett-Koehler, 1996); *Managing the Unknowable: Strategic Boundaries between Order and*

Chaos in Organizations, by Ralph Stacey (San Francisco: Jossey-Bass, 1992); *Weaving Complexity and Business: Engaging the Soul at Work,* by Roger Lewin and Birute Regine (New York: Texere, 2001); and *The New Pioneers: The Men and Women Who Are Transforming the Workplace and the Marketplace,* by Tom Petzinger (New York: Simon & Schuster, 1999).

18. Rupert Sheldrake, *The Presence of the Past: Morphic Resonance and the Habits of Nature* (Rochester, VT: Park Street Press, 1995).

19. Ron Pevny, "Vision Quests: Learning to Live Centered in the Soul," in *Spirit at Work Newsletter* (January 2004): 1, 7.

20. Personal communication, June 15, 2005.

21. James Hillman says that each of us has the seeds of our Soul's Code, our spiritual DNA, implanted in us before we are born and that the work of our life on Earth is to discover what our Soul's Code is. Evidence of our Soul's Code always shows up in early childhood. James Hillman, *Soul's Code: In Search of Character and Calling* (New York: Warner Books, 1997).

22. Lance Secretan, *Inspire! What Great Leaders Do* (Hoboken, NJ: Wiley, 2004), 53.

23. Ibid., 59.

24. Conley, *The Rebel Rules,* 44.

25. Retrieved from http://literati.net/Thurman/index.htm.

26. Kenny Moore, "Kenny Moore Held a Funeral and Everybody Came," *Fast Company,* no. 79 (February 2004): 30.

27. Robert Catell and Kenny Moore, with Glenn Rifkin, *The CEO and the Monk: One Company's Journey to Profit and Purpose* (New York: Wiley, 2004), 181–182.

28. Marcus Buckingham and Donald Clifton, *Now Discover Your Strengths* (New York: Free Press, 2001).

29. Lois Sekerak Hogan, "The Edge of All Our Possibility: A Labor Day Reflection." Unpublished.

CHAPTER 4

1. Marcus Buckingham and Donald Clifton, *Now Discover Your Strengths* (New York: Free Press, 2001).

2. Ibid., 8.

3. Ibid., 25.

4. Ibid., 26.

5. Peter Russell, *The Global Brain Awakens: Our Next Evolutionary Leap* (Palo Alto, CA: Global Brain, 1995).

6. Liam Pleven, "Remote Chance of Bird-Flu Pandemic Spawns Murky Outlook for Life Insurers." *Wall Street Journal,* April 4, 2006, C6.

7. Ibid.

8. Margaret Wheatley, *Finding Our Way: Leadership for an Uncertain Time* (San Francisco: Berrett-Koehler, 2005), 126.

9. Stirling Kelso, Joseph Manez, and Jennifer Pollock, "Data Dump," *Fast Company* (April 2006): 29–30.

10. Ibid., 30.

11. Ibid., 30.

12. Robert Rivlin and Karen Gravelle, *Deciphering the Senses: The Expanding World of Human Perception* (New York: Simon & Schuster, 1984), 159.

13. Carl Jung, *Analytical Psychology: Its Theory and Practice—The Tavistock Lectures* (New York: Pantheon Books, 1968), 14–15.

14. Joann Stein, personal communication, March 22, 2006.

15. Marcia Emery, *Intuition Workbook: An Expert's Guide to Unlocking the Wisdom of Your Subconscious Mind* (Englewood Cliffs, NJ: Prentice-Hall, 1994), xvii.

16. As quoted in Patricia Garfield, *Creative Dreaming* (New York: Ballantine Books, 1974), 42.

17. Emery, *Intuition Workbook,* 159.

18. Ibid.

19. F. A. Keule, as reported during a convention, 1890, retrieved from http://www.herownroom.com/famousdreams.htm.

20. Carmen Brickner, personal communication, March 20, 2006.

21. My thanks to Perry Pascarella, who pointed out this story. The quote is retrieved from http://www.geocities.com/madhukar_shukla/crebook/08.html.

22. Paula Raines, J.D., Ph.D., personal communication, March 19, 2006.

23. As quoted in Stephen LaBerge and Howard Reingold, *Exploring the World of Lucid Dreaming* (New York: Ballantine Books, 1990), 10.

24. Jung, *Analytical Psychology.*

25. Carmen Brickner, personal communication, March 20, 2006.

26. Mark Rosenberg, personal communication, March 21, 2006.

27. An excellent resource for understanding and working with dreams is http://www.lucidity.com, created by Stephen LaBerge.

28. Malcolm Gladwell, *Blink: The Power of Thinking without Thinking* (New York: Little, Brown, 2005), 11.

29. Ibid., p. 23.

30. In quantum physics there is a phenomenon called "subtle dependence on initial conditions." This is also known as the "Butterfly Effect," since it posits that a very small factor can cause significant effects on a larger system; for example, a butterfly flapping its wings in Kansas can cause a typhoon in Hong Kong.

31. Gladwell, *Blink,* pp. 33–34.

32. Rupert Sheldrake, online telepathy experiment, retrieved from http://www.sheldrake.org/experiments/oltnew/start.html.

33. All the quotations in this section are from a telephone interview with Tony Visconti on December 29, 2005.

34. Tony Visconti says that he continues to be in touch with his spirit guides, but back then, they were the only kind of guidance that he had. Now he has many more tools for understanding and creating the future.

35. See Question 1 in Tony Visconti's email interview in Appendix B for a description of the relevance of the Lobsang Rampa books.

36. Patricia Aburdene, ASAW Authors Teleconference interview, December 9, 2005.

37. Willis Harman, *An Incomplete Guide to the Future* (New York: Norton, 1979).

38. Willis Harman. *Creative Work: The Constructive Role of Business in Transforming Society* (Indianapolis: Knowledge Systems, Inc., 1990). This book was extremely significant to me in formulating my own thinking about spirituality in the workplace, which I originally defined as an individual phenomenon that was very personal and private. After reading this book, I came to see that what I was sensing was a small part of a much bigger trend and that business has a key role to play in helping the world to move toward a more humanistic, ecological, peaceful, and balanced paradigm.

39. John Renesch, *Getting to the Better Future: How Business Can Lead the Way to New Possibilities* (San Francisco: New Business Books, 2000), 9.

40. Ibid., 10–11 (italics in the original).

41. John Renesch, "Epilogue: The Great Dream," retrieved from www.renesch.com.

42. Renesch, *Getting to the Better Future,* 115–120.

43. Ibid., 116.

44. Renesch, "Epilogue: The Great Dream."

45. John Renesch, personal correspondence, March 29, 2006.

46. Lao Tsu, *Tao Te Ching,* translated by Gia-Fu Feng and Jane English (New York: Vintage Books, 1972), verse 37.

47. Judi Neal, "Business Leader Disseminates Spiritual Wisdom: Tami Simon, CEO of Sounds True," e-doc available on http://www.amazon.com.

48. Gladwell, *Blink,* 43–44.

CHAPTER 5

1. Lance Secretan, *Inspirational Leadership: Destiny, Calling and Cause* (Toronto, Canada: Macmillan Canada, 1999).

2. Tony Visconti, telephone interview, December 29, 2006.

3. Dave Thompson, Liner notes for *Marc Bolan & T. Rex: Twentieth Century Boy: The Ultimate Collection* (Santa Monica, CA: Universal Music Enterprises, 2002), 1.

4. Jerry Wennstrom, *The Inspired Heart: An Artist's Journey of Transformation* (Boulder, CO: Sentient Publications, 2002).

5. Ibid., 183.

6. Ibid., 181.

7. Walter Bruggemann, *The Prophetic Imagination,* 2nd ed. (Minneapolis: Fortress Press, 2001), 40.

8. Retrieved from http://www.raptureready.com/faq/faq369.html.

9. Jeffrey Satinover, *The Quantum Brain: The Search for Freedom and the Next Generation of Man* (New York: Wiley, 2001), 14. Italics in original.

10. Ibid., p. 24.

11. Laurence Gonzales, *Deep Survival: Who Lives, Who Dies, and Why* (New York: Norton, 2003), 39.

12. Ibid., 41.

13. Ibid., 41.

14. Ibid., 85.

15. Chip Conley, *The Rebel Rules: Daring to Be Yourself in Business* (New York: Simon & Schuster, 2001), 75.

16. Joel Barker, *Paradigms: The Business of Discovering the Future* (New York: Harper Collins, 1992), 74.

17. Julia Cameron, *The Artist's Way: A Spiritual Path to Higher Creativity* (New York: Jeremy Tarcher, 2002).

18. *Webster's New World Compact School and Office Dictionary* (New York: Simon & Schuster, 1982), 278.

19. Gonzales, *Deep Survival,* 180.

20. Jack Gibb, *Trust: A New View of Personal and Organizational Development* (Los Angeles: Guild of Tutors Press, 1978).

21. Martin Seligman, *Authentic Happiness* (New York: Free Press, 2002), 4. The study quoted by Seligman was undertaken by D. Danner, D. Snowdon, and W. Friesen, "Positive Emotions in Early Life and Longevity: Findings from the Nun Study," *Journal of Personality and Social Psychology* 80: 804–813.

22. Ibid., 9–10.

23. Ibid., 23.

24. Ibid., 40.

25. Martin Seligman. *Learned Optimism* (New York: Knopf, 1991).

26. Conley, *The Rebel Rules,* 76.

27. Ibid.

28. Ibid., 79.

29. Ibid., 80.

30. Wayne Dyer, *The Power of Intention: Learning to Co-create Your World Your Way* (Carlsbad, CA: Hay House, 2004).

31. Ibid., 3.

32. Carlos Castaneda, *The Active Side of Infinity* (New York: Harper Perennial, 2000), quoted in Wayne Dyer, *The Power of Intention* (Carlsbad, CA: Hay House, 2004), 4.

33. Ibid.

34. Lynne McTaggart, *The Field: The Quest for the Secret Force of the Universe* (New York: Harper Perennial, 2002), xiii.

35. Ibid., 19.

36. Ibid., 111.

37. Ibid., 113.

38. Ibid., 116.

39. Tijn Touber, "The Amazing Promises of the Zero Point Field," *Ode* (November 2003): 43.

40. Shakti Gawain, *Creative Visualization* (Mill Valley, CA: Whatever Publishing, 1978), 13.

41. Ibid., 35.

42. Gregg Braden, *The Isaiah Effect: Decoding the Lost Science of Prayer and Prophecy* (New York: Three Rivers Press, 2000), 25.

43. Ibid., 168.

44. Patricia Garfield, *Creative Dreaming* (New York: Ballantine Books, 1974), 81.

45. Ibid., 83.

46. Ibid., 83.

47. G. William Domhoff, *Senoi Dream Theory: Myth, Scientific Method, and the Dreamwork Movement* (2003). Retrieved at http://dreamresearch.net/Library/senoi.html.

48. Jack Canfield, Mark Victor Hansen, and Les Hewitt, *The Power of Focus: How to Hit Your Business, Personal and Financial Targets with Absolute Certainty* (Deerfield Beach, FL: Health Communications, 2000), 79.

49. Robert Louis Stevenson, "A Chapter on Dreams," *Memories and Portraits, Random Memories, Memories of Himself* (New York: Scribner, 1925).

50. Canfield, Hansen, and Hewitt, *The Power of Focus*, 33.

51. Ibid., 76–78.

52. Gawain, *Creative Visualization,* 134–137.

53. Peter Senge, C. Otto Sharmer, Joseph Jaworksi, and Betty Sue Flowers, *Presence: An Exploration of Profound Change in People, Organizations, and Society* (New York: Currency Doubleday, 2004), 103.

54. Ibid.

55. Mihalyi Csikzentmihalyi, *Flow: The Psychology of Optimal Experience* (New York: Harper & Row, 1990), 4.

56. Ibid., 74.

57. Malcolm Gladwell, *The Tipping Point: How Little Things Can Make a Big Difference* (New York: Back Bay Books, 2002).

58. Ibid., 43.

59. Ibid., 45–46.

60. Ibid., 48–49.

61. Lance Secretan, *ONE: The Art and Practice of Conscious Leadership* (Caledon, Ontario, Canada: The Secretan Center, 2006).

62. Peter Russell, *The Global Brain Awakens: Our Next Evolutionary Leap* (Palo Alto, CA: Global Brain, 1995).

63. Richard Barrett, *Building a Values-Driven Organization: A Whole System Approach to Cultural Transformation* (Boston: Butterworth-Heinemann, 2006), 13–14.

64. Judi Neal, *Creating Enlightened Organizations: A Practical Guide for Implementing Spirit at Work* (East Haven, CT: Spirit at Work Publishing, 2006).

65. David Gerson and Gail Straub, *Empowerment: The Art of Creating Your Life as You Want It* (New York: Delta Trade Paperbacks, 1989), 6.

66. Sue Annis Hammond, *The Thin Book of Appreciative Inquiry* (Plano, TX: Kodiak Consulting, 1996), 20–21.

67. Sue Annis Hammond and Cathy Royal (eds.), *Lessons from the Field: Applying Appreciative Inquiry* (Plano, TX: Practical Press, 1998), 12.

68. Andrew Harvey, *Hidden Journey: A Spiritual Awakening* (New York: Penguin, 1992).

69. Andrew Harvey and Mark Matousek, *Dialogues with a Modern Mystic* (Wheaton, IL: Theosophical Publishing House, 1994), 17.

70. All definitions of "bless" in this section are from *Webster's New World Compact School Dictionary* (New York: Simon & Schuster, 1982), 48.

CHAPTER 6

1. Dan Ruben, "Earth, Spirit and Work," *Spirit at Work Newsletter* (December 1998), 4.

2. Ibid.

3. Ken Wilber, Foreword to Arjuna Ardagh, *The Translucent Evolution: How People Just Like You Are Waking Up and Changing the World* (Novato, CA: New World Library, 2005).

4. John Byrne, *Informed Consent* (New York: McGraw-Hill, 1995).

5. You can learn more about Deborah Cox's work at http://www.ignitespirit.com.

6. Reiki is a practice of energy healing that uses the imagery of symbols to improve the energy of a person or a system.

7. Pat Sullivan, *Work with Meaning, Work with Joy: Bringing Your Spirit to Any Job* (Lanham, MD: Sheed & Ward, 2003).

8. Mary Ann Vlahac, personal communication during a series of interviews between 2002 and 2006. I wrote an article about her titled "Sunsets in the Boardroom" (available as an e-doc on www.Amazon.com) that describes her nature-based practices when she worked for Peoples Bank.

9. Jennifer Laabs, "Balancing Spirituality and Work," *Personnel Journal* 74, no. 9 (September 18, 1995): 60.

10. Barry Heermann, *Noble Purpose: Igniting Extraordinary Passion for Life and Work* (Fairfax, VA: QSU Publishing, 2004).

11. Steven Jobs, "You've Got to Find What You Love, Jobs Says," *Stanford Report,* June 14, 2005. Retrieved from http://news-service.stanford.edu/news/2005/june15/jobs-061505.html 3/23/06.

12. James Collins and Jerry Porras, *Built to Last: Successful Habits of Visionary Companies* (San Francisco: HarperBusiness, 1997). See chapter 3, "More Than Profits," 46–79, for more information on how to "preserve the core."

13. Don Petersen, quoted in ibid., 52.

14. Henry Ford, quoted in ibid., 53.

15. More information about the Kripalu Consultant Collaborative can be found at http://www.spiritintheworkplace.com.

16. Robert Ott, Colleen Kelly, and Marlow Hotchkiss, *LAKES: A Journey of Heroes* (Webster, NY: Xerox Corporation and Living Systems, 1997), 234.

17. Ibid., 235.

18. "Sikorsky Strike Spikes State Unemployment Numbers," *Newsday,* April 20, 2006. Retrieved online at http://www.newsday.com/news/local/wire/connecticut/ny-bc-ct-brf—connecticutjo0420apr20,0,1501682.story?coll = ny-region-apconnecticut.

19. Tom Brown, *Anatomy of Fire* (Lexington, KY: Management General), e-book retrieved from http://www.anatomyoffire.com, chapter 2, 3.

20. *Merriam-Webster Online Dictionary,* retrieved from http://www.m-w.com/cgi-bin/dictionary?va = doomsayer.

21. Jack Gibb, *Trust: A New View of Personal and Organizational Development* (Los Angeles: Guild of Tutors Press, 1978).

22. Dee Hock, *One from Many: VISA and the Rise of the Chaordic Organization* (San Francisco: Berrett-Koehler, 2005), 208.

23. Ibid., 210.

24. Ibid.

25. Arjuna Ardagh, *The Translucent Revolution: How People Just Like You Are Waking Up and Changing the World* (Novato, CA: New World Library, 2005).

26. Barry Heermann, *Noble Purpose: Igniting Extraordinary Passion in Life and Work* (Fairfax, VA: QSU Publishing, 2004).

27. Srikumar Rao, *Are You Ready to Succeed? Unconventional Strategies for Achieving Personal Mastery in Business and Life* (New York: Hyperion, 2006).

28. Richard Barrett, *Building a Values Driven Organization: A Whole System Approach to Cultural Transformation* (Boston: Butterworth-Heinemann, 2006).

29. Lance Secretan, *ONE: The Art and Practice of Conscious Leadership* (Caledon, Ontario, Canada: The Secretan Center, 2006).

30. Details about the International Spirit at Work Award and case studies about the honorees are on the Association for Spirit at Work Web site at http://www.spiritatwork.org.

CHAPTER 7

1. This scenario is a composite based on innovative practices from several ideas, as well as on images I had while meditating on the future with the idea of bringing this organizational design into the present.

2. Sounds True, in Boulder, Colorado, has a policy of allowing dogs in the workplace as long as they are well-behaved toward humans and toward other canines and as long as no one in the work area has allergies to dogs.

3. This building design is similar to that of the Johnson & Johnson corporate headquarters, in New Brunswick, New Jersey.

4. Rob Rabbin is a wonderful writer on spirituality in the workplace. This mention is to honor him for his work and to make reference to his article "Vice President of Corporate

Consciousness," *Spirit at Work Newsletter* (East Haven, CT: Association for Spirit at Work), October 1997.

5. J.-Robert Ouimet explains how Spiritual Support Groups work in his dissertation summary titled "The Golden Book," available at http://www.our-project.org.

6. More and more organizations have meditation rooms or silence rooms. They include Ouimet-Tomasso, ANZ Bank, Pfizer, and Rodale Press.

7. Johnson & Johnson has a program just like this in its New Brunswick, New Jersey, corporate headquarters.

8. Times of India, an International Spirit at Work Award recipient, states, in its award application, "The organization structure is consumer focused and the customer is seen as God. Everyone in the organization joins together to provide an offering to this God (customer) with the best possible news and views, of highest quality at fastest speed. The organization is not solely governed by profits. The aim of the organization is to make employees and stakeholders happy and achieve their highest potential by using the organization as a platform for self-actualization."

9. This section is modeled on some of the practices of SAS, a major software company in Cary, North Carolina.

10. This description is based on the shaman character Jason Hand in Richard Whiteley's book *The Corporate Shaman: A Business Fable* (New York: HarperCollins, 2002).

11. Peter Vaill, *Learning as a Way of Being: Strategies for Survival in a World of Permanent White Water* (San Francisco: Jossey-Bass, 1997).

12. George Land and Beth Jarman, *Breakpoint and Beyond: Mastering the Future—Today* (New York: HarperBusiness, 1993), 5.

13. Ibid., 17–23.

14. Malcolm Gladwell, *The Tipping Point: How Little Things Can Make a Big Difference* (New York: Little, Brown, 2002), 9.

15. This process is described by Elisabet Sartouris in an interview in Paul Ray and Sherry Anderson, *The Cultural Creatives: How 50 Million People Are Changing the World* (New York: Harmony Books, 2000), 266.

16. Rosabeth Moss Kanter, *Men and Women of the Corporation* (New York: Basic Books, 1993).

17. Paul Ray and Sherry Anderson, *The Cultural Creatives: How 50 Million People Are Changing the World* (New York: Harmony Books, 2000).

18. The Alliance of Organizational Systems Designers, in Winston-Salem, North Carolina, estimates that a critical mass of early adopters of between 5 and 10 percent is enough to create organizational acceptance and implementation of a designed organizational change process. From notes taken at OSD Advanced Course Training for Executives and Internal OSD Consultants, January 1993.

19. Joann Lublin, "A CEO Talks about His Company's Innovative Pay Ideas. Free Ice Cream, Anyone?" *Wall Street Journal*, April 10, 2006, R6.

20. Ibid.

21. Ibid.

22. Ibid.

23. Ibid.

24. This case study is based on an interview for an article by Judi Neal titled "Business Leader Disseminates Spiritual Wisdom: Tami Simon, CEO of Sounds True," published as an e-doc on http://www.amazon.com, March 2003.

25. John Cowan, *Small Decencies: Reflection and Meditations on Being Human at Work* (New York: HarperBusiness, 1992), 1–3.

26. John Carreyrou, Jo Wrighton, and Alessandra Galloni, "Financier's Fall: How Banker's Life, Full of Intrigue, Ended in Murder," *Wall Street Journal,* April 14, 2005, A1, A12.

27. Ibid., A12.

28. Ibid.

29. Ibid.

30. Jean Houston, *Jump Time: Shaping Your Future in a World of Radical Change* (New York: Jeremy P. Tarcher/Putnam, 2000).

31. John Renesch, *Getting to the Better Future: A Matter of Conscious Choosing* (San Francisco: NewBusinessBooks, 2000).

32. Gary Zukav, *Soul Stories* (New York: Fireside, 2000).

33. Peter Russell, *The Global Brain Awakens: Our Next Evolutionary Leap* (Palo Alto, CA: Global Brain, 1995).

34. John Renesch, interview, April 1, 2006.

35. Teilhard de Chardin, *The Future of Man* (New York: Image, 2004), 11–12.

36. Ibid., 12.

APPENDIX C

1. Marcus Buckingham and Donald Clifton, *Now Discover Your Strengths* (New York: Free Press, 2001).

INDEX

About the Author

JUDI NEAL is Founder and Executive Director of The Association for Spirit at Work, a non-profit association of people and organizations interested in the study and practice of spirituality in the workplace. She previously served in management at Honeywell and is Professor Emeritus in the management department at the University of New Haven. She is also President of Neal & Associates, a consulting firm that supports enlightened organizations, and, as Founder of the International Spirit at Work Awards, she has helped to increase awareness about organizations that nurture the human spirit. Past Chair of the "Management, Spirituality and Religion" Interest Group of the Academy of Management and Past President of the Eastern Academy of Management, she organizes and participates in conferences on spirituality in the workplace and has published many articles and book chapters in the field.